FREE TO BELIEVE

TRACEY JERALD

Sigrid ♡

FREE TO BELIEVE

Design a love
beyond your
wildest dreams.

xoxo,

Tracey
Gordol

Copyright © 2019 by Tracey Jerald

ISBN: 978-1-7324461-8-2 (eBook)

ISBN: 978-1-7324461-9-9 (Paperback)

Editor: One Love Editing (http://oneloveediting.com)

Copy Edits: Virginia Tesi Carey

Cover Design: Amy Queau – QDesign (https://www.qcoverdesign.com)

For Linda Russell.
The only person I know who could help me get through writing this book while I had a concussion. I wanted to curl into a ball and cry so many times, but you kept reminding me there was a story to be told. You have my gratitude and my love for this and so many other reasons.
I am so blessed to have you in my life.

THE LEGEND OF AMARYLLIS

There are variations regarding the legend of how amaryllis flowers came to be. Generally, the tale is told like this:

Amaryllis, a shy nymph, fell deeply in love with Alteo, a shepherd with great strength and beauty, but her love was not returned. He was too obsessed with his gardens to pay much attention to her.

Amaryllis hoped to win Alteo over by giving him the one thing he wanted most, a flower so unique it had never existed in the world before. She sought advice from the oracle Delphi and carefully followed his instructions. She dressed in white, and for thirty nights, appeared on Alteo's doorstep, piercing her heart with a golden arrow.

When Alteo finally opened his eyes to what was before him, he saw only a striking crimson flower that sprung from the blood of Amaryllis's heart.

It's not surprising the amaryllis has come to be the symbol of pride, determination, and radiant beauty. What's also not surprising is somehow, someway, we all bleed a little bit while we're falling in love.

PROLOGUE

EMILY

When I was a child, all I knew was that love died. Repeatedly, it was torn from me brutally. When I saw my parents die, I realized love respected nothing; not pleading, not tears, not begging.

So, I became silent.

I holed up my heart.

When my Aunt Dee—the person who saved the modicum of goodness in me—died, I realized some hard truths.

I am the catalyst for death, betrayal, and heartbreak. When someone tries to penetrate the walls I frantically hold up around me, they inevitably end up getting hurt. Some even die.

All because of love.

And I've never forgotten it.

It's easier to live behind the barrier I've created. It's not made out of steel or armor. It's made out of silence.

If I don't give in to the shattering need inside of me, I can't hurt anyone else.

I live inside my heart wanting. Watching. Wishing.

I hear what's said about me: that I'm cold, a challenge, a bitch, an ice queen.

I'm none of those things.

I'm petrified that due to the promise I made, I'm only allowed to let so many people in. To add another might mean any of them could die.

So, I've shut off my need for love. I deny the fact there's something more out there.

Because I believe if I give in to the longing to fill the void that lives in the core of my body and catastrophe strikes again, I'll never forgive myself.

1

EMILY

I wear his ring not caring I will never love the man I agreed to marry. I see the concern in my family's faces. They think I don't see the lies behind his eyes or that he'll miraculously change? They think I'm so blinded by the pretty words that fall from his lips that I think they will become truth? Maybe they believe I actually think our once instant attraction will flame into a passion so deep that it will burn away their lingering doubt? Maybe they think he's taken root in my heart? Will he permanently open the fortress doors I've hidden behind since I was a child?

They couldn't be more wrong. I know I'll never love him.

It's why I agreed to marry him.

"Bryan, I know you made these reservations a while ago." Running a weary hand down my blonde curls, I sigh. "I just had two bridezillas who were booked at the same time. They wanted the exact same gown and realized that in the middle of the salon and—"

Bryan rudely interrupts me. "Em, I don't have time to listen to this crap. I have to get back to my patients. Maybe we'd have a chance to discuss this over dinner, but since you're canceling again, we can talk about it at some other time." He quickly disconnects the call.

With a choked sound, I toss my cell on the table next to me before reaching down to brush Mugsy's, my very elderly dog, ears. "Oh, Mugs. What did I get myself into?" I murmur.

When did my carefully controlled life degenerate to this?

Through the restored stained-glass windows that stream beams of color into my personal workspace, light winks off the diamond that rests on the third finger of my left hand. The ring on my finger symbolizing a relationship I don't know how to handle. It's too ostentatious, too weighty, too suppressing.

I'm not sure how much more I can bear. I may have signed up for a loveless marriage, but I didn't sign up to have my soul destroyed. And every moment I'm engaged to the esteemed Dr. Bryan Moser, I feel like another pigment of the color of my life is being stripped away.

I need to figure out what to do about it.

I met Bryan a little more than a year ago after he performed a life-saving surgery on one of my younger sisters, Corinna. I was blindsided by his interest—he literally grabbed me into his arms after telling me my sister was going to live and drowned me in a kiss so completely unexpected, I had no choice but to respond.

Bryan and I had a whirlwind courtship and an even faster engagement. When he slid the ring on my finger, he assured me I could have all the time in the world I wanted to plan our wedding.

"Maybe that's when I should have known, Mugs. Does it seem like to you Bryan just wants a fiancée to parade around to his doctor friends when it suits him?"

My old dog just looks up at me and scoots back farther, a sure sign he wants me to rub him down.

Chuckling, I give the job my full attention even as my mind drifts. Should I end my engagement, or should I try to find a way to make this work?

Bryan had pursued me, just like my father had gone after my mother, with a single-mindedness that brooked no argument. My parents were made for each other. They died for each other.

Or with each other. My father's illegal activities had my mother killed, but then he died alongside her.

But unlike with my parents, Bryan's pursuit of me played a large part in putting a dent in my defenses. He was charming, he was charismatic, he was incredibly intelligent—much like the stories about my parents that my Aunt Dee used to try to comfort me with when I first came into her care. Only, Bryan was determined to infiltrate my life. He was determined to consume it—to consume me. And by doing so, he's driving me further and further away, deeper into my already closed-off heart. And I never thought that was possible.

Burying my nose into Mugsy's neck, I inhale his familiar scent. "I have all I need with you, Mugs. Strong, loyal, and true. Never giving up when things get rough." Tipping his muzzle up, I smile. "If life were a fairy tale, I'd choose you. I wouldn't care about your looks, your age, or your profession if you could love me the way you do."

I'm rewarded with a lick on the underside of my chin, causing me to laugh.

Standing, I reward him with the one thing I know he can't resist. "Let's go, baby. It's time for a treat."

Mugsy ambles slowly to his feet and follows me to where I keep his precious dog biscuits.

DRIVING with my dog securely latched in the back of my Rover after he spent all afternoon napping in my private studio, I head home after an exhausting day. I really want to pour myself a glass of pinot noir, munch on a plate of cheese and crackers, and just curl up on my couch with my sketch pad. Fortunately, the drive from Amaryllis Events—my family's wedding-and event-planning business—to our family's compound of houses is hardly more than a mile.

Pulling into my driveway, I rest my head against the steering wheel. My home—which was once the servant's quarters on the enormous farm we bought over a decade ago for a steal— is nestled in between Cassidy and Phil's homes. Kind of the way our rooms used to be in the tiny trailer we were raised in, with Dee on one side of me and Cassidy, Phil on the other.

Taking in the contrast between the weathered brick, cedar shingles, and barn wood, I sigh when I realize this is why I work as hard as I do. So I—we—could fulfill the dream we had on a rainy night in a trailer just outside of Charleston. Today just happened to be one of those days where I wish I could delegate and not spend hours placating brides who demand I find them the right kind of wine to drink while shopping and who blame me when I can't get a dress on time because they left finding their wedding gown to the absolute last minute.

When I graduated with a degree in fine arts from the University of Charleston, I dreamed one day I'd design dresses so stunning my name would fall from people's lips in reverence. And while I've made a mark in fashion by the design of the amaryllis lace Ali trademarked for me years ago, and a few of my gowns have landed on the pages of bridal magazines, I haven't found that missing "it" to drive people to select Amaryllis Designs over some of the more established names in the business: Monique Lhuillier, Pronovinas, Hailey Paige, Reem Acra, Rivini.

Unclipping Mugs's harness, he lumbers down from the back seat. An ache of sadness washes over me. It seems like just yesterday he would have leapt from the car with all his might, chasing some animal only he could see. Now, he patiently trots up to my back steps waiting for me to unlock the door, his days of terrorizing the squirrels over.

The house line is ringing as I enter the foyer. Closing the door behind me, I hurriedly step past Mugs, who stops inconveniently to lap at his water bowl. Snatching it up before the last ring, I let out a breathless "Hello?"

My older sister Cassidy's amused voice comes through the line. "Did I interrupt anything?"

"Not unless you consider my almost tripping over the dog to answer your call."

"Ahh. I just wanted to check in and see how things ended up downstairs today. I heard you had quite an interesting appointment."

"Give me a minute to open a bottle of wine and I'll tell you all about it," I grunt.

Cass makes a sound. "That bad?"

"Jesus, Cass. I swear to God, I thought they were going to tear the damn dress in half. It wasn't until I screamed that if they ripped it they'd be buying both that dress *plus* whatever dress they both ended up choosing that they both settled down." Tucking the phone under my chin, I uncork the bottle of wine. I snag a glass from my cabinet. Using more than a generous hand pouring into the thin crystal, I fill my glass before taking a sip. "That was before the insults started." The memory gives me a headache. "Scheduling error or not, no more dual appointments. These two were supposedly best friends since they were three, for Christ's sake."

"It could be worse," she offers.

"How?" I demand.

"They could have been playing tug-o'-war with the groom."

I think about that for a moment. "I think that might have gone better." The musical laughter on the other end of the phone does much to relieve my frustration.

"Why don't you come over and have dinner with us? This way you won't be suffering your own company. Not to mention your own cooking," she tacks on dryly.

"Normally, I'd take you up on that offer, but I canceled dinner with Bryan so I can just relax."

"Hmmm."

I bristle. "What's that supposed to mean?"

"Nothing."

"Cass..." I warn, an edge to my voice.

She lets out a sigh. "I'm...concerned. You don't seem happy, Em. To be honest, I'm beginning to wonder if you were happier before you started dating Bryan."

"I'm...content."

"What a lukewarm word for someone who used to laugh so hard she'd spit her drink out because she found such joy in life."

"It's undignified for a doctor's wife to do that." The words are out of my mouth before I realize I'm saying them.

"Em..." Cass begins, but I cut her off.

"I'm fine, Cass. I'm perfectly fine." Or I will be once I decide whether I want to live the rest of my life with a diamond on my finger and an anvil of stress where my heart should have been.

"Listen, I really just want to go relax. We'll talk more tomorrow, okay?"

She hesitates before agreeing. "Okay. I love you."

"Back at you. Night."

Tossing the phone to the counter, I pick up the glass. The three-carat diamond Bryan coolly slid on my finger mocks me as I lift the glass to my lips.

I can't look at it anymore.

Placing the glass back on the counter, I tug it off my finger. Just the weight of it coming off my hand seems to release a burden inside of me. I place it on the counter next to my glass of wine. I look down at my naked hand and realize the ring hasn't had time to brand me by leaving an indentation on my skin.

A voice inside me whispers, *It's as if it was never there.*

Shaking my head, I do what I do best in times of stress. Without sliding the ring back on my hand, I go back to the mudroom where Mugsy has curled into his doggie bed. My heart breaks knowing I likely don't have much time left with him. I crouch down and whisper so quietly so I don't disturb him, "You've been my one true love, old man." His tail thumps up and down a few times, but he doesn't stir.

Picking up the bag I dropped earlier, I take it into my rarely used kitchen. Seeing the diamond on the counter, I can't help but shudder a little at the idea of sliding it back on my finger. On paper, Bryan is perfect. He's a brilliant surgeon. He's intellectually stimulating. He's gorgeous. And I'll be forever indebted to him for saving Corinna's life last year. Yet even though I know I'll never give over that side of me that I've long buried, there's still something else. Another part of him that's been showing up more and more as of late. I can't quite put my finger on it yet. As much as I've always been a loner, there are things about him that are driving me even deeper into myself.

Pulling out my personal sketch journal, I flip to the last page and begin to speak using the language I know best using one of the charcoal pencils I always keep handy.

Before I even touch the charcoal pencil to the paper, I think back to our first date. Bryan picked me up in his Mercedes and we drove to Westport for dinner on the water. Our conversation was certainly unique; Corinna had just come home from the hospital from her surgery, so we talked a good deal about her procedure and her outlook. My initial comfort with Bryan had a lot to do with his connection to my family and the fact we had a very important point of interest in common already.

As time passed, our interests diverged. I thought that was a benefit. While my blood didn't run hot for him, we had a lot to talk about. At first our disagreements made our relationship seem livelier, more animated. Then after Bryan proposed, it was as if he no longer had to hold up a facade.

It's as if he felt his arrogance, his superiority, and even sometimes his cruelty was bought and paid for.

In my head, I can hear Dee whisper, *You deserve more.*

Do I? I wonder. Or do I just deserve to finish this life with a little piece of happiness even if it never equals love?

With a jagged sigh, I begin sketching to unburden my mind while I contemplate what the best course of action truly is.

Is being alone really so much worse than being with someone for all the wrong reasons?

2

EMILY

I brood for a long time before needing the haven of my second floor. Even though it's late, I fortunately don't have any clients until early afternoon, so I still have time to decompress.

Finishing the last of my wine, I stand up and call for Mugsy. When he doesn't come to me, I go in search of him. He's still in his bed by the door. I frown. More and more, he's been sleeping downstairs. Grabbing a blanket, I cover him with it. I crouch down and rub my face next to his. "Sleep tight, my handsome man."

He licks my face.

"I'll see you in the morning unless you need to go out before then." Standing, I walk over to the kitchen stove and leave the light on in case Mugsy needs it.

Once I reach the second floor of my home, some of my stress leaches out from me. Here's where I spend hours when I'm at home alone, either in my converted climate-controlled attic, where racks of vintage designer clothing I've collected hang waiting to be worn by me or one of my family members, or in my art space. Filled with light, it takes up the space over my three-car garage and contains an industrial-size sewing machine and multiple shelves filled with the most luxurious fabric I can get my hands on. In reality, the house is way too huge for one person, but I need the storage. We just can't keep all of this at the mansion where we operate Amaryllis Events.

I don't linger, but I do wander through the rooms, appreciating the bold colors of the materials against the gray walls. Everything pops against the gray better, even white. They taught me that in design school. And when Cass, Phil, and I were living in Aunt Dee's old trailer, I didn't have the room to set up an all-gray studio. With a small smile of remembrance, I remember running down to Publix to get boxes, Hobby Lobby to get Styrofoam, and the cheapest light gray fabric they had at JoAnn's just so I could set up a corner of my room with a makeshift studio.

Even if I'll never be one of the greats, I've still come so far. And I appreciate that. I really do. It's just hard to not want more when it's all I can have.

Even once I'm in bed, it's a while before I find sleep. Tossing and turning, I deliberate not just Bryan but the past and how it's influenced my future. I know the longer I'm engaged to him, the more I'm pulling into myself and away from those who care about me because I can sense their concern about my growing unhappiness. And that is the absolute last thing I want. I think about the life I was born into, the life led, and the life I've been blessed with.

After my parents were shot and killed in front of me when I was seven, I shut down inside. I went from being a vivacious, spoiled little princess living in a row of matched suburban McMansions to living in a trailer in the middle of nowhere South Carolina. Aunt Dee, God rest her soul, used the microscopic income she earned plus the little money left over after settling my parents' estate to create a warm home for me. It was safe. It had food. It had love. But what she didn't have money for was more extensive therapy.

And Lord knows I needed it. Then. Now, I have everything under control.

I was barely seven when it happened. One moment, I was happily dressing my new dolls in my playroom at one end of the house. The next, men dressed in all black with ski masks were dragging me down our long carpeted hall with a hand clamped over my mouth to muffle my screams. Yanking me by my hair and arms, they threw me in front of my father. Words I didn't understand were spat at him as they forced me to my knees. My little body shivered as I felt a heavy weight jammed against the back of my neck, cold and brutal. I didn't understand what was happening. And then I looked to the side and screamed. And screamed.

My mother's body lay on the ground not moving. A pool of red began to spread out beneath her.

"No!" I screamed. "Mommy!" Shoving away from the cold metal, uncaring what could happen, I scrambled over to her. My hands landed in the stickiness. "Mommy, we have to get you help!" My mommy was supposed to be beautiful in ball gowns and jewels. She wasn't supposed to be bruised and hurt. I started screaming again.

"Shh, Emily. Hush now. It'll—" She paused to cough, a little trickle of blood coming out of her nose. I used my shirt to wipe it away. "—be okay."

"Promise?"

The next thing I knew I was being dragged back, this time in front of the bad men. I heard my mother's whisper. "Don't let them hurt Emily, Stephen." Then I saw her head fall to the side.

Looking ill, my father whispered, "I'm sorry. I'm so sorry." Right before he looked over my head and said, "Do it."

At the time, I thought he meant for them to shoot him. During the years that passed, Aunt Dee confessed the police believed my father meant to buy his own life with mine. As he had my mother's. But my own actions saved my life.

Throwing myself forward, I spread myself in front of my father and shrieked, "Noooo! You can't take him too!" Right before a whistle whizzed past me and hit my father with a thud.

"What disgusts me is your beautiful little girl was willing to sacrifice herself to save you. She is worth saving. You are not." The killer, whose face I never saw but whose eyes I would never forget, pulled me away from my father and mother. "You know how to call emergency, yes?" he asked in a heavily accented voice.

Gasping for my next breath, I nodded.

"Then go call them now." Turning me toward the kitchen, I gave him one more look. "Go, now."

I turned and ran. But when my slippery feet hit the kitchen tile, I slipped as I came to an abrupt stop. Miss Meg's body was on the floor much like Mommy's was. I let out a wail of pain even as I picked up the phone to dial 911.

"911, what's your emergency?"

"Help..." It was all I could whisper.

"I'm sorry, I can't hear you. Please speak up."

"Help me, please. Come now."

Those were the last words I would speak for almost four years.

The rest was a blur—a movie played on fast forward. I remember the front door splintering as the police swarmed the house, but I hardly remember being picked up and taken from my home. I remember they brought me glass after glass of water in the police station—but I don't remember how long I was there. I vaguely remember being woken from an unwitting slumber on a cot one of the policewomen found to find my Aunt Dee standing in front of me, her hand clasped over her mouth with tears streaming down her face. She knelt by my side and stroked the bloodstained hair away from my face. "We'll get through this, Emily. I promise you."

I blinked at her, all my words gone in the last pleas I made on the phone. I became silent in a world that no longer deserved my voice because silence doesn't argue. Maybe my silence may have saved the people I loved. Silence doesn't hurt.

"Go back to sleep, baby. I have to deal with the police before we can...well, before we can move forward," she said brusquely.

Obeying, I closed my eyes.

That time of my life is as deeply branded on my heart as my amaryllis tattoo is now inked on my back.

Aunt Dee tried anything to get me to talk. After more than a year, I still hadn't spoken a single word. Using all her limited resources, Aunt Dee brought me to multiple therapists who ultimately concluded I would talk when I was ready. But she wasn't satisfied with that. Aunt Dee tried taking me to church. She'd tried sending me to school. She tried bringing me around other children who I could see were happy just so I understood life went on.

I needed the bond of other survivors to be able to actually have the courage to take the steps to move on.

The day I would meet my future "brother" and "sister" is so vivid in my memory, I could sketch it blindfolded. One cool Sunday, Aunt Dee reluctantly cajoled me into going to a deserted park. By then, it had been more than two years since my parents were killed. I remember lagging behind when I heard her gasp, "Oh, my dear sweet God in heaven." Then she was running as fast as she could toward the farthest slide in the park.

A young voice shouted out, "Stay away!" but she didn't listen. She never did when it came to her heart. It was what I first resented about her and then loved the most about her. When she died, it was what my heart most grieved about her—her willingness to open her heart to love.

Aunt Dee gentled Phil and Cassidy. "It will be more comfortable to come stay with us tonight. We'll get you a warm meal. You can sleep in a bed. I promise nothing will happen to you." But it wasn't until both of their eyes met mine and they waited for me to pass judgment, that Phil reluctantly relented.

"All right." Sliding out from where he was hiding, he reached back for Cassidy, who was trembling but visibly relieved. Picking up her tiny, battered body in his arms, he agreed. "But just for one night."

"One night, son. We'll get a good meal in you and see what you need," Dee promised. When three heads swung toward me, I did the only thing I could. I nodded.

What Phil, Cassidy, and it turns out I needed were each other.

And Dee somehow made things work. For about five years, we lived together, scrimped by together, healed together, and loved one another. We became a family; survivors, all of us. And then the day came when we had to figure out how to go on without Dee.

Standing over her grave, I whispered, "Life hurts a lot worse than death."

"No, it doesn't, Em," Phil whispered back.

"Yes, it does. Particularly if you happen to love me," I said, before I dropped the flowers I was holding on the ground and walked away sobbing.

After Dee died, we fought to stay together emotionally as well as physically in one of the hardest battles we would ever face: the threat of being separated. Phil was a legal adult, but Cassidy and I were only fifteen. We tried to remain in Phil's care until that avenue was shut down to us. Standing before the judge to become legally emancipated, I will never forget his parting words: "I hope I'm not making the biggest mistake of my life by allowing this to occur. You have no idea for the life you are in for. And I'm afraid you'll be back in my courtroom for some other reason."

Looking back, it's no wonder the void Dee left us with could only be filled by the love of three more "sisters"—Ali, Corinna, and Holly. The love she taught us to have for one another was just that huge. But to this day, there is no love that has thawed the ice around my heart since she died.

I let out my fear the only way I knew how. Not through words, but through art.

When I was a child, the pencil drawings were rudimentary, but as my mind became clearer and my fingers stronger, the images became almost photogenic memories of my terror. And later, the moments of joy as we built our family together: Aunt Dee, Phil, Cassidy, and me. Later the sketches included Ali, Corinna, and Holly.

The images I cherish above all others are the ones I drew of my mother bejeweled in a ball gown right before she leaned down to kiss me good night as a child. And then there's the one on Aunt Dee's face when I finally told her I loved her—words I'd been thinking in my head for years and were the first ones I said after my self-imposed silence.

And a few nights, a few years later, both women died.

Just like everyone who dares to love me dies.

It's on that thought that I finally fall asleep. But my nightmares follow me, reminding me of the deal I bargained for after Dee's death.

So, instead of dreaming of my parents' murder or Dee's waxy face, I scream in my head as Phil, Cass, Ali, Cori, and Holly all fall to the specter of death who believes I dare too much when I love.

Because I believed.

3

EMILY

The next day, it's more of the same. This time one of the same brides from yesterday—the one who was in an argument with her best friend over one of my original designs —came back to see me, wanting me to include transporting her dress to France for her wedding. Free—with my stylist services included. While I'm happy to accommodate the request, I hate wasting valuable time explaining if she wants me to transport the dress and be her stylist for her wedding day, it needs to be understood there will be an additional charge.

Slyly, she taunts me with "I bet if I went with the Reem Acra dress, they'd have a designer in their Paris store who could help me. *Gratis.*" She adds the last little bit in French as if that's going to intimidate me.

Yes, it's a direct hit to my professional pride, but I refuse to let that show. Standing from behind my mahogany desk, I close the design book in front of me. "Of course, that's your choice. However, I can't guarantee the dress will be here after today."

"What do you mean?" the bride, Lara, screeches.

I find some small pleasure in dangling this knowledge in front of her after the sanctimonious attitude I've dealt with for two days.

"Your friend Susan also left me a message earlier still expressing her interest in this particular dress. If you're deciding against it..." My voice trails off.

"You can't sell my dress out from under me!"

"Actually—" I shrug. "—I can. We don't have a signed contract."

This is the part of my business I would happily toss over the fence to someone if I could find that right person who could convey the feeling I want my brides to understand about my designs. I want to spend hours lost in my studio creating and not dealing with pretentious brides who feel that just because they're about to drop anywhere between ten to twenty grand on a dress, I should genuflect at their feet. Part of me would rather give my dresses away to someone who would appreciate them for what they are—art.

Despite my misgivings about my engagement, it wasn't just excuses I was giving to Bryan last night. I am physically drained each night I drag myself home. I'm not only expected to sell dresses, I have to design for next season as well. That means studying market trends across all fashion and wedding business areas. I have to look at every trend from flowers, to cake selection, to shoes, to colors, to shapes before I can sit down and design what I think will sell. It takes a lot of time on top of the day-to-day operations of the salon.

And the more time I spend in this room of gray, the more I feel my soul disappearing.

Especially with brides like Lara Fredericks.

"Daddy! She can't do that." A perfectly manicured hand smacks down on top of my design book. I want to slap at it, but I manage to refrain. "Do something to stop her!"

A portly man, dressed impeccably in this season's Ralph Lauren Purple Label suit, leans forward in his seat. "Ms. Freeman, can't I leave a check with you for the full amount of the dress for a few days? This way, Lara can make up her mind without any of the pressure she's obviously feeling."

A small part of me feels for this man having such an atrocious spawn of Satan as a daughter. The other part of me recognizes she's a creature of his own making. There's a small part of me that wonders if I would have been like her had my parents lived—a spoiled society princess. Instead of voicing my opinions about his daughter, I ask politely, "Mr. Fredericks, I understand you run a business that's traded on the Exchange? Your assistant mentioned it when she called to schedule the appointment."

He brightens. "Why yes, I do. How clever of you to remember." Lara frowns.

Leaning forward a bit, I ask him, "If someone was interested in investing in your company, wouldn't you make sure the contracts were signed—particularly if you had an exact offer from a similar competitor who had an equal reputation?"

His eyes narrow at how neatly I've boxed him into his own corner. But he doesn't disagree. "Touché, Ms. Freeman."

"Daddy?" The panic in Lara's voice is now unmistakable.

"I'm sorry, sweetheart, but Ms. Freeman is right. You have to make a decision, or you risk losing the dress. If we have to pay extra for her services in France"—he eyes me shrewdly—"then I think they'll be worth it."

She recoils as if he slapped her. "But...I need more time. And you said you'd get it for me!"

He shakes his head. "Ms. Freeman has a buyer for this dress, Lara. If you don't want it..."

"But I might!" she cries. "I'm just not sure yet."

He shifts forward and stands. "Then it looks like you can compliment Susan on wearing the dress when you're her matron of honor."

She looks at him in a daze. "You're really not going to get her to hold the dress for me. I can't believe you. Wait till I tell Mother."

I stand to my full height. In the sky-high heels I'm wearing, I'm towering at just under six feet. "Buying a wedding dress is an enormous commitment, Ms. Fredericks. If you're not ready to purchase this dress, then maybe Reem Acra is the designer for you." I can't believe these words are coming out of my mouth. I should be trying to convince this bride I'm the designer to make all her dreams come true. But I just can't put forth the effort to do so; I don't have it in me anymore. I don't seem to have the energy for much these days except existing. The glint of my own diamond engagement ring I snagged as I walked out of my house catches my eye as father and daughter continue to argue in front of me.

Briefly, I wonder where they went—the hopes I locked up so tightly in the vault of my heart. It isn't that Bryan broke through the walls I built around my heart. If anything, he's shored up the bricks so they're more fortified than ever. I feel trapped inside myself, unable to escape with no sign of rescue.

I'd wonder if this vacant ache is how the average person feels when they're "in love" if I didn't see the proof to the contrary every day with the relationships my siblings have: Phil and Jason, Cassidy with Caleb, Ali and Keene, and Corinna with Colby.

Corinna once asked me what I wanted in a relationship. I realized I couldn't tell her the truth: that I wanted to know I wasn't a danger to someone by loving them. In the smallest part of me that I still have hope in, I want to believe love could exist for someone like me. So, I made up something about how maybe I could find the dream we execute for our clients every day: happiness. During the nights when I can't sleep, I'm beginning to wonder if they aren't the same thing.

"I'll take it." I'm brought abruptly out of my wandering musing by Lara's voice.

"You will?" I gracefully sit down, when all I want to do is fall down in my chair. The price tag on this dress is astronomical. I hand stitched every bead onto it. It's one of a kind.

An Emily Freeman Original.

"Yes. Since Daddy has agreed to pay additional for your services"—my bride can't help the sneer in her voice—"I suppose we'll add that on as well."

James Fredericks rolls his eyes at his daughter. "What my daughter is trying to say, Ms. Freeman, is we'd be delighted if you would adjust the price of the gown that will undoubtedly look gorgeous on my daughter and accommodate its transportation—as well as your own—to France for her wedding in four months."

Lara Fredericks flaps her hand at her father. "Will that do? Now Susan can't have my dress?" she demands.

Reaching into my desk, I pull out one of Ali's ironclad contracts. "The minute we have all parties sign this document and your father's payment clears."

James Fredericks gives me a wry look. "Do you take American Express?"

I grin. "For an additional three-percent fee."

Shoulders shaking, he reaches for his wallet. "It's worth it. Trust me."

4

EMILY

"I can't believe you managed to sell a twenty-thousand-dollar dress and tack on first-class travel to Paris!" Ali exclaims. She's flipping through the contracts. I practically danced into her office once the Fredericks left and after I called Susan Simon's family to let them know the dress sold earlier in the day. Once my ears stopped ringing, I decided to celebrate my biggest dress sale to date. "Hell, if you didn't sell that dress soon, I was debating buying it and holding on to it for Kalie."

Having just taken a drink of coffee, I spit it out, turning my head at the last minute to avoid the precious contracts lying on Ali's desk. "Jesus, Ali. She's not even two yet. Were you planning on having me alter it for something?"

"Nope. I was going to hold on to it for her wedding."

Helpless to do anything but laugh, I barely manage to get out, "I can just picture Keene's reaction."

Ali grins. "I was planning on storing it at Phil's."

We're a mess when Cassidy strolls into the room. Older than I am by about six months, my "big" sister is the tiniest of all of us in stature. Yet every time I see her, it still amazes me to witness what love has done to her. Before, Cass was fairly timid, needing us to fight her battles for her. Now, she's this pint-sized warrior ready to take on the world. "I'm more curious how you managed to sell the dress in question to one of the bridezillas that had you threatening no more dual bridal appointments."

"I'm still standing by that," I grumble.

My sisters laugh. Cassidy sits down in the chair across from me. Frowning, she looks at Ali. "You know there's coffee on your floor."

Ali points at me. "You can thank Em for that. Phil isn't around, and she just avoided the contracts on my desk."

Cassidy's head snaps toward me, likely remembering the rest of our conversation last night. The room takes on a recently familiar tension. I know my family wants to intercede because they believe I'm making a colossal mistake, but they love me. They're respecting my decisions and my choices. I sigh. I'm going to have to let them in on some of my thoughts before they both worry themselves to death. Twirling the diamond around my finger agitatedly, I admit, "I'm not so sure..." before I'm interrupted from behind.

"If you finish that with 'about my engagement,' I promise I won't bitch for a month if you spit on me at dinner," Phil says from behind us, and I twist around to see my brother; he looks like an eager kid about to be told he's getting ice cream for dinner. "And if you follow it up with 'I'm breaking the engagement,' I'll take you shoe shopping."

Holly pushes past him into Ali's office. "I'll take you to the fabric store."

My lips part in surprise. Do none of my family members like my fiancé? Before I have time to process that thought, the shock I feel is compounded when Corinna adds on, "When I was sick, I said to you to find your happy, Em. Don't settle for something just because you think you have to."

"You are the last person I expected to hear this from," I say boldly to Corinna.

"Why? I know he was my doctor and all, but he's not more important than you are to me. Please, put an end to this farce before you're so far in you can't get out." Pushing her way into the room past Phil, she leans against the wall in her trademark chef's coat and jeans. Her own diamond sparkles against her left hand.

"What if I love him?" I ask curiously. I don't, but I'm curious about their intervention efforts.

"Then we wouldn't be sitting here trying to save your happily ever after," Holly says gently.

I snort. I can't help it. "Like I believe in those."

"That's why we're here," Phil interjects smoothly.

"To make me want to buy into something that's full of shit?" I demand. It's not, and I know it. But I can't ever have it.

Ever.

"No, to prevent you from buying into something worse than shit," Ali says.

"What's worse than that?"

"A life filled with nothing."

I don't have an answer to that.

"Em, honey. Do you remember why you said 'yes'?" Cassidy asks me.

I stay quiet. I have my reasons, but I can't share them.

She reaches out her hand. I take a hold of it with all the strength I'd grab onto a rope being tossed to me if I was drowning. Because I think I am. "Did you ever want to say 'no'?"

Yes. The thought whispers through my mind. I never wanted to get engaged, but I allowed myself to be talked into it. Pulling my hand from Cassidy's, I tug at the ring on my other hand. Placing it on Ali's desk, I admit, "All the time."

A sharp collective breath is let out in the room. Phil moves into the cramped office to squat in front of me. "You should give him back the ring, Em. You're not happy."

I whisper aloud the one fear that I haven't voiced aloud, the one thought I never admitted to anyone until just now. "What if this is the only shot I've got at anything close to what you all have?"

"I don't believe that for one second," Cassidy says fiercely.

"But how do you know?" I whisper.

"None of us do, Em. I just have to have faith there's something glorious out there waiting. At least," Holly adds, "that's what I keep telling myself."

"But you won't find it if you're hiding," Corinna says firmly. "I should know."

"Or if you're running," Ali adds.

"Or if you're afraid," Cassidy says.

"You just have to know we're always here for you no matter what happens. And if you are meant to be single, so be it. But be single and be fabulously happy, not engaged and miserable," Phil concludes.

I swallow hard. The diamond sitting on Ali's desk mocks me as it stares back at me. I can't keep it. I have to talk to Bryan and end this engagement. It's a farce, a mockery in the face of what I know marriage should be.

Running a hand through my curls, I let out a shaky laugh. "Hell, I thought I was coming in here to celebrate selling the most expensive dress in our inventory and getting a trip to Paris out of it to boot. I didn't think I was coming in to celebrate changing the course of my life at the same time."

Standing, Phil reaches down for my hand to pull me to my feet. With my heels, we're almost the same height. Hugging me hard, he announces, "You're turning into Cassidy with your multitasking."

I pull back in horror. "Bite your tongue."

The room erupts in laughter, which Cassidy takes good-naturedly. "What am I supposed to do now?" Should I celebrate or end my engagement? Something of what I'm thinking must show on my face because Phil shakes his head before pulling me close.

"You can do anything you set your heart to, Em. I'm so damn proud of you."

5

EMILY

"Bryan," I say firmly. "I need to actually talk with you. The benefit is hardly the proper place for it."

"What happened? Did you not sell a dress? Poor baby," he says snidely. "Some of us actually had real work to do today, so forgive me if I'm not sympathetic about your little job."

I pull the phone away from my ear. Doing so, I realize I never put my ring back on earlier from Ali's office. Wriggling, I shove my hand into the pocket of my dress and pull it out. Letting it fall out of my hand, it clatters onto the side table in my studio where I had been enjoying a glass of wine and sketching with Mugsy at my feet. He looks up at me and whines.

"Don't tell me it's got anything to do with that dog of yours, Emily, or I swear, I won't be held accountable for what I'm about to say," Bryan adds.

And just like that, the order of what's right and true in my life clicks back into place. And there's no room for him in it. This egotistical man with the overinflated opinion of himself isn't worth the time it takes for our conversation, let alone the respect I'm trying to afford him by ending our engagement in person. I don't know whatever it was in my mind that ever made me think Bryan's twisted righteousness was worth settling for. But suddenly, my eyes are wide open. Even if I don't believe in happily ever after, it's an atrocity to a respected union. And trust me, I see marriages of those kind come through my door every day that have longevity.

Even if I was the last woman on Earth responsible for repopulating the planet, this man wouldn't be enough for me.

"What would you say?" Hitting Speaker, I put the phone down and pick up the ancient leather sketchbook where I turn the page. I close my eyes before placing the charcoal to paper, beginning a new picture of Bryan. I imagine him sitting in his office with his tie undone, jacket off, his blond hair falling forward as he stands up slowly, trying to intimidate me even though I can't see him.

"I'd have told you to put that mutt down long ago, Emily. You don't need that albatross around your neck as you're trying to run a business and plan our wedding." His voice comes through clearly.

"Hmm," I respond absentmindedly as I sketch the disturbed features I've seen directed at me all too often. I use the charcoal to ruthlessly erase him from my memory. Getting him permanently out of my life can't happen soon enough.

The rollers of the studio door creak as Bryan's blathering on about how he's made a new friend who's a vet who can take care of my little problem. Corinna enters, her mouth agape. Her eyes turn the dark chocolate color that indicates her temper's about to fly, but I shake my head. I don't want her to blast him; I want that pleasure all for myself. Holding up my finger to my lips, I silence my little sister. "That's extremely...educational, Bryan. But no, I think I'll keep my dog."

"You'll regret that decision, Emily," he warns me. Like I'm a schoolgirl instead of a thirty-three-year-old woman who has lived through more horror than he's ever seen in his operating room.

"I highly doubt that. As I was saying, we need to talk. It won't be tonight. Do you have a better time?" I'm firm in not attending the fundraiser with my soon-to-be-ex fiancé.

"You can make an appointment with my secretary," he tells me right before he hangs up. And Corinna explodes.

"Holy shit, Em. If the great Dr. Bryan Moser talks to you like that regularly and you don't end the engagement, I swear to God, I'm having one of the guys from Colby's team kidnap you until you realize what a real man is like. He talked to me like that once, *once*, and I almost found a new doctor," Corinna snaps as she stalks forward. Corinna's recent medical issues actually led to my introduction to Bryan.

I hold up the hand still not wearing the ring. "Please, give me some credit, Cori. I just wanted to see how far he'd go. Isn't it a bit uncouth to end an engagement over the phone?"

Cori stops so suddenly her sneakers catch on the hardwood floors causing a loud *screech* in the room. "Uncouth?" She snickers. "Well, sorry about the lecture, then. You know that was really for Dr. Douchebag."

I'm amused despite myself. "Is the nickname new or something you all have been calling Bryan behind my back?"

Corinna sits at the end of the chaise I've been relaxing on. "He's always had his moments where he's exhibited prima donna behavior. Then again, what doctor doesn't?"

Silently, I agree with her. "When did the rest of the family start calling him that?"

"About a week after you got engaged to him," she admits cheerfully, her spectacular eyes turning back to their normal golden color as she relaxes. "Hand me your wine."

After she takes the extended glass and swallows, I ask, "And you didn't feel it was your place to say anything?"

She shakes her head as she hands me the glass back. "Not until today when we talked it out in Ali's office. I realized part of the reason you were dithering back and forth was because you feel some sort of debt to him because of me."

Nailed it. "It's hard not to, Cori. He did save your life."

"Something a number of doctors could have done if I had spoken up to the family about my medical condition before it reached a critical point, Em. Bryan was my doctor. Sure, he's brilliant at what he does, but it wasn't like he was the one person on the planet who had a compatible organ and he donated it. Stop feeling indebted to him for saving my life. There's only one person I credit with that."

"Who's that?" I ask, genuinely curious.

"Colby. He saved my heart. Without that, I really didn't have a life worth fighting for. Is that the kind of love you have with Bryan?"

I let out the giggle-snort I've been suppressing anytime someone used the words "Bryan" and "love" in the same sentence over the last three months since I said yes to what must have been the coldest engagement proposal ever.

"What's so funny, Em?" Corinna's confusion is written all over her face.

"You're assuming I love Bryan." I'm outright laughing at this point. It feels so good to admit this to someone and not feel the weight of guilt along with it.

"You don't?" I shake my head. "Then why did you say yes?" she demands.

"Too many reasons, but none of them are love." I shrug. "Obviously I made an error. Now, I'm just trying to figure out how to get out of it as best as I can."

"Want my advice?" Corinna offers as she stands.

"Sure."

"The man may be a genius when it comes to being a doctor, and he can hold a social mask long enough to not be a dick with his patients, most of the time. But eventually, masks crumble. And a man with his ego isn't going to take well to having it squashed. Break the engagement in a public place. Better yet, take one of us with you." Her voice is concerned.

Slowly her words penetrate. "You think he's capable of..."

She holds up her hands. "I don't know. I've just been in the kitchen working while going over all the times he's acted like an asshole while I was his patient. It occurred to me every time he was more than your average dick—like around the time I thought of canceling my surgery—was because I challenged his ego. I don't want to be right, but I'd hate worse if I'm wrong."

What's tragic is when I add Corinna's words with the man who wanted me to put my dog down because he's become burdensome, I'm coming up with an answer that causes my stomach to churn. Covering my response with my typical calmness, I take a sip of wine before putting the glass down. "Okay. I'll figure out when I can head down to his place. I'm pretty sure I have a few things I left the last time I stayed there."

"Good." Corinna stands and begins to make her way toward the open door. Pausing, she turns around to ask, "When was the last time you did that anyway?"

Without thinking, I answer, "Three, four months ago. Why?"

The huge smile that crosses her face should give me warning that what's going to come out of her mouth is going to be completely inappropriate. Instead, I stupidly take a sip of wine and almost choke when she says, "Jesus, Em. If I'd known that, I would have given you batteries for your vibrator on your birthday instead of a gift card to the fabric store."

"Get out of here!" I sputter. Corinna winks before she makes her way out the door. But she does bring up an excellent point. I won't regret being able to find someone who stimulates me sexually a hell of a lot more than Bryan did in bed.

My smile fading, I turn back to capturing what will soon be my past on a sketch pad that already holds so many memories of it. I settle more comfortably on my chaise. Mugsy stirs at my feet. People throw the word love around when it comes to the emotions between a man and a woman like it's the blessed balm to soothe any hurt. Right—I snort a little in my glass before I freeze.

No, Em, I chide myself. *It's okay to be yourself again. You don't have to be someone else's perfect answer anymore. Not that you ever were.*

It's amazing what guilt and extreme gratitude can lead you to. I met Bryan because he performed a life-saving operation on Corinna. Afterward, he swept me off my feet by laying a hell of a kiss on me in front of my whole family. Shock, charm, and disarm.

He's used the tactic many times since we've been together. It's what made outsiders think we were bound for a lifetime of happiness. Rolling my eyes, I keep drawing in the details of the picture I was working on before Cori walked in the room. Yet, I know if I continue down this path, I would be bound for a life sentence in a prison I can't escape. Even something as important as sex in a relationship as new as ours is so mediocre, it hasn't happened in months. I'm grateful I don't have to lie there pretending an interest while he pumps away and leaves me hanging.

I guess my need for a family to call my own outweighed my common sense.

Long ago, Cori drunkenly suggested she, Holly, and I get married and become sister wives. When Holly—equally drunk—asked about the sex, Cori said vibrators were our answer. They don't know how prophetic their words were. I've gotten off more to my vibrator in the time I've been with Bryan than I have to the man himself.

I add details to my sketch only I would remember: the way Bryan's fists turn white when he's frustrated, the way his jaw clenches, the way his eyes narrow. I can't quite capture the way his jaw ticks, nor can I capture the initial bite down of his teeth.

Laying aside the charcoal and the sketchbook when I'm done, I close my eyes. I can see the scene I drew in my head so clearly. It was a few months ago. I'd spent the night at the vet with Mugsy, and Bryan had been livid I didn't put him down at that time.

I reach for my phone. Before I can think about it, I shoot off a text to Bryan. *We need to talk. As soon as possible.* Before I can think about it, I hit Send. Shivering, I reach down and stroke my baby's ears. "We'll see if he responds, Mugs," I say as I drift off to sleep.

Not long after my dreams begin, I can hear my Aunt Dee whisper to me, "If you believe in yourself, Emily, you can survive anything." I just wish I could.

Believe.

The thing is, I believe. I believe in a promise I made by Dee's graveside. And I'll hold steadfast to it as long as I can.

With the diamond lying on my desk and my heart unburdened, I dream of brilliant gowns that are flooded in red.

6

EMILY

The next morning, I jolt awake still in the same clothes from yesterday. On the rare occasion this happens, I expect to see one of my siblings, like Phil or Cass. I certainly don't expect to see all of my siblings, each one of them wearing expressions ranging from disgust to abject fury.

Oh no. This can't be good.

"What happened?" I ask warily. I sit up bracing myself for whatever blow they're about to deliver.

"Do you have any wine around here?" Corinna asks, as she searches my studio for the wine I keep on hand for prospective brides.

"Screw the wine, Cori. She might need the whiskey for this," Ali counters. Brushing past me, she drops a kiss on my cheek. Of all my adopted sisters, we're the two who most closely resemble each other. But that's where our similarities end. While we're both blonde-haired and blue-eyed, Ali is outspoken and opinionated where I'm often introspective and contemplative. It makes her an exceptional attorney and an even better advocate for our family.

"Might? I think you're being kind, Ali," Phil drawls. He wraps his arms around me and squeezes me hard.

"Which is why what we have to tell you is utterly infuriating." Cassidy comes up next to us just in time to hear Phil's comment. In her hands is the *Darien Times* newspaper. "You might want to lie back down for this."

Still sitting on my chaise, Phil drops on one side of me, Cassidy the other. Ali slides into her usual spot against the wall. Holly and Corinna collapse against the heap of floor pillows I have around the room. Mugsy ambles over toward them. "What's happened? Did we get a bad review or something?" I nod, the paper clutched in Cassidy's hands.

Ali's comment of "Tell her what a raging bastard he really is. She deserves to know" sets clanging off inside my head. The last time she had that vicious look on her face, she was trying to protect Cassidy from Keene—her husband who happens to be Cassidy's biological brother—whose less than stellar behavior as he assimilated himself to finding his long-lost sister left our family with a huge rift.

I shift toward Corinna, who looks ready to commit murder. Her hands are clenched so tightly in her lap, her knuckles are white. "What? Is it Colby?" I demand. My nails scrape against my jeans.

I feel a large hand cover my right one. "No, sweetheart. It isn't Colby." Phil's face is filled with a combination of barely leashed anger and an overwhelming sympathy.

"Oh, for God's sake. Just give her the paper so she knows what kind of asshole she's engaged to," Holly snaps. "Once again, a picture is worth a thousand words."

Cassidy silently hands me the folded newspaper flipped open to the Arts and Entertainment section. It appears last night's hospital benefit had media coverage. And there's my soon-to-be ex-fiancé on the cover with his arms wrapped around another woman, his head buried in her hair.

Surprisingly, I'm not jealous. I'm...relieved if I have to be honest. I've been fighting myself looking for an excuse to end our engagement, but I shouldn't have needed one. Yet, Bryan just handed it to me whether he meant to or not. I feel like I should send the photographer a bouquet of flowers or maybe one of Corinna's cakes.

Then I get a glimpse of the caption. And my eyes narrow dangerously.

Dr. Bryan Moser and his date, Dr. Corey Whitacre, as they enter the fund-raiser for the new children's wing of Greenwich Hospital. Dr. Whitacre, who heads Pediatric Orthopedics, is wearing an original design by local designer Emily Freeman of Amaryllis Designs, a subsidiary of award-winning local wedding and event planners, Amaryllis Events.

"What the hell?" I shout. Slapping the paper in Phil's lap with enough force to cause him to groan out in pain, I push myself to my feet.

There's a stillness in the room. "Em, did you and Bryan break up?" Cassidy asks.

"No!" I shout. "I told Cori last night I thought it was tacky to do it over the phone. I was planning on going to talk to him about it today."

Looks pass between my siblings faster than a Ping-Pong ball at an Olympic match. "So, this anger is about the cheating?" Phil chooses his words carefully.

"I'm pissed because he called me last night to ask me if I was making it to that damn fund-raiser. I'm pissed because he hung up on me when I said I couldn't make it. I'm livid," I screech, "because that bastard once again tried to tell me to put my dog down because he was an 'albatross.' And I hadn't even sent the asshole a text yet to tell him we needed to talk until after that photo was taken. So, has he been fucking around on me? Yes, I'm pissed about that. And what the hell is that about me designing that dress?" I throw my hand toward Phil's lap, who cowers back in fear. "I don't recognize that woman, and I'm damn certain I'd remember anyone I've done a custom design for. I'm done. Completely done." I let out a ragged breath. "Now, who's staying here while I shower and get ready, and is driving me to that cocksucker's condo to shove this damn ring somewhere he'll need one of his esteemed colleagues to remove it?"

Five hands go shooting in the air simultaneously. I toss the ring back on the table without another word. Striding out of my studio, I call over my shoulder, "Someone make some damn coffee. I'll be down soon."

"On it," Corinna calls back.

Stomping up the stairs, I wonder where I can shove Dr. Moser's engagement ring that it will cause the most pain.

7

EMILY

Quickly getting ready, I throw on one of the spare outfits I keep at the office just in case something like last night occurs. Slipping into a blue Joan Vass dress with a pair of Stuart Weitzman boots, I slide on a silver Tiffany ring on my left ring finger.

God, it feels so damn good to not put on that fucking diamond.

I know I should have ended the engagement long ago, but I told myself my nerves would settle and that Bryan and I would have a comfortable marriage. I snort out loud. How comfortable would it have been with three in our bed? Asshole.

I talked myself into thinking he was a good man. I thought he was solid, stable, conscientious. Now, with the stunt he pulled last night thrown in my face, I'm again reminded of the toddleresque move he pulled right before Corinna's surgery where he refused to talk to her because she couldn't make it to the phone.

So, was it our engagement that became problematic and this was his quick way of disposing of it, or was he just punishing me for bad behavior? Either way, I don't care. He just gave me the final push I need to cut him loose and be done.

After heading downstairs, I stop in my studio to snatch up the ring. I catch sight of Mugsy lying near the window. Fierce bitterness fills me as I remember what my veterinarian said about certain types of pet owners who would have put their pets down long before I did. Bryan would have done that. Mugsy would have been disposable to him.

Bastard.

"You're not disposable to me, Mugs. You're irreplaceable," I say aloud. My throat becomes tight, and I hurry out away from my studio before I have to spend time repairing my makeup.

When I walk into Corinna's kitchen, I call out, "We have to take the Rover. We won't fit into any of your cars."

Corinna hands me my coffee. Taking a sip, I want to tell everyone to get out while I have an intimate moment with my drink. In the time I was upstairs, she made homemade caramel. "Tell me you didn't give these heathens"—I wave my arm to encompass our brother and sisters—"any of this caramel."

Corinna laughs. "There's a full jar in the fridge for you to take home later. I did let Phil lick the spoon though. He looked so pathetic."

"I am pathetic," Phil pipes in.

"At least you're owning it now. That's the first step—admitting you need help," Ali says dryly.

"That won't stop him from begging for your drink by the time we hit the road, Em," Cassidy predicts. Sweeping up the offending newspaper, she slips it into her bag. Narrowing her eyes at the ring I casually tossed on the counter, she says, "I can't believe he pulled the wool over our eyes."

Swallowing another drink of coffee, I shake my head. "Did he? I was remembering upstairs when Corinna was conflicted about him operating on her because of his attitude. He prettied up his apology and we all let it go. Maybe we should have paid more attention then."

Holly pipes in. "That's a good point, Em. And when has he hung out with the family since then unless you forced him to?" Murmurs of assent go around the room.

"And I'm not blameless. I jumped in too fast, said yes too quick," I say with disgust.

"Why did you?" Ali asks. The others look at me expectantly.

I open my mouth and close it a few times. I never talk about them, but maybe it's time to. "My parents had a whirlwind courtship, I was told. Apparently my father took one look at my mother and fell head over heels in love with her," I say quietly. You could hear a pin drop in the room it's that silent. "When Bryan kissed me that first time, it was like oh, wow. I thought maybe this could be the start of something. Obviously I was wrong."

"Or maybe you were completely right," Holly observes. Everyone, especially me, looks at her in shock.

"What do you mean?" I ask confused.

"You don't talk about them a lot, so we don't know about what your day-to-day life was like, Em. But in the end? Your father was a selfish prick who was willing to sacrifice the people he was supposed to love in order to save himself." She nods toward Cassidy's bag. "Sounds like another egomaniac we all now hate."

Shock holds me immobile. I can't move as I process her words because they're true. Once again, Holly's keen eye has seen below the layers into the heart and soul of a situation.

How many times over the last year have I mentally compared Bryan to my father? But unlike my mother, I was trying to find myself before I would never be lost. I just hadn't got there.

Until now.

Putting down my cup, I tip my chin up. "Holly?" My voice comes out cool and composed. Just like the ice princess I've been accused of being.

"Yes?" she replies warily.

"You are one hundred percent right. Now"—my voice hardens —"let's go officially break my engagement."

TURNING off Old Church Road in Greenwich, Phil parks my Land Rover next to Bryan's Mercedes. While I admire the design of the early-twentieth-century Victorian unit, deep in my heart, I knew there wasn't a chance in hell I was leaving my home on the family's farm to move here. Yet another bone of contention between me and Bryan that we'd argued over quite frequently.

Pulling his spare key from my bag, I gesture to my family to follow me. We march together as one force to the wraparound porch in front of Bryan's unit. I insert my key, twist, and step inside.

I almost take a header on the suit jacket. Phil catches me as I slip backward. "Whoa. Are you okay?"

My heartbeat picks up as my eyes follow the jacket my boots are tangled up in to the line of clothes leading toward the back hall where Bryan's master bedroom lies. Holding on to Phil's hand, I carefully step out of the twisted mess I've left of Bryan's suit coat. "Okay? No. I don't think that's the right word right now."

He asks, "Why not?" just as Holly goes, "Oh, shit."

She moved farther into the room, and she's holding up something. A dress.

Well, I guess that just confirmed the cheating question. Son of a bitch. I step closer. "That's the same dress from last night. I can't tell if it's mine or if it's a fake." I let out a huge sigh. It looks almost identical to one I designed, but my brain is going a million miles in a million different directions. I have to do one thing at a time. And right now, becoming free is most important. "I'll be just a few minutes. Take the dress with us. I'll want to look at it at some point. And see if you can find my shit in the hall closet. Maybe there's a bag we can use to get it out of here."

"What? He never even gave you a drawer?" Ali exclaims, heading toward the closet.

"I never was here long enough." Stalking off down the hallway toward Bryan's room, I'm in a fury. To me, there is no greater disrespect than cheating. It's essentially the living death of a relationship versus the kind of death I'm used to.

The kind that ends with a body in a casket.

When, I'm right outside Bryan's bedroom door, I raise my hand to knock when I hear a long, low moan. Yeah, to hell with the nice route. Throwing open the door, I'm careful to not let it slam.

I find my soon-to-be ex gripping the headboard of his bed while one of his esteemed colleagues is trailing her tongue over his cock. Calmly, I call out, "I'm surprised you can find it, Dr. Whitacre. I often found it has a problem of disappearing at inopportune times."

"Fuck, Emily." Bryan kicks his bedmate in the shoulder as he scrambles to cover himself. "It's not—"

"What I'm thinking?" I smirk. "Please. Have a decent-size pair of balls for once, Bryan. Own up to the fact you were enjoying a lovely morning screw before you have to get to the office."

"But Em, I thought you were engaged to him?" Corinna comes up behind me, pretend shock in her voice. "I mean, after all, he gave you a ring and everything."

I shake my head in mock sadness. "Don't you see, Cori? I refused to follow all my doctor's orders, so I guess he decided to take on another candidate for the clinical trial."

"Hmm. Well, we're done out there."

Bryan's face, which was pale before, flames in anger. "You brought your family into my home? How dare you!" He steps forward and yanks the sheet with him, exposing Dr. Whitacre's nakedness. She screeches as she scrambles to cover herself with pillows. "Bryan, damnit!"

Ignoring her, I focus on him. "No, the better question is how dare you? You have no moral high ground whatsoever. You're a pig of a human being, Bryan. A disgusting excuse for a man."

Shifting his focus to Corinna, he mutters bitterly, "I saved your life."

"And now I'm making sure Em has the rest of hers to live. Without you," Corinna adds. "I think in the long term, we'll all be better off without you in them."

"In case you're wondering, Bryan, we're through." I turn to leave when I feel his hand grip my arm.

"This was nothing—" he begins, but I cut him off. I'm pleased to hear a small whimper of sound from behind him. Maybe Dr. Whitacre will get out while she still can.

"Wrong." His eyes narrow on me. I rip my arm away as his fingers start to tighten. I'm almost certain there will be a bruise later. I don't give him the satisfaction of rubbing it. "I think you're a dick for the way you treat women. And not just me." My eyes drift over to where Dr. Whitacre is covering herself with pillows. "Good luck," I tell her sincerely. "You'll need it. The ring is on your kitchen bar. And don't try to say I didn't return it. If I know Ali, she's likely taken pictures."

Turning, I leave—disgusted and disillusioned. Another relationship dead.

What a shock.

My siblings don't say anything as I lead the way back to my Rover.

Not until Ali climbs into the far back seat, muttering, "I don't quite think this is over."

I turn my head. "What makes you say that?"

"Not now. Later, once I check up on a few things." Her eyes have gone unfocused.

Turning back in my seat, I face forward as Phil drives us back to Collyer.

I have no idea that the clusterfuck Bryan perpetrated is about to alter the course of my life.

8

EMILY

Ali was right. There were more repercussions than just the end of my engagement.

Things are starting to settle back to our old normal. I've heard nothing from Bryan, much to my relief. Slowly, I'm releasing the tension that's had me strung so tight I didn't realize I was this close to snapping. So, it's a pleasure to be eating Corinna's baked goods while joking around the conference room table after a weekend birthday party we planned and catered.

My sister's guys—Caleb, Keene, and Colby—are telling Phil's husband, Jason, about a case they just wrapped up for their investigative firm, Hudson Investigations.

"So, this guy decided he really doesn't want to have us digging into him," Caleb says with a benevolent smile. "It doesn't look good for a politician to have those kinds of secrets exposed."

Keene's sexy grin isn't anywhere as polite. Then again, he never is. "I have little doubt we'd find something to nail him with six ways from Sunday."

I roll my eyes. "Always so in tune with your sensitive side, Keene."

He leans back in his chair, crossing his hands over his lean stomach. "Only with those I love, Em. The rest of the world can go to hell."

"And that's why we don't let him in on client negotiations," Colby pipes in, amused. He reaches for one of Corinna's brownies on a platter in the center of the table.

"Colby, it's a miracle you're as healthy as you are living with Corinna. I say that as a doctor, mind you," Jason muses. "How can you live with all of those sweets all the time?"

"Oh, Cori doesn't bake like this at home. Only on special occasions. Our only indulgence is her caramel coffee."

I can't help but smile. "She made me a fresh jar the other morning."

Keene levels his green-eyed stare on me. "Bad thing letting me know that. If you find it missing, just know it's likely I've broken into your house to steal it. You won't be upset by that, will you?"

I'm laughing even as I shake my head. "If we knew years ago the way to tame you was to feed you sweets, Keene, we'd have asked Jason"—I nod to my other brother-in-law—"to set up a glucose mainline for you."

"I'm not as much fun when I'm tamed," he says dryly.

"I don't know about that, baby," I hear from behind me. I spin around and see Ali stride in with a file folder in her hand. "I think you're fun all the time."

There are moments in time when despite your own personal anguish, joy shines through. Seeing the softening of Keene's face every time he looks at my sister is one of those.

She's tapping the folder impatiently on her hip. "What's that?" I ask curiously.

"If I'm not mistaken, it's a way to potentially bring down people for what they did to you without more than a few phone calls," she says softly.

"I just want this over. We can just let this go. It will be okay." Eventually my pride will heal.

"This isn't solely because of you, Em," Ali says quietly. Sitting next to me, she slides the file over. "We actually could sue whomever made the dress for copyright infringement."

"What?" I open the folder. Inside is a contract. "What's this?" My voice trails off as I start to flip through the stack of papers and photos.

"I went through our files. While the dress Dr. Whitacre was wearing was your design, she isn't the one who bought the dress from us. That's the original contract from the Texan oil baron's wife who commissioned the dress—a referral from Danielle Madison." Ali mentions our family friend and a world-famous supermodel whom I've designed formal gowns for. I nod and she continues. "I figured in your shock, you might not have remembered who commissioned the dress." Ali has an unusually freakish genius brain we heavily rely upon. "I pulled up the contract and it explicitly states we don't have the right to reproduce that dress for over a year. That year isn't up for another four months, Em," she concludes.

Shit. This is huge. "I don't understand? Why would this have to do..." And then I freeze. I'm holding the pictures from the article that ousted Bryan and Dr. Whitacre.

"Those are the originals from the *Darien Times*, yes. I contacted the newspaper. I checked our files and saw there was no record of ever selling a dress to Dr. Whitacre. When I mentioned they might need to print a retraction, they were adamant Dr. Whitacre said it was an original. I demanded copies of the photos. They were all too happy to provide them."

"Where's the dress?" I demand.

"My office. Remember? I grabbed it on our way out the other morning," Ali says. "I put it away because I figured you wouldn't want to see it."

I sure as shit want to see it now. "Is there a magnifying glass in here?" I demand.

"Will an antique one work?" Jason asks, jumping up.

"I don't care. I just need something." There are certain marks I put on every original design that only the family and original design owners know about. Somewhere on the dress, there will be a hand-stitched amaryllis. My initials will also be sewn in somehow, either using beading, stitching, scratches on leather—something. Finally, there will be a dress number somewhere marked on the dress. Each dress has it hidden in a separate location.

Ali leaves the room and is back a few moments later with a white garbage bag. I use my nails to tear into it. I want to touch this dress as much as I want to go back to the hours while we were waiting to see if Corinna was going to live or die, but I have to know.

This isn't about retribution; this is about our family pride.

The room is eerily quiet as I sweep over the dress carefully using the magnifying glass. I remember the design. When I made the dress for Harper to wear to her daughter's wedding, she was thrilled I was able to make it flow so effortlessly into her daughter's theme. She was an absolute treasure to work with. Part of me is hoping she found another dress she loved more and this truly is the original.

The amaryllis should be on the outside of the left hip. It's not there.

Strike one.

That doesn't mean the stitching didn't come out, Em. Look for your initials in the hem where the beading touches the floor. This takes much longer and requires me looking through the hem at every single angle. I don't see it. All I see are flowers.

Strike two.

My anger increases as I look for the dress number. In this case, it should be stitched right under my initials with the beading as an overlay.

Strike three.

"It's a fake." I'm seething. I carefully lay down the magnifying glass before gathering the photos to hand them to Ali. "Find out where it was made and sue them all."

"Oh, it will be my absolute pleasure." Ali's cobalt-blue eyes are shining.

∾

It didn't take long for Ali—with the assistance of Caleb's brother-in-law Jared—to file a copyright infringement suit naming Dr. Bryan Moser and Dr. Corey Whitacre as the key witnesses.

Anticipating his reaction when he was served to appear in federal district court, Caleb and Keene arranged for their company to provide security both at Amaryllis Events and at the farm. Ali wasn't fazed in the least. She merely looked at her watch and said, "I give it twenty-four hours before either his attorney—or hers—contacts us to make a deal."

It ended up being Dr. Whitacre's attorney who did.

We are all silent as she follows her attorney into the conference room. "My client has something to say before we get down to business. Corey." He nods.

She clears her throat. Her face is haunted. "I apologize. He told me things had ended..."

Cutting her off before she can go any further, I raise my hand. "That's not why we're here today."

Her head drops. "That's not the kind of person I am," she whispers.

My eyes go to Colby's in the corner. He shakes his head. While I won't discuss Bryan, I will give her this. "It may not be you, but it is him. My advice?" Her head comes up, and I see her eyes are rimmed with red tears. "Find yourself again, Dr. Whitacre. Then move on."

She nods. Taking a deep breath, she says, "Bryan told me he had a special dress for me to wear..."

Corey Whitacre was a fountain of knowledge. By the time she was done being questioned, I figured out the timeline as to when this occurred. I now feel more foolish than ever because this was ultimately my fault.

About a month ago, I left Bryan in my studio fuming over an argument we had about my lack of understanding of what was involved in being a surgeon's wife when a frantic bride came in due to a torn train. My portfolio was lying on my desk—a mistake I'll never make ever again. As I was frantically sewing up the bride's dress, Bryan must have lifted the sketch.

I don't know what made him do it. I may never know. But if I'm infuriated with him, I'm disgusted with myself. My sketches are my heart and soul. I shouldn't have been so careless.

Before Dr. Whitacre left, she stopped in front of me. "I am truly, sorry, Ms. Freeman. For everything."

Knowing she likely has the least to be apologetic for, I nod. "Thank you for helping us."

"Come on, Corey." Her attorney lays a proprietary hand on her back. Holly, who's been standing next to me, elbows me in the ribs. No, I'm not immune to the vibe there. With time, maybe Dr. Whitacre will heal enough to see what's waiting for her.

After the conference room doors close, I let out a sigh of relief. "What's next?"

Ali leans back in her chair. "With the information Dr. Whitacre was able to provide to us about where she went for her fittings, we sic the guys on the money trail. Then, if we can't settle, we go before the judge."

I mull that over for a few minutes. "She didn't deserve for that to happen to her."

Ali glares. "Neither did you."

"It was my mistake in leaving my portfolio out," I admit quietly.

"In front of someone you were supposed to be able to trust? No judge is going to fault you for that." Ali stands and stretches. "This won't see the inside of a courtroom."

"How do you know?" My other siblings are in various states of relaxation around the room.

"Because—" Ali smiles knowingly. "—Dr. Moser won't like the repercussions if I go forward with the suit."

~

ALI WASN'T WRONG.

Once she had all the evidence in her hands, the news media picked up the case and it became public. Very public. There's both a curse and a blessing to small-town newspapers.

Greenwich Hospital found out and called their head of neurology in before the board and advised he was under suspension for failing to conduct himself in accordance with the ethical standards outlined in his contract. Pending the outcome of the investigation, he would either be reinstated or terminated.

As Caleb had an acquaintance who sits on the hospital board, he let him know Bryan panicked in the meeting. Ali was contacted within a few days by Bryan's attorney. In it was a detailed statement of the actions Bryan had committed when he stole my dress design. It contained the name of the designer who was previously accused of copying my work in the past with no proof. And now we have a notarized statement that can bring that son of a bitch down. There was also a terse apology at the bottom that I dismissed immediately because it was likely something Bryan's attorney recommended.

Ali turned the lawsuit focus toward the designer with guns blazing.

I don't know what to feel other than disgust I was taken in by such a man combined with an overwhelming relief that I could put this in the past and move on.

But to what, I have no idea.

9

JAKE

"Jenna, will you turn down your music so I can talk with you?" I yell from the bottom of the stairs. I can almost guarantee there's no way she heard me. *"Jenna!"* I yell at the top of my lungs.

Shit, if I have to listen to Lady Gaga one more time on repeat singing about taking someone home, I might hang myself by my guitar strap. I lower my head to the newel post. Whoever said raising a teenage daughter was easy was obviously taking large amounts of drugs to numb their senses. Raising Jenna is the hardest thing I've ever done. The second being the day Jenna's mother decided she no longer wanted to be burdened with a husband or daughter.

I can't blame Jenna for her bitterness; I'm filled with it myself. It's why I decided to take my cousin and her fiancé up on their offer to borrow their home on Nantucket. I applied for a teaching position on the island, making us one of its approximate 10,000 permanent year-round residents.

Jenna couldn't be more pissed.

I uprooted us right before her senior year of high school, but things were getting bad at home when I made that call. Right before the end of the school year, I had been contacted by the Loudoun

County Sherriff's Office because my little girl was at a party drunk and stoned off her ass. When I called her mother to discuss the situation, Michelle couldn't be bothered. She was too busy trying to settle down with her new lover.

Now, I was dealing with a sixteen-year-old who felt betrayed by her mother, hated me because I uprooted the only life she knew, and had barely any support system. I had a little more than a year left with the little girl I cradled in my arms seconds after her mother pushed her out before she left to go to college—providing she could get her act together to get in.

Stomping up the stairs, my own frustration boils over. "I swear to God, Jenna, if that music isn't turned down by the time I reach your room, I'm confiscating everything that plays music in this house and chucking it out the window."

Suddenly the music volume turns to a reasonable level and the door to her suite flies open. "Does that mean your music shit too, Dad?" she asks hopefully.

But now I've forgotten about the music.

"What the hell did you do to your hair?" I bellow. My daughter's perfectly golden locks are an array of color with magenta being the featured color.

She smirks. "Relax. It's color chalk. It'll come out as soon as I wash it."

I get right in her face. "Then go wash it. You have to go to work soon."

She rolls her eyes. "I spent hours doing this. There isn't a chance I'm changing it."

"Must you fight me on everything?"

"You're the one who brought me to this hellhole."

I snort. "Yeah because living in this house is such a hardship."

"I'll admit, Dani has good taste. Everything else about this island pretty much sucks."

I scoff. "Except for your new hair?"

She grins, and for just a moment, I have my little girl back. I want to put her crazy-ass hair in pigtails and turn time back about ten years to an age when she thought I hung the moon in her sky. "Come on, you have to admit, it's pretty damn cool."

The fact she did all this without clearing it with me aside, she did an incredible job. "I refuse to admit a thing." I give her a mock glare. "As long as it washes out," I caution sternly.

You'd think I just handed her the world. "You mean it? I can keep it in?" Her excitement is palpable.

"As long as it truly is chalk, Jenna. You know how I feel about lying."

"It is, Dad. Hold on." She races back into her room. Coming back with the packaging, she shows me that it may take a few washes due to the lightness of her natural hair, but in fact the chalk is washable. I give up the small battle to win the war of finding my daughter's heart after I crushed it a few months earlier.

"Just promise me you'll ask next time? What if you had a college interview or something?"

Jenna laughs. The sound is the music that warms my soul. "Chill, Dad. My hair won't be a problem where I want to go."

I swallow hard. I can't believe we're actually having this conversation with some semblance of calm. "So, you've been thinking about it?"

Turning, she walks into her room and flops back on her queen-size bed. I cringe when I imagine washing the sheets with the hair chalk covering them. Jenna's books and sketch pads cover practically every surface. "Thinking about it? It's all I've thought of."

Finding an open space, I sit on the edge of the bed. Laying my hand on hers, I ask, "So, where did you decide?" UMass wouldn't be hard for her to get into. Wellesley might be a stretch, I muse. So would Brown. Lord knows, she's as talented as I am at music, so maybe NYU or Juilliard?

"I'm going to go to Rhode Island School of Design for their apparel design program. You know RISD, right?" she announces proudly.

She would have shocked me less if she hit me with a two-by-four. Fashion? My torn T-shirt and Army-pant-wearing daughter wants to go to school for fashion? What a load of crap. "Like hell you are!" I roar.

"Dad!"

~

JENNA and I continue to argue until she storms off. After she hops on her scooter to go to work, I head to the basement of my cousin's house. I need music therapy right now desperately.

Luckily, when Dani moved in, the old cinema that used to be here was converted to a music space both her fiancé and I could happily spend every waking moment in. Sitting down at the perfectly tuned baby grand piano, I warm up my hands by playing run after run of scales. Up and down the beautiful ivory keys, my fingers fly at a speed indicative of my mood. Sometimes it's languid and slow, sometimes it's bouncy and joyful. Today, my fingers are crashing down on the keys like I'm trying to drill them through the handcrafted base that holds them.

Soon, I'm lost in the wonders of Chopin and Schubert. My emotions begin to settle when my phone buzzes on top of the piano indicating a FaceTime call. I slam my hands down in the middle of Chopin's 12 Etudes, Op. 10: No.12 In C Minor. There's only one person who persistently wants to FaceTime me.

"What do you want, Danielle? Still having problems convincing your favorite designer to make your latest red-carpet fashion statement for you?" I snap rudely.

"No, but I wouldn't ask her. She's having some personal problems. Anyway, did I interrupt you in the middle of playing with your toys in the music room again?" she coos. Most men would be brought to their knees by the sheer beauty of the woman on the other end of the line. To me, supermodel Danielle Madison has been, and always will be, a royal pain in my ass. Then again, when you're raised next door to each other by fathers who are twins, it's more like having an annoying younger sister you just can't get rid of.

"It's been a day," I grit out. "Jenna is trying my last nerve, and we still have almost two months before school starts."

"What happened?" she asks, her brow lowering to a V.

Dani loves Jenna as much as if she were her own, so I know the concern is genuine. I recount our conversation including her latest whim about becoming a fashion designer when she's never expressed any sort of interest in it before. When I get to that part of the story, Dani's face goes blank.

"Jake, you know I love to disagree with you just for the sake of it. But..." Her voice trails off.

An unsettled feeling lodges in my stomach. "What is it?"

"She's been interested in design for a while. I have hundreds of emails from Jenna about the business."

I gape at her. "She can always talk with me!" I exclaim.

Dani looks at me knowingly. "How did you react to the hair chalk?"

My lips press together.

"Did you know that people at her job have been doing this for months and have been on her case because she hasn't tried it yet? Did you know she's petrified to ask you to change anything about how she looks because she's afraid you only see her as a little girl and won't let her grow up? I've said this before, Jake. She's maturing. Changing. She has questions. Now she's coming to me with them."

That unsettled feeling in my gut just exploded into a rancid nausea threatening my lunch from coming back up. "What do I do, Dani?"

She shakes her head. "I can't work that out for you. All I can do is be there for both of you the way I am now. The way I always will be."

I lean my elbows on the keys of the piano and a discordant sound comes out. Resting my eyes in the heels of my hand, I whisper, "Thanks."

"I wasn't just calling to say hi though."

Pulling one hand away, I catch Dani biting her lower lip—a sure tell. "What did you do?"

"That designer with the problems I was telling you about? She needs a place to get away for a little while." Lord help me. This is the last thing I need right now.

I jump to my feet. "Oh, come on! You promised until Jenna and I worked things out, there would be no renting of the apartment to any strangers."

"I'm not renting it, and this person isn't a stranger. She's a wonderful person. She's just taken a lot of hard knocks lately."

"Just like everyone else in the world," I say bitterly. "So, in addition to a hormonal teenage girl..."

"Young woman," Dani corrects me irritably.

"Young woman," I parrot in her higher-pitched voice. Reverting to my own, I continue. "I now need to look out for a woman who's emotionally unstable?"

"You don't have to look out for her at all, Jacob. All you have to do is make certain the apartment above the garage is in working order," Dani says irritably. "Emily is certainly able to look out for herself."

"If that's the case, then why is she coming here?" I counter.

"She's very...self-contained. I don't even know the full story. Yet. Have a good day, cousin." She moves her hand to disconnect.

"Hey, wait. When is she coming?" I yell frantically before she can press the red telephone icon ending our call.

"Anytime now. I left her arrival open for her."

"And a pain in the ass for me? How generous of you," I bite out.

"Whatever works. See you soon." She hangs up before I can say anything else.

If my phone hadn't just been replaced, I'd throw it across the room. Instead, I slam my hands back on the ivory and black keys in front of me and pick up where I left off. Chopin was certainly getting a workout tonight.

10

EMILY

"I wish you'd kept the ring," Holly grumbles. She's sitting on my bed watching me pack.

"Why? I don't need a tangible reminder of that asshole in my life." I'm holding a pile of carefully folded shirts that I place in my Coach duffle bag. "What the hell kind of clothing am I going to need on Nantucket?" I gripe aloud.

Holly shrugs. "It's an island, Em. Beachwear?"

I frown. "It's an island off the coast of Massachusetts, Hols. It's not exactly the tropics."

Holly flops back on my bed and pulls out her phone. Letting out a screech, she exclaims, "Holy shit, Em! How are you supposed to get a tan? If it hits eighty, you'll be lucky."

Mentally adding a few sweaters and jeans to my ever-growing pile of clothes, I head back to my closet. "Do you think I'll need a dress for anything?" I call out.

"For what? The island is mostly casual, isn't it?"

"How the hell am I supposed to know?" I grumble. "I've never been there." I come out with three pairs of Tieks—only the best ballet flats on the planet—and a stack of leggings in every color imaginable. "I wish you guys would come with me."

Holly's face softens. Rolling off the bed, she comes to me and wraps her arms around me. "I wish we could. Maybe we can come up for some of the time once wedding season starts to slow down a bit."

I lean into her. "I feel like I'm deserting you all."

"Em, most of your work is done. Your brides all picked out their dresses months ago. Yes, it sucks you won't be here for the fittings, but we hired a seamstress to cover for you. You need to get away to deal with everything. It hasn't been an easy few weeks for you."

No, it hasn't.

Between finding out about Bryan's infidelity, breaking my engagement, and suing the designer who was reproducing my designs from the sketches Bryan gave them, my nerves are completely shot.

And that was before I received a phone call that could change my life.

The CEO and president of the Council of Fashion Designers of America, Inc., Wesley Barnes, called our offices a few days ago. He'd heard through a mutual acquaintance about Amaryllis Designs once again suing over copyright infringement over my designs. While thoroughly disgusted by the events in general, he said if people were willing to steal my work, there must be something worth stealing. After reviewing a portfolio pulled together by his assistant, he was recommending I join fifty other CFDA artists in displaying a collection at Bridal New York Fashion Week.

I fell out of my office chair with a thud.

"Ms. Freeman, in truth, you will be replacing the designer who stole your designs." I gasped in shock at the way karma was rewarding me. "Our attorneys spoke with your sister. We all find it in our best interest to present a united front in eliminating this individual from the CFDA community swiftly and with consequences." While I absorbed that, Barnes continued. "You will be taking over his space at the Skylight at Moynihan Station, which has already been reserved. Your company will need to absorb that cost. There's no time left to make other arrangements. It's going to be tight enough getting your designs completed as it is." Pausing, he asked me, "Are you ready to take this next step in your career?"

From my position on the floor, the pride on my family's faces radiated at me as they all nodded frantically. Cassidy brushed tears from her cheeks. Phil had his arms wrapped around her. They knew from the moment I enrolled at the University of Charleston, this had been my dream. I'd just never believed it could come true. "Yes, sir. I am."

"The only creative control you will have will be over the presentation of your own designs and your model selection," he warned me. "Is this how you want your debut to begin?"

"Sir, I just want a chance to prove I can do it. I'll make it work," I said confidently at the time.

Now, less than forty-eight hours later, I'm strung so tight someone could probably use me to play a song. But yesterday I realized I can't be here right now. I have to get find some peace in order to find my creative spark before I'm mired under the weight of my emotions.

"How are you getting everything you need to the island anyway? You're not driving alone, are you?" Holly frets.

I shake my head. "Caleb offered his company jet to fly me there. The guys asked around their office. One of their analysts is actually planning on heading to Cape Cod next week on vacation. I offered to pay him to drive my stuff up and then transport it over on the ferry. Caleb is being his usual awesome self and giving him an extra few days of comp time to help me out."

"That's cool. What about transportation when you're first on the island? It's larger than you think."

"Dani said she'd have her place stocked with groceries and food for Mugsy. I sent her a list. It's not like I cook anyway."

"You at least do that better than you sing."

I throw a pillow at her, but I can't contradict her. I know I have a terrible voice. At least I can throw a salad together. No one—and I do mean no one—wants to hear me carry a tune.

"Seriously, though, what about day-to-day things? What about internet? What about coffee?" She jumps to her knees. "Em, what are you going to do if you can't get coffee?"

"There are bikes, Hols. You know, with baskets and whatnot? It's only eight miles to the center of town," I say absentmindedly.

"I'm sorry, did you turn into Ali overnight? Eight miles? Are you crazy? That's *sixteen miles* to get a cup of coffee until you get your car. Are you sure you can't load your car on the plane?"

"Maybe they have Uber?" I say weakly.

"Or maybe you should bite the bullet and bring a Keurig with you," she retorts.

Corinna strolls in with Ali and Cassidy right behind her. "Relax, both of you. Em, after you talked to her, Dani forgot a few things and tried to call you. Since she couldn't reach you, she pinged me. I have a rundown about life on Nantucket. They have Uber. They have cabs. And after I laughed over the idea of Em cooking, she said she'll make sure there's a Keurig at the apartment. Em will survive."

Corinna continues. "Dani also said to tell you there's a heated pool on the property and not to forget a swimsuit. You might not want to dive into the Atlantic without a wetsuit, but the pool should be perfect to swim in."

"Bathing suit, check." I head back into my regular closet and grab a few bikinis, cover-ups, and flip-flops. I drop the new items on the bed and fall facedown on top of them. "Ugh. I feel like I'm going away forever, when I'm really just going for a few months."

Cassidy rubs my back. "It's not like we're not just a call away whenever you need us, Em."

I blow a curl out of my face so I can see her more fully. "Why don't each of you come with me? For a week at a time?"

Ali laughs from my easy chair in the corner. "Maybe later in the summer, one or two of us can make it up. I'm sure you'll settle in just fine."

"I'm not." Right now, I trust the members of my family. That's it. Everyone else I have good reason to be wary of. Though we've become friends through the work we do together for her red-carpet events, even Dani and her generosity are leaving me out of sorts.

"Don't let what Bryan did close you off to the world, Em," Corinna says softly. "Those mistakes are his for being an asshole, not yours for wanting something more."

I laugh, but it comes out a bitter, wretched sound. "I have little belief at this point that I can find love without destroying it."

"You haven't looked around the room," Cassidy says firmly. "We all love you, and we're not going anywhere. And if Phil were here, he'd say the same thing."

I open my mouth and then close it, unable to tell them the real reason why I can love them safely. That reason is written on the back of a drawing hidden away in a safe in my closet. The vow I took if God would just stop stealing the people I love away from me. I knew then the love—the sheer overwhelming love my adopted brother and sisters have given to me—is something I knew I could never live without. They are the ones who get to see the real me—the woman who spits her drink when she laughs too hard, can't sing worth a damn so does it at the top of her lungs, and thinks the best color is the rainbow. They're the ones who know I'd rather capture a lifelong memory in a drawing than a picture. They know my biggest regrets, my smallest fears, and they love me anyway.

But they don't know I bargained my future happiness for it.

So, I settle for the truth.

"I'm going to be so lost without you all."

Suddenly, my body is smooshed into the bed as each one of my sisters climbs on top of me in some way. We look like a pack of football players in a huddle after a loose ball. "Love you, Em." Cassidy tugs one of my curls.

"Love you both," Ali murmurs from where she's lying across us.

"Love you all," Corinna calls out cheerfully. She's diagonal over Ali, but her boobs might be smothering Cassidy.

"Love you always," Holly calls from her perch on top.

I don't say it, but I feel it so strongly my heart's about to burst. And for just a moment, the walls I've carefully built are lowered and the silence around my heart isn't painful. It's comforting as the bonds of sisterhood fill it.

We're all smooshed together still when Ali says, "Jesus, I hope no one farts. I've got three asses in my face."

And with that, we collapse with laughter.

How on earth am I supposed to find my balance without them when I've never been my best except with them?

11

JAKE

Dani called back to let me know her pain-in-the-ass friend is supposed to be arriving today along with what seems like a million other tourists who want to take refuge on Nantucket. Her orders to go buy her friend supplies royally pissed me off. Apparently either this chick is a model or she has no cooking skills whatsoever because there is no real food in addition to having to purchase yogurt, fruit, and fresh vegetables, some cheese and wine. I also had to purchase single-serving Keurig cups. Which of course meant buying a Keurig. And dog food that cost as much as the entire grocery bill.

Jesus, I bet it's some kind of yap-yap dog that's going to keep me up all hours of the night. Just what I need.

Lugging all of the bags up the garage steps, I stop dead in my tracks when I see two suitcases, a large black duffle, and an oversized slouchy bag sitting outside the door. Glancing at my watch, I mutter, "Shit." She's already here.

Dropping all the bags near her luggage, I wander along the porch that wraps around the garage apartment. I don't find Dani's mystery guest seated at either the table and chairs nor the lounger I spent most of yesterday scrubbing down with Jenna's reluctant help. Lifting my hand to shade my eyes from the sun's overwhelming glare, I spot a lone figure on the sand.

Well, as long as she's occupied for a few minutes, I might as well bring in the groceries. Turning, I stomp back along the deck. When I get to the door, I sigh in disgust. It looks like I'll have to carry in her ladyship's bags before I can bring in anything. Using the set of keys I plan on turning over before returning to my regularly scheduled life of arguing with my daughter and then taking it out on my music, I unlock the side door to the apartment.

Memories assail me the minute I cross the threshold. Leaning against the jamb, I wonder how many times Michelle, Jenna, and I stayed here before our lives disintegrated. Ten? Twenty? Does it really matter now? Except as I cross to the bedroom with the first two bags, I can see the scuff marks made by Jenna's exersaucer when she was a baby. I remember being horrified and Dani just laughing, saying it gave the room character. Squatting down, I run my fingers over the floors, which have been re-stained but never buffed out.

"I sure as hell hope you can explain who you are. Otherwise, I'm pressing Send to call the police," a cold voice says from the doorway. "I was told by the owner no one should be in this apartment when I got here."

Lifting my head, I see a woman who's dressed like she belongs on a runway right next to my cousin. Two words scream through my brain: high maintenance. It doesn't matter she's wearing shredded jeans and a studded tank top, I recognize the sunglasses on her eyes as Armani since Dani did a photoshoot for them last year. "Couldn't be bothered to pick up a bag on your way in, lady?" I bite out as I push to my feet.

If anything, her voice gets colder. "Not when I'm uncertain who you are and what you're doing."

"The groceries didn't give it away?" Dani said some of her friends weren't the brightest. This must be one of them. "Let me spell it out for you. This is a onetime delivery of food for you and your mutt." I strain my eyes to get a look at her dog, but I can't hear it, which I suppose is a good sign.

It's boiling outside by Nantucket summer standards, but I feel like I'm in the middle of one of our coldest winters in this room with this woman. "If you let me know the amount you spent, I will be happy to pay you cash for your troubles right now."

I shake my head in disgust. "Dani already took care of everything." I expect to see the ice around her thaw. Instead she frowns, either upset or disturbed, I can't tell. Frankly, I don't care.

"I'll have to contact her. That was—unexpected," she says softly. Turning around, she moves back toward the door. Picking up her last two bags, she places them on the couch and begins rooting through one of them.

"No problem," I say sarcastically. "I'll just grab the food."

She pulls out an object and pops it open. I catch the glint of a mirror as the sunlight reflects off it. Oh, dear God. Is she checking her makeup? I make a mental note to keep Jenna as far away from this person as humanely possible. Grabbing handfuls of bags in my fists, including the brand-new Keurig, I turn just in time to hear a loud snap as it closes. Suddenly, sunglasses have been replaced by red glasses frames that display the darkest blue eyes I've ever seen.

And they're looking at me in disgust.

I realize I must have voiced some of my thoughts out loud when she says, "No, I wanted to be able to see what I was doing. Now, if you'll give me my keys, I'm more than capable of putting away all of the stuff and settling in. Oh, but don't let me be so rude," she adds snidely. Reaching into her monstrosity of a purse, she pulls out several bills. Folding them, she shoves them into my hands. "There's your tip for being half of a human and doing me a favor. Since my car with the rest of my stuff won't be delivered until next week, I have no way of getting around the island." I'm frozen in shock—whether that's because she has more crap or because she's so brittle, I don't know —but she moves to the door and grabs the rest of the groceries. After moving them toward the kitchen, she comes back and holds out her hand. "Now, hand over the keys and get out. I'll be sure to tell the homeowner and your employer what a fabulous job you did with your delivery."

Holy shit. She has no idea who I am. No wonder she was so hostile when she first came in. I can almost see the humor in the situation now. "Listen, Ms...." I wait for her to supply her last name because I can't remember if Dani ever gave it to me or not.

Her stony face says reveals nothing.

I clear my throat. "Right. I should probably tell you—" I don't have a chance to say more because she cuts me off.

"Can I have the keys please?"

I pull them from my pocket and hold them out to her, face up on my palm. Taking them, she slides them into her pocket. "Again, I appreciate your assistance." Moving to the door, she stands by it.

Shaking my head, I walk through the door. I'm on the other side of the threshold when I give her what I think will be something for her to think on. "Has anyone told you you're a complete icy bitch?"

It takes her less than a half a second to reply. "All the damn time."

Right before she slams the door in my face.

"I can't believe you were such a jackass to Emily," Dani screeches in my ear hours later.

"She threatened to have me arrested," I protest. I take a pull of the beer I'm drinking as I sit on the back deck admiring the view of the Atlantic Ocean at sunset. It stirs something in me, the swirling orange, pinks, and red hues of the sky. It almost makes me feel like grabbing my sax from downstairs and letting loose with some Coltrane. It's full of soul. But I haven't picked up that instrument in more years than I care to count. The sax requires a certain combination of feeling.

And they're not inspired by the ice brick living next door.

"Listen, you dick, I just found out what's really going on. You have no idea of the crap she's been through in the past few weeks, so cut her some slack."

Curious, I ask, "Why don't you tell me?"

"Because it's not my story to tell. Would you want someone going around telling stories about me? About you? About Jenna?"

"Hell no," I say emphatically.

"Then let me just say she has good reason to be wary of the world in general—men especially." The disgust in Dani's voice reminds me of all the phone calls we shared when she was first starting out in the modeling business. I frown. Maybe a photographer got handsy with her? Someone wanted to sleep with her for a job? I know Dani went through her fair share of bullshit when she was first starting out. My protective instincts kick in.

"Fine. I'll go apologize." If I had a choice, I think I'd rather let Jenna dye her hair permanently the colors it was this morning. I lift my beer to my lips.

"How about just not going out of your way to be a complete asshole?" Dani suggests. "Besides, I can't believe Em had that severe of a reaction once you told her who you were."

I pause in the act of drinking. Shit, this is going to go downhill. "I think there's more than a little misconception between your friend Emily and I."

There's a deathly quiet on the other end of the line. "What do you mean?" Her voice is lethal. Kind of like the way it got when we were kids and I cut off all her Barbie dolls' hair.

"I never introduced myself to your friend." Sliding my hand into my pocket, I finger the hundred dollars Emily gave me. "I kind of got sidetracked."

A soft feminine voice with a hint of a drawl comes from behind me. "Is that before or after you called me an icy bitch, Jacob?" I whirl around to find Emily has added a loose sweatshirt on top of the outfit she was wearing earlier. "After I talked with Dani and found out who you were, I figured I'd make amends." A dark smile crosses her face. "Then again, maybe I don't need to after all."

12

EMILY

So, this is Dani's cousin Jacob Madison. Now that I'm getting a good look at him, I can the see the Madison genes breed true. He's disturbingly good-looking with a chiseled jawline and blond hair that's obviously had his hands run through it, tempting a woman to sink her own hands in there.

Too bad he's a man and I've mentally sworn them off for the foreseeable future while I figure out who the hell I am again under the impossible pressure of designing a collection to knock Fashion Week on its ass.

When I have the chance to design clothes for her, Dani talks openly about the love she has for Brendan and her immediate family. And all of them were thrilled when Brendan asked her to marry him earlier this year in their home in Nashville. But during one of our fittings, Dani's admitted to being worried about the relationship between her cousin and his teenage daughter. I'm beginning to understand why. If her niece is anything like my adopted sisters were at that age, then her brusque father must seem like an overbearing pain in the ass.

"I just came to reimburse you—Dani—for the groceries and coffee maker." Holding out a stack of twenties, I march straight forward. I ignore the tingling of my body as his hand scrapes against mine when he accepts the money. "It was generous, but I pay my own way."

"Dani, I'll call you back," he mutters into the phone. He arches a brow. "I suppose I should offer an apology."

"Not if you don't mean it." I change the subject. "Are there any rules I need to know while I stay here?"

His eyes narrow. They're a beautiful shade of mahogany brown with long, dark lashes that contrast with his sun-tipped hair. My artist's mind is already taking note of the details of his face.

God, he's got one hell of a face.

I frown. I shouldn't be noticing it. Not after everything.

"Like what?" His voice is about as welcoming as the iceberg was to the *Titanic*.

I sigh. "Like, can I walk my dog without a leash on the beach? What are the rules about parking? Is there anything I need to avoid on the property?"

"Most of the beach on the island is private, including ours. While there is technically a leash law, as long as it's your property, your little yap-yap dog can be off the leash as long as you have it under control." Jake's voice is full of derision.

I'm vaguely amused. "You think I have a dog that's going to disturb you?"

"I'm almost certain of it," he concludes.

"Why's that?"

"Because just your being here is bound to be a pain in the ass."

Now, I'm half-amused, half-offended. "How do you handle regular renters?"

"I don't. And Danielle promised me there would be none of those until we were gone."

"I see." And I truly do. "Then if you could answer the question about parking?"

"If you plan on renting a car, then park on the right side of the garage. It's filled with junk, but at least you won't block me in." Turning his back to me, he stalks off down the wraparound deck.

"I didn't have any other questions, thanks!" I call out. He pauses, turns, and stalks back to me.

"Listen, lady. I didn't want you here. We have family issues we're trying to work out. Just stay out of my way and maybe we'll be able to endure your visit while you recover from the broken nail you're dealing with this week."

Holding up my hands, I show off my perfectly polished nails.

"Well, damn. It must have been a really rough week," he drawls. "What happened? Get into a fight over a man?"

His snarky words strike a little too close to home. "Actually, I ended my engagement to a lying, cheating bastard who also stole from me." Ignoring the chastised look on his face, I shrug. "I guess I'm so shallow it was probably my fault though, right?"

"Emily..." There's sympathy in his voice I neither need nor want.

"Please." My tone is derisive. I can't resist saying, "Why don't we keep your own little brand of sunshine in your corner and I'll stay in mine?"

Turning, I start to walk down the stairs that head toward the garage apartment. I hear him call out, "If you need anything, let me know!"

Hell might freeze over before I ask this man for help. I just flick my hand over my shoulder as I cross the decking that connects our two properties. Even through my own stress, I haven't forgot the life lessons my aunt taught me. Be strong. Be courteous. Be polite unless you absolutely can't. Because kindness is free and can set about a chain reaction of events.

What is it about Jacob Madison that drives me over the edge away from those lessons?

13

JAKE

It seems my luck with women is consistent this week. I'm on the outs with my cousin, my daughter, *and* my new neighbor. Dani hasn't returned my calls since she hung up on me after finding out I was an asshole for no other reason than I was put out. Jenna is still pissed over my reaction to her announcement. Since then, the only words I've received are in writing and directly pertain to her work schedule. I let out a harsh breath in pace with the slapping of my feet in the hard sand. I have no idea what to do other than tell Jenna that I've looked at RISD and ask her what she plans on doing if she can't make it as a designer.

It's a pipe dream. It's fantastical. Sure, she's an amazing artist, but a designer? That takes a practicality and a cutthroat attitude I'm not sure exists in my baby girl.

Churning my legs harder, I disrupt a flock of shore birds as I pound past. It's early morning and the beach is deserted. I'm taking advantage of this incredible weather to get in a workout before I have to suffer the evil dread-mill in the harsh winter months.

Coming to Nantucket was both a good and miserable decision. It got me and Jenna out of the rut we were in, but it's put us smack in the middle of other memories. I feel like I'm battling so much pain on so many sides, there's not enough happiness to combat it. Do I capitulate under the whims of my daughter in order to work our way back to us? Should I just give in?

No, I tell myself firmly, picking up my stride. Jenna has to demonstrate why she wants this as much as why she'd want any other school. And somehow, I feel like this is just another test of hers, another button to push to see how far she can aggravate me. *Be strong. Set the example for her now*, I lecture myself as I huff in another breath. This way she won't be so flighty with her decisions.

Not like her mother.

Pausing, I drop my hands to my knees and pant. Marriage to Michelle wasn't perfect—not by a long shot. We were too young when she got pregnant. I was barely twenty-one; Michelle had just turned twenty. But I thought we were in love. I knew with a little hard work, we could make it as a little family.

But while I grew up the very second Jenna was put into my arms, my dreams of becoming a professional musician being put aside in order to support my family, Michelle never did. After the initial newness wore off, she wanted the life we had before. She wanted the man she'd met who seduced her with his saxophone from behind the bright lights of the stage. She wanted the man who would croon to her alone in a room full of strangers.

I had no clue she began to seek that attention out while I was home watching Jenna. She claimed she was going to work, to school, to mommy support groups. She wasn't lying about work or school; it would have been hard to lie about those as I took care of the bills. But God, was I a fucking fool. I believed her when she said all the mommies drank glasses of wine to alleviate their stress. Michelle was so much happier, so our little world was.

This went on for years until the night Jenna got so sick she had to go to the hospital.

I spent hours trying to get a hold of my wife. I tried the few of her friends I knew. They all clucked sympathetically about Michelle but did tell me to get Jenna to the hospital immediately. After all, a fever of 104 was nothing to joke around about in a child.

I was in the hospital for four hours when the text came in. It was from Michelle's best friend. It was a photo captioned with *I'm sorry*. So was I when I saw a close-up of my wife sitting on a local bar top where my ex-bandmate had his tongue shoved down her throat. The betrayal burned like I swallowed battery acid. I remember typing back two words—*How long?*—before pressing Send. Then I put the phone away and focused on the small blonde girl in the bed. Because ultimately, it didn't matter.

My marriage was over. All that mattered was Jenna.

Another rotation of doctors came through before I ever heard from my "wife." Her frantic entrance into the ER sent everyone into a tailspin. Quietly, so as not to disturb our daughter, I told her, "I'd use this time to go home and pack your shit. Leave a forwarding address. Touch one thing I bought, touch one thing of Jenna's, and I'll eviscerate you in court before I divorce you."

"I fell asleep on Tay's sofa, Jake..." she started. Whipping out my phone, I hissed, "That's so obvious. Now get out so I can care for my daughter."

We were twenty-seven and twenty-six respectively. Since that time, I can only count a handful of times Michelle's had contact with Jenna. It hasn't been because I've prevented it. It's because Michelle's been on her own path finding who she is. As Jenna's grown older, she gets a cynical look in her eyes when she talks about her mother.

Dani's stepped in to become the strong female role model in Jenna's life. Standing to my full height, I scrub my hands over my face. I shouldn't be surprised she wants to go into fashion, should I? After all, when your cousin is the most famous fashion model on the planet, you're bound to absorb some of that. I let out a harsh sigh.

"It's too beautiful a morning to start it out poorly. So, I'll say good morning and excuse me." The third woman whom I've managed to piss off starts to move past me to avoid the crashing waves. I blink. Emily has a backless tank, sports bra, and running shorts on. I almost trip over my feet in the sand as I see the length of her legs eating up the distance, a steely, fixed determination on her face. Jesus, watching her is incredible. Then I almost fall over for a completely different reason. Laughter starts low in my gut, and it takes everything in me not to let it out.

Completely ruining her sophisticated look, her curls are pulled into two pigtails that are dancing around her head. I can't help but grin, especially when I look down and see the dog next to her.

This isn't a yap-yap dog. This is a beloved family member.

"Good morning, Emily." I drop to a knee. "Hey, old man." He walks up to me and gives my face a lick. "Oh, you're such a good boy, aren't you." Emily's cool demeanor falls away, and her perfect stride falters. I frown. "Are you okay?" Despite her confidence running, sand is challenging to run in even for experienced runners.

"I'm fine, Jacob. I'm just...never mind. We'll leave you to your morning. Come on, Mugs." She turns to take off, but I make a snap decision. Maybe I can mend one of my problems.

"Do you mind if I run with you for a few?" I ask casually. Her head snaps around so fast one of her pigtails slaps her in her face. I have to hold back the smile threatening my face.

"Go ahead and laugh. Everyone else makes fun of me for running with pigtails," she grumbles. Turning, she starts off down the beach at a pace comfortable for her dog to trot next to her. Since she didn't say no, I follow after them.

We jog in companionable silence for a few moments before I break it. "Who makes fun of your pigtails?" I actually think they're kind of cute. They're not at all what I expected out of the woman who displayed such cool hauteur a few days ago.

Her breathing steady, she replies, "Phil openly laughs at me. Ali rolls her eyes. Cass, Cori, and Holly just giggle. But it's the only way I can get through this torture." When her watch beeps a few moments later, she lets out a whoop of excitement. Slightly under her breath she mutters, "Now I can get them all off my back."

"Who?" I find I'm mildly curious about this friend of Dani's.

"My family." She bends over and stretches her hamstrings.

I mentally go over what she said while I'm distracted by the tug of her tight shorts against her ass. No one had a classification. "You're married? I thought you said you were engaged? Are those your kids?"

Snorting from her upside-down position, she lifts her head so it's perpendicular to the ground. "Not married. And not likely to be."

"Then who are all those people?" Really, she doesn't owe me an answer, but curiosity has me hoping she'll tell me. If anything it's a distraction from thoughts I should absolutely not be having.

Straightening, Em reaches my shoulder. She must be five nine, maybe five ten. Now that I think about it, she's a lot shorter than my cousin. At six foot two inches tall, I'm barely an inch taller than Dani. "My brother and sisters," she relents.

Suddenly, the ache I was developing flees in my frustration. If she's so close to her family, why isn't she staying with one of them? Why is she invading my space? Emily's frozen in place. It isn't until she opens her mouth and the ice princess reappears that I realize once again my internal filter has failed me.

"I didn't stay with them because I actually live with them on an enormous farm. I couldn't stay there due to some personal and professional reasons. But trust me, I'd have stayed in a No-Tell Motel off I-95 if I thought I wouldn't be judged." Turning, she begins striding down the beach, her long legs eating up the distance quickly. Mugs takes off after her, darting in and out of the water at the shoreline like a little puppy.

"Emily!" I call out.

As she runs through the flock of shore birds, she throws up a bird of her own.

And I have to admit, I deserve it.

So much for making amends with my new neighbor, I think glumly as I kick at the sand. Deciding to give Emily the respite she needs, I walk back the mile to the stairs leading from the house to the beach.

Later as I stand naked under the shower, I wonder if I should make a peace offering by driving my new neighbor into town to get groceries. There's no way what I bought will last her more than just a few days. While I'm there, I can drop by to see Jenna at work. But soon, I'm absorbed in maintenance around the property and completely lose track of time.

By the time I remember to go ask her if she needs anything,

there's no answer at her door. Letting out a sigh, I turn around and head back to the main house. Heading down to the music room, I sit down with my guitar and start strumming out some chords before letting the music carry me away.

But I can't get dancing blonde curls and dark blue eyes out of my mind.

14

EMILY

I shouldn't have run so far today. Despite my enjoyment of being able to lord it over Phil during a FaceTime call earlier, I'm tired. Then I realized I only gave Dani a list of minimal dairy items to tide me over for a few days not knowing what would be available here locally to my liking. Groaning, I open the refrigerator. I have nothing to eat for dinner, not even yogurt. I'm going to have to head into town or call around to see if a local merchant will deliver.

Leaving Mugsy resting in a pile of blankets on the couch, I debate my choices. I could walk, but I know I won't be able to carry the groceries home. I look up the Uber prices and practically choke. There's something in my upbringing from Aunt Dee that, despite the wealth I enjoy now, won't allow me to pay that much for an eight-mile ride. Talk about highway robbery! Now I begin to understand the reason why Holly was so worried about me without my Rover.

It looks like walking is going to be my only choice, because I refuse to pay the exorbitant prices to have some coffee creamer, brick cheese, and milk delivered. I'm equally unwilling to ask Jacob for a favor after the attitude he persistently throws at me. God, I can't wait for my vehicle to be back at my disposal.

I head down the stairs to the gravel driveway when through the window, I spy an old bike in the garage. I'm sure I can bike the eight miles into town. Right? I mean, Nantucket is an island and islands are flat. I should be able to handle this with no problem at all. Walking around the side of the garage, I test the doorknob. It smoothly opens. Excellent.

I make my way over to the bike and pull it from the pile. I navigate it around a Honda Pilot, praying I don't ding the paint. Successfully getting it outside, I give it a critical overview. It looks like it just needs to be cleaned up with a metric ton of Lysol wipes. Then, I can lose myself in the glorious view from somewhere other than this apartment.

THE INVENTOR of the bicycle should be brought back to life and shot to death in front of a firing squad.

I have no idea what I was thinking. The directions on my iPhone said thirty-nine minutes. It's now been closer to an hour and ten minutes. Since I've started, cars have driven by me at unusually high rates of speed, cursed at me from their convertible tops, and flicked me off out of their moon roofs. I hope and pray one of those assholes is on a bike once my Rover arrives in a few days. Then we'll just see who gets the last laugh.

I'm just turning off the Sconset Bike Path and onto Sparks Avenue when disaster strikes. The chain breaks on my only mode of transportation. The chain whips against my calf, causing me to yelp in pain and go careening off the path. Luckily, I don't fall off even though the pain I'm now feeling is excruciating. Sitting down on the sidewalk, I assess the damage.

Shit, I'm bleeding.

Rooting around in my over-the-shoulder purse for a tissue, I yell toward the sky, "Oh, for fuck's sake! This is how you want to play? Fine. I'll walk all the miles home. My food will probably be rancid by then, but who the hell cares?" Pushing to my feet, I wince at what I know will be a massive bruise on my shin by the end of the day, if not by the end of the hour.

Hobbling, I push the offending mode of transportation the last two-tenths of a mile to the Stop and Shop parking lot. And it's there I see it. Rising up over the metal shopping carts like some oasis in the desert. A storefront called Sacred Grinds.

There is no way in hell that place doesn't sell coffee.

With a new purpose for making it across the parking lot, I ignore the pain in my body. I disregard the blood trickling down into my ballet flats. I shove that evil piece of scrap metal to the curb and stride inside. I'm a woman on a mission.

The air is scented with the most glorious sounds and smells ever. I hear the grind and hiss of the espresso machine. My nose lifts as freshly ground beans make their way into what has to be an exceptional cup of coffee. It has to be. After the day I've had, if it sucks, I might just cry.

And then I spot it sitting by the barista.

A large jar of caramel.

Mine.

I don't care how much I have to pay.

"Holy crap! I mean excuse me, ma'am. Are you okay?" A young woman with some of the most extraordinary colored hair I've ever seen comes racing around the counter. She's holding a first aid kit and a bunch of wet towels. "You're bleeding into your shoe!" she exclaims.

I'm so dazed by seeing the first possibility of happiness since I stepped foot on this island, I offer her a distracted "Hmm?"

"Maybe you hit your head too. Jeez. I'm the only one working. I wonder if I should call my dad. He would know what to do." She worries her bottom lip back and forth between her teeth.

Realizing I'm about to see a teen meltdown if I don't get it together, I offer her a smile. "I'm okay, sweetheart. Really. Thank you for being so concerned." Looking down at my leg, I shake my head ruefully. "I was biking into town, and at the last minute, the chain on my bike snapped. Do you mind if I..." I gesture to the first aid kit.

"Oh no! Of course not. Help yourself. Can I get you something to drink while you're cleaning up?" This girl is so sweet, I just want to bundle her up and bring her back to Connecticut with me. She reminds me a lot of my sisters at that age.

"If it involves caffeine, cream, and is drenched in caramel sauce, you've got a winner." I wink at her.

"Then you absolutely want our Love Me Brew. It's all of that plus shaved chocolate on top." The young barista moves behind the counter and washes her hands. Looking over at me past her colorful mane of hair, she tells me, "We sell the caramel by the jar if you like it."

I glance upward. "This is my reward for dealing with that death trap, isn't it? Thank you, Lord."

The girl laughs.

Quickly and painfully, I apply antiseptic to my leg and follow it with antibiotic ointment and a rather large bandage. Soon, a gorgeous drink is being placed in front of me with a small silver creamer server with extra caramel. Touched by the unexpected gesture, I beam.

"I figure you were wounded and could use some love on the side."

Taking my first sip, I moan aloud. "I haven't had coffee this good since I left home. My sister is the only other person I know who makes coffee this amazing."

She grins before standing and heading to the back. "I'll just leave you to...hey! What's my old bike doing out there?"

Standing, I hobble over to the window. "Your old bike? That's the piece of shit—excuse my language—that broke down on me? I found it in the garage of the apartment I'm staying in."

The barista's brow lowers. "Emily?"

I jerk back in confusion and end up banging my leg under the table. Wincing, I ask, "How do you know my name?"

She lets out a series of giggles before holding out her hand. "I'm Jenna. Jenna Madison. Dani's cousin. She told you were going to be coming, but I haven't had a chance to pop by to say hi. I believe you met my dad a few days ago."

No. Freaking. Way. This is Dani's youngest cousin? Studying her face, I can see the same high cheekbones and lush lips that grace her famous cousin. But... "Jenna, please tell me that hair isn't permanent," I beg of her.

She laughs. "Nope. It's just hair color chalk. But thank you for asking versus yelling at me like Dad did. Say, why were you biking into town anyway? Why didn't you just ask Dad for a ride?"

As my face goes blank while I try to think of a polite way of explaining I would sooner ride the bike again, Jenna just laughs. "Oh, this is going to be priceless. Are you up for a little fun, Emily?"

I think about it. For about half a heartbeat. "Just tell me we don't have to walk home and I can get a few groceries."

"Whatever we can put in the basket of my Vespa."

I groan.

"It has two seats, Emily."

My face brightens. "Will it get the caramel home safe?"

"Not only that, we can probably get you another coffee to go."

I hold out my hand. "Jenna, you've got yourself a deal." I have no idea what kind of trouble Jenna plans on stirring up for her father, but just being around this delightful girl reminds me so much of the antics of my own family, I can't help but be pulled in by her natural enthusiasm and charm.

"How much longer till you're done for the day?"

A girl yells from the back. "Hey, Jenna! Thanks for covering my break. You can clock out whenever."

She looks at me and shrugs.

"Then how about you ring me up for my two drinks, a huge jar of that caramel sauce, and let's go get some groceries." My leg is throbbing. "And maybe some Tylenol."

Giving me a sympathetic smile, she says, "Deal. Hey, what are you having for dinner tonight?"

I think briefly of what's in my fridge. "Probably a salad. Why?"

With a wicked smile, she tells me, "Not anymore," right before she goes behind the counter to ring up my purchases.

"Lynne! I'm out."

"See you tomorrow!"

Soon we're on our way. Before we go, Jenna takes a picture of the bike and uploads it to Dani with the caption *It's sad when Em has to take this to get to town. I'll be taking her home. Don't worry.*

I burst out laughing as we stroll into Stop and Shop.

Maybe I wouldn't be laughing so hard if I knew what was in store for me later that evening.

15

JAKE

I'm in the middle of playing the guitar along with a song Brendan wrote for his latest album when I get an incoming text. Opening it up, I see it's a forward from Jenna to Dani. It's a picture of a rusted-out, piece-of-shit bike of Jenna's that Dani is constantly reminding me to get rid of. Next to it is a picture of a bleeding leg being bandaged by a woman with blonde curls. *I can see you're really helping to welcome my guest if this is how you helped her get into town for supplies,* followed by a bunch of orange-faced swearing emojis. I don't have to guess how pissed Dani is. I'll deal with that later.

I'm insanely curious how Emily and Jenna managed to hook up. I also have to admit to wondering how Emily got along with my cantankerous teenager.

I don't have to wait long to find out.

My phone rings. Jenna, for all she's pissed at me, knows the rules: call before leaving work. "Hey, Dad. You'll never believe who I ran into at work."

My voice is dry when I reply, "Bet I can."

"Dani got to you already, huh? Well, good. You should be ashamed for not asking Em if she needed anything." I pull the phone away, wondering if I'm talking to an alien. I'm being schooled on manners from my sixteen-year-old daughter, who would sooner turn up the volume on her Bluetooth speakers than have a meaningful conversation. "Anyway, Em and I are on our way home."

Em? The Ice Queen and my daughter bonded so quickly Jenna feels comfortable enough to shorten her name? This bears some thought, but right now my concern is first and always my daughter's safety.

"Jenna," I say firmly as I lay my guitar aside. "You know the rules. No double riders on the Vespa."

"Dad, she's hurt. I'm not making her wait for you to get here when I can be home in ten minutes. Besides, she has to let Mugsy out soon," Jenna argues.

I grit my teeth. I can see the manipulation in this all the way from Cape Cod. Jenna's trying to prove to me she can ride double, and she's using Emily to do it. The problem is, she's not wrong. If Emily is hurt, this is the quickest way to get her home. "This is not the end of this discussion, Jenna. Get you and Emily home safely. If you're here in less than fifteen minutes because you're speeding, you'll lose the scooter. Do you understand?"

"Perfectly. Oh, and I invited Em to dinner." She disconnects before I can voice any protest.

Great. Just fucking great. Knowing I can get one more song out, I put down my acoustic guitar and plug in the electric Les Paul. The notes to "Dream On" start rippling from my fingers. Soon, I'm lost back in a time where there weren't any responsibilities. Arguments happened over set lists. There was nothing but the music and losing myself in the power of my fingers moving up and down the fret board.

TWENTY-FIVE MINUTES LATER, I'm in the kitchen stirring the sauce for the pasta I had defrosted earlier when I hear the front door open. Normally, Jenna just escapes to her room after calling out a greeting, but today, I hear two voices headed in my direction. When I hear Jenna yell, "Dad, a little help?" I drop the spoon, splattering sauce everywhere, and go rushing into the foyer.

Jenna is helping a limping Emily while trying to carry a few bags from Stop and Shop. "Stop, Jenna. It's not that bad," Emily protests. Her navy blue eyes narrow as she catches sight of me. "See? I can walk on my own." Lifting her chin as she removes her arm from around my daughter's shoulders, she manages a step or two before she stumbles. "Crap," she mutters.

I rush forward and catch her before she falls. My arms grip her small waist. Her curls brush against my chin. The smell of mint and something else tantalizes me as I catch her weight against me. Against my will, my body responds like it hasn't in too long.

Far too long if this standoffish woman is doing it for me.

Her arms clutch my forearms in a death grip. "I'm perfectly fine, thank you." Unlike her body, which is so wobbly it was about to face-plant in the foyer, her voice comes out cold as an iceberg. Hell, even if she tried, I bet her voice wouldn't rise above this modulated tone. It's damn annoying.

Rather like the woman herself.

"Dad!" Jenna exclaims. "Em's bleeding again. Do you think we can avoid staining the floors and get her some bandages?" She drops the bags she's holding onto the floor.

Holding Emily away from my body, I run my gaze downward. While the wound on her leg isn't gushing, it's bled through the bandage that's wrapped around it. Ouch. That must have hurt like hell. Without thinking, I sweep her up in my arms and stride toward the kitchen with Jenna hard on my heels. "Please put me down. I can handle this on my own," Emily says stiffly.

"Just be quiet. We keep the medical supplies in there."

"Isn't there a first aid kit in my apartment?" she says haughtily. I'm equally affronted and amused by the fact she'd rather be anywhere than in my arms or my home. *Lady, the feeling is entirely mutual.*

Since the table is already set for dinner, I plop Emily on top of the counter. "Stay," I order her.

"I'm not a dog." She shifts and a ripple of pain crosses her face, but just as quickly it's gone and a mask of blankness drops down. I almost admire her for the way she's able to hide her emotions. Holding Emily's gaze, I ask, "Jenna, do any of Emily's groceries have to be refrigerated?"

"Yeah, Dad. Practically all of them."

"Why don't you give Jenna your keys and she can bring everything up for you? Maybe let your dog out?" I suggest. A war happens in those blue eyes. Finally, she nods.

"Jenna, they're in my purse. Go ahead and grab them."

Jenna roots around in a small handbag slung over her shoulder. "Got 'em. Do you want your coffee here or at your house, Em?"

"My place, please. Thanks for getting it from the scooter, sweetie," Emily says quietly.

"Be right back." Jenna rushes out. The front door slams behind her, sealing Emily and me in a heightened tension.

Emily goes to slide off the counter, but I cage her in before she can. "I'm serious, Emily. I want to check out that leg." Guilt prompts me to admit, "It's my fault you got hurt."

"If you mean because of the bike, I'll admit you should have warned me to not use it. However, your hospitality, or lack thereof, is certainly not a problem. Part of my borrowing the apartment wasn't entertainment. In fact, I'd prefer to be alone."

I frown, worried about Jenna first, last, always. "Does that include my daughter?"

Emily scowls. "Of course not. Your daughter is sweet and caring. She dropped whatever it was she was doing at work today to help me."

I can't help but laugh. "She's normally like Satan's prodigy these days," I admit.

And suddenly it's me who is wobbly on their feet as Emily truly smiles. The brilliance of it reminds me of how I feel when I hear an old song on the radio I haven't heard in forever. It's the thrill of hitting the F# above C5 on an alto sax. It's the heat of playing in front of a live crowd.

The cadence of my heart picks up. What the hell is happening?

"How old is she, sixteen?" I nod in response, unable to respond. Emily's smile is pure mischief. "We were a lot worse. Trust me."

I back away and move toward the pantry closet to retrieve the first aid kit. If she keeps smiling when I'm this near her, I'm going to do something monumentally stupid.

Like kiss her.

With my back turned, I ask, "Your family?" as I slip into the large pantry. Pulling the kit from the floor, I make my way back to her.

She's contemplative. "It's not a hard question."

"It is if you knew my family," she murmurs. I pull over a chair from the dining room table before I get to work. As I unwrap the gauze from her leg, I wince as I see the bruising already starting to climb up her leg.

"Jesus, Emily, are you certain it's not broken?"

She sets her curls dancing as she shakes her head. "I don't think so. I can walk on it. Besides, I have too much to do for it to be broken."

"Like what? You're supposed to be on vacation," I challenge her.

"Not really," she says evasively. "I'm supposed to be working on a project while I'm here. I just had too many distractions at home."

"I hope it doesn't require walking for the next few days. Jenna might have to be the one to walk your dog for you." My voice is grim as I carefully remove the blood-soaked pads. The jagged cut doesn't look exceptionally deep, but the fact it's bleeding after more than an hour is still concerning me. "How well did you clean this out?"

She grimaces. "About as well as I could handle with the alcohol wipes from Sacred Grinds' first aid kit."

"Hate to break it to you, but I'm going to have to do a more thorough job than that."

"Great. It's a good thing I'm not back at home eating, then," she says resignedly.

I tip my head to the side. "What does that have to do with anything?"

"Because my family is a bunch of foodies. We love to eat. Except I can't cook worth a damn. So, if I can't work out for the next few days..." I cut her off.

"Probably closer to a week."

She nods. "A week, then. Then it's best if I don't overindulge."

I frown. "If you're not modeling, do you have to be so careful with your intake? Dani doesn't worry about it."

She stills. "You think I'm a model," she says carefully.

"I know I've seen your face before, I just can't figure out where," I admit.

She chuckles. "I'm not a model. I don't have the figure for it."

Without looking up from what I'm doing, I mutter under my breath, "Your figure's just fine." It's too much to hope she hasn't heard me when her sharp inhale of breath tells me she has.

Divine intervention saves me. The front door flies open and Jenna comes bursting back in. "Oh my, God. Em! It's you! Seriously? Dani didn't tell me *you* were coming to stay!"

Emily's exhaustion shows briefly on her delicate face. By the time Jenna reaches her, there's a different person in front of me. Gone is the cold, argumentative woman who confronted me on the deck and on the beach. Her exhaustion and pain are hidden behind a dazzling smile that doesn't quite reach her eyes. Even as I use cotton balls to rub hydrogen peroxide into her wound, she doesn't let Jenna see her pain. No, instead she's rapidly answering questions after question while I quickly bandage her leg.

It isn't until I'm cleaning up, that I catch a few words like "pattern," "lace," and "show." Frustrated with the bunch of non-answers I've received up until now, I fold my arms across my chest and interrupt their conversation. "What is it you do, exactly, Emily?"

It's Jenna who answers. Laughing, she points at Em and says, "I can't believe you don't recognize her from the pictures with Dani when they did the article of Best Dressed People in *People* magazine. The eggplant dress? That was Em's design. She's Amaryllis Designs!" Jenna's practically bouncing as she announces that information.

Em just shrugs.

Suddenly it hits me like a two-by-four. The spread in *People* was huge. It was an exposé on Danielle's life as a high-in-demand model, the girlfriend of country's hottest superstar, and their efforts to bring a spotlight to children's cancer research—something they've become passionate about since Brendan's nephew was diagnosed with a very rare form of leukemia. As my mind flips back through the article, I remember a sidebar where Dani was dressed for a red-carpet event in a purple-colored gown. There was an Instagram photo of her getting ready with her stylist. I didn't pay much attention then. But if memory—and my daughter's enthusiasm—is correct, that woman just got finished being bandaged on my kitchen counter.

Mentally, I groan. The woman who I've done nothing but antagonize is Emily Freeman. Dani talks about her incessantly. Not only is she the woman Dani hopes to convince to make all of her future gowns, she's the sister of the woman who competed with Brendan on *Caketastic*, a Food Network show he went on to raise awareness for his nephew's condition. Emily's also recently become an obsession of my daughter's as she's blathered on about fashion in an attempt to convince me she's done her research for a career in design.

I give her outfit a once-over. I know nothing about women's clothes, but Emily—even disheveled from her biking disaster today —still looks incredibly put together with a loose see-through T-shirt, a tight camisole, and very short flowered shorts. Not to mention flats that I know damn well by their turquoise sole cost more than my first guitar.

While I'm mentally kicking myself in the ass, I don't let that show. Instead I drawl, "If you'd been wearing something more stylish like cowboy boots with that outfit, we could have avoided this whole disaster."

Perversely enjoying as the practiced smile falls from her face, Emily hisses, "Too bad they're coming with my Rover in a few days. Then we could have avoided this mess altogether."

A Rover? Jesus Christ. Jenna looks delighted with Emily's news whereas I'm groaning. Here I've been talking to Jenna that most designers don't make much money, and my uninvited guest drives a car that probably equals my salary as a teacher for next year.

Great. Just great.

16
_____

EMILY

"**A**re you all right?" Ali demands as I FaceTime my family from the back deck after I indulged in a bubble bath when I got back to my apartment. Mugsy's head is in my lap. I absentmindedly stroke his ears as I recall the events of the day.

Needless to say, I didn't stay for dinner over at the main house after another battle with Jacob Madison. Jenna was upset, and I hated leaving her that way. I explained I really wasn't up to it because of my leg, but the reality was I just couldn't be around her father for another minute.

I really don't want to shatter Jenna's illusions about her father. He might look like something out of my deepest fantasies and have a voice that makes my toes curl, but damn if he doesn't drive me insane every time he opens his mouth.

It's too bad when he opens it, regardless if it's to say something insulting, the sound alone makes my stomach quiver.

"I'm as fine as I can be, Ali." I stretch a bit while the iPad propped up on the table shows my family shoving each other to try to get in front of the screen at the main house at the farm. "I'm sore and my leg hurts." I frown down at it. Ali yelled at me earlier for not putting ice on it sooner. The cold is brutal, but I know the throbbing feeling right now will help me ultimately heal faster.

Cassidy pipes in. "I'd say get a glass of wine and forget about the day, but I'm not sure if that would help."

"We'll call Jason in a few to make sure it won't start the bleeding again," Phil yells from where he's been relegated to the back so my sisters can see.

I sigh in exasperation. "If he's working, don't bother him. I don't think my leg's going to fall off overnight. Dani's cousin had a look at it."

There's silence on their end of the line. "Really?" Corinna's drawl is the most pronounced of all of ours. Its honeyed sound can either be soothing or grating. Right now, it's like fingernails running down a chalkboard.

"Jacob is a royal pain in the ass with a daughter who reminds me of all of you when you were sixteen." Raucous laughter bursts out from several members of my family. "He grates on my last nerve." Not a lie. Even though I have an uncontrollable urge to sketch him. "I don't understand quite how Dani doesn't murder him, Cori. I think Keene would have welcomed me more graciously."

Ali's wiping tears from her cheeks. "That says a lot."

Holly grins. "I bet you went all haughty royal on him, didn't you?"

Corinna snickers. "That's a sucker bet. I'm not taking that." Holly sticks her tongue out.

Phil stands up and reaches over for the iPad much to my sisters' protests. "Children, calm down. I would like to actually find out how our Em is doing and not roast her tonight." My heart melts a little at the uncommon show of brotherly concern when Phil tacks on, "We can save that for when she's feeling better."

I roll my eyes. "I'm totally feeling the love here, people."

Phil sits back down and flashes me a grin. "You wouldn't have us any other way."

True. "Can someone at least pretend to feel some sympathy? I'm sitting here in pain, and I want to finish this call so I can go drink some wine. If I'm even allowed to," I pout petulantly.

"Yeah, baby. I'll ping Jace when I'm done talking with you. Now, honestly, how are you?" The look of concern on Phil's face makes my heart melt even as my stomach starts to knot.

I push a hand through my wet curls. "One minute I'm so exhausted, I don't care where I am or what I'm doing. The next, I'm so angry about everything, all I want to do is scream. I can't find my balance." *Nor can I find an outlet as I haven't picked up a single chalk to design since I got here days ago*, I think to myself.

Phil purses his lips thoughtfully. "I don't know whether we should tell you everything or not now."

The feeling in my stomach is now closer to feeling like someone has put it through a meat grinder. "Better you tell me now than I find out, Phillip," I warn him.

"Here, talk to Cass."

Shit.

"Cassidy, tell me what the hell is going on. Right. Now," I demand.

My older sister takes a deep breath. "The thing is..."

Ali interrupts her, lifting a yellow manila envelope on the table. "These are the days I hate my job."

I hazard a guess. "Patrick?" I say, naming the designer whose place I took at Fashion Week.

"Got it in one," Ali says grimly. "Turns out he decided to coun-tersue for defamation of character. His lawyers are arguing that you only went after him because of his spot in the lineup, not the designs."

I cut her off. What a load of crap. "What does this mean for me, Ali?"

"It means I have to tread more carefully in my arguments, but ultimately nothing against the case," Ali says patiently. "Because of the fact Patrick's a lying shit who stole your proprietary information and sold them for gain. Which we have him on cold."

"Great," I mutter. "Has there been any word from the CFDA attorneys involved?" Maybe I don't need to be worrying about finding my creative juices if they're going to yank my first Fashion Week out from under me.

Ali nods. "Regardless of what happens with Patrick—which I'm handling—what he did to you still was grounds for the actions they took. The show is still on. In fact, your name appearing in the newspaper—" She upends the manila folder. I can't even count the number of clippings that fall out. "—is just generating more free publicity for the show every time they call for comment. They think it's going to be the most highly attended fashion show next to Reem Acra's." Her cobalt-blue eyes gleam. "So, I hope whatever you're working on is going to rock the runway."

"Yeah, no pressure there." Now the throbbing has moved from my leg to my head and my heart.

Cassidy's face appears square in the feed. "Em, is everything okay?"

"It's fine, Cass. Everything's just fine." In fact, it's so fine, I think the last time I felt this empty hollowness was when Aunt Dee passed away.

"Well, this should cheer you up. Phil's on his phone with Jason, and judging by the hand gestures, I say you're good for a couple of glasses of wine." Cassidy turns the video toward Phil, who's pantomiming drinking with his thumb and pinky finger out. He then holds up two fingers and a thumbs-up.

"If I'm translating big brother correctly, Jason is telling him you're good for two glasses of wine, no more," Cassidy says wryly. She laughs as Phil applauds her correct charades interpretation.

"Trust me, unless it was going to kill me, I was planning on drinking anyway."

Joining my family in laughter, I feel an easement in my soul. Maybe burying all of these emotions isn't the answer. It wasn't when my parents died nor when Dee did. Tonight, I'll grab my journal and draw out my wounds in order to shine a light on them. Maybe they won't end up being the designs that wind up in the show, but maybe it will be the first step to healing. To finding my soul.

And believing in myself again enough to knock the fashion world on its ass.

17

JAKE

Dinner with Jenna once Emily left the house was cold and silent. She couldn't believe I was so rude to not encourage her to stay, not only because she was staying on our property but because she was injured. The last words she said to me before grabbing her food and stomping off to her room cut deep. "That's not how I was raised to treat people. By you."

Damn, if my soon-to-be seventeen-year-old didn't just call me out. And she was one hundred percent correct.

I go out through the kitchen onto the back deck. From where I'm standing, I can see Em sitting at the little table with a leather-bound sketchbook in hand. On the table next to her is a glass of wine. Frowning, I wonder if she should be drinking. I quickly make a call to a local doctor on the island, explaining what happened and what steps I took to treat her injury. He also makes arrangements to come out later in the week to look at her leg to check for any infection.

Feeling marginally better, I go back inside and call up to Jenna that I'll be right back. I grit my teeth when I don't get any response. I don't imagine the reception is going to be much better where I'm headed either. Picking up the disposable container I filled with spaghetti and homemade meat sauce earlier, I head out through the kitchen and down the porch stairs. I cross the walkway between our decks and quickly climb the stairs.

About four steps from the top, I feel two sets of eyes watching me. One's probably salivating from the smell, and the other's likely out for my blood. Waving the proverbial white flag, I address them both. "I brought you some spaghetti." It's her dog who welcomes me with a few thumps of his tail.

Emily chortles. "Did your daughter make you?"

"No, Ms. Smart-Ass. I did this all on my own without guidance from my cousin or my daughter, thank you very much." I hold the covered container out to her.

Emily places her sketchbook on the table, facedown. Lifting the lid, she sniffs what was supposed to be our shared meal inside. "This smells delicious. Homemade?" she asks, surprised.

"Just the sauce. It's not that hard to do." I reach a hand out to touch her sketchbook and am rewarded by having my hand slapped. Hard. "What the hell was that for?"

"No one looks in that sketchbook. Ever," she says flatly.

"How do you make your designs, then, if no one can see them?" Now that I know who she is, I'm curious about the process.

"That isn't my design sketchbook. This book has never been looked at by another human. If I thought it had without my permission, I'd burn it." Whoa. I'm taken aback at the utter desolation on the beautiful face in front of me. But as quickly as it appears, it disappears without a trace. "If you really want to talk to me about design, there's a black leather folder on the coffee table. Grab that and a fork and maybe I'll tell you."

"Using me since I'm here?"

"Whatever works."

I nod at her almost empty glass of wine. "Need a refill?"

She shakes her head. "My brother-in-law called earlier on his break from the ER. Two glasses are my limit. But can you do one more thing?" She holds up a bag of melting ice. I wince, thinking I should offer one of our less messy ice packs. "Can you dump this for me? I'm beginning to feel like Mugsy had an accident on me." As she shifts, her face takes on a cast of pain that doesn't disappear. Tears start to form. I reach for her wineglass and shove it into her hand.

"Drink," I order.

Letting out a choked laugh, she does. "Trying to get me drunk, Jacob?"

"Jake, okay? Every time you call me Jacob, I feel like I'm being schooled by my parents for something I did to Dani."

She grins and my body reacts the same way it did in my kitchen. "Word of advice? Never tell a woman those things, Jake. It leaves her with great ammunition for later."

Shaking my head with silent laughter, I head for the back door. "I'll be right back, Emily."

"Em." I turn around.

"Excuse me?"

"The only people who called me Emily are gone from my life. Everyone else calls me Em."

"Em," I say softly. It suits her right now with her curls dancing in the ocean breeze.

"Jake?"

"Yes." I'm distracted by the picture she's making against the setting sun.

"Are you cleaning my floor since that bag of ice is leaking all over it?"

Shit. Rushing to the sink, I pretend to not hear her bark of laughter. But after how I left everything earlier, I kind of don't mind being the reason she's laughing right now.

"Recognize this dress?" Em's stuffed herself with pasta. Recovering the rest which she claims she'll eat for days, she's just opened the leather portfolio I brought out for her and after flipping through a few drawings, pulls out a charcoal sketch.

She passes it to me, and I almost drop it. It's the dress Dani wore to the Country Music Awards with Brendan. It's the purple one that was featured in *People* magazine. Here in my hands is the black-and-white drawing that started it all. "Wow." Even though I'm still skeptical about Jenna going into the business, I have to admit it's kind of a thrill to imagine this drawing went from Em's talented brain and fingers to a seamstress somewhere to be worn by my cousin.

Passing the sketch back, I watch as Emily slides it carefully back into the leather portfolio. "Tell me how it goes from that to the final product." I'm genuinely curious. "How did you get the inspiration for it?"

She tilts her head. "Do you study the legends?"

"Musical ones, sure." I toss her a quick grin.

She rolls her eyes. "I mean the Greeks, the Romans, the Egyptians. Those kinds of legends. Historical."

"A little bit. I assume you have?"

Her face blanks when she answers, "Yes. Quite a bit, actually."

"Did you study them in school?" I ask casually. I don't know where she went just then, but I know Emily isn't sitting with me right now. And oddly, I want her back.

Nodding her head, she sets her curls dancing. "I did. It was my minor in college. Actually, I did a dual minor in business and history."

I sigh. "This is a conversation I wish someone would have with my daughter."

"You don't discuss college? And Dani's mentioned you're a teacher?" Her voice is laced with surprise.

"We 'discuss' college all the time. The problem is making her understand there's an element of practicality behind her chosen field."

"Which is?"

Wryly, I admit, "Fashion."

"Ahh. I begin to understand. I'm happy to talk with her, anytime."

"Maybe you should talk to me first. Just so I have an idea of what you'll be telling her." Suddenly I have an image of Emily telling Jenna all about the glorious parties and jet-setting around the globe. Emily lets out a sound that's a half giggle, half snort that I find utterly charming.

"I'm assuming you don't want to hear about the parts where your cousin has to strip naked for me several times."

I shudder. "Please. It was bad enough when I had all of my friends hitting on her during high school." I perk up. "But if you want to take my cousin out of the picture and embellish on that for me, who am I to argue?"

Emily lets out a bark of laughter that startles Mugsy. He howls awake from what must have been a great puppy dream.

"Come here, old man. There's nothing wrong with your mama. She's just having some fun." Mugsy ambles toward me. Sniffing at my hand, he sits down on his hindquarters before scooting back. He knocks his head into my hand several times. Bewildered, I look at Em to see her lips parted in surprise.

"He wants you to pet his ears. No, actually, it's more like a demand to," she muses. I begin stroking his silky ears, and Emily's face softens. "Normally, it's one of my family members doing exactly what you're doing. He's so spoiled." She holds out her hand, and Mugsy leans forward and gives her a lick. She scratches under his chin.

Our faces are so close, I can smell the mint of her hair mixed with the ocean breeze. I never realized the combination would be so alluring. Clearing my throat, I ask, "How did you get him?"

"He found us. One night, he was starving and was begging for food. We didn't have much, but what we had, we gave to him."

"He was lucky." The words are out of my mouth before I know I'm going to say them. Em's lips part in surprise. "I mean, he could have wound up at a shelter, or..."

"Or worse," Em finishes grimly. Abruptly, she says, "I was engaged."

I stop stroking Mugsy, who whines. Resuming, I ask, "So you said. When did it end?"

"Last week."

"Jesus." No wonder she wanted to get away. "I'm sorry."

"I'm not."

"Oh." What am I supposed to say to that? Mugsy settles down on the deck between us and lets out a sigh. Without him to distract me, I ask the inevitable. "Why?"

"Part of it was because I found out he was a lying, cheating dick. Part of it was he stole from me. But there's a part that I haven't said out loud. He changed from when we first met. By the time I ended things, he was an utter asshole. I don't know why I let it go on as long as I did." Pausing, she takes a deep breath. "He wanted me to put down my dog since he was so old." Her voice in the dusk of the night is laced with well-earned bitterness that I understand all too well. "I don't know you yet, Jake. Everything I do, I know from Dani. And we didn't get off on the right foot, but you do have one good point. You just spent more time petting my dog in the time you've been sitting here than in the year I was with my ex."

I choose my words carefully before I respond. "I think you're well rid of the schmuck."

One heartbeat. Two.

Then Emily agrees. "That seems to be the consensus."

"Now, give me a crash course on fashion so I can go home and seem like an authority to my daughter."

"Please. That would take more than just a single conversation."

I let out a mock sigh. "What will it take?"

"A lobotomy because I think your interest in fashion is about zero."

"You'd be right," I admit. "But apparently, I have a pretty important woman to impress, so I'd better start learning."

That tips her lips into a lazy grin. "That's a good answer, Dad." The urge to tangle my fingers in the back of her hair and kiss her in the sunset is overwhelming.

Emily begins talking about all of the meticulous details about how she created Dani's gown. Long after the sun goes down, I realize Emily's not only incredibly talented, she's focused and driven, with a brilliant brain and an attention for detail.

Maybe Dani knew what she was doing by sending her here. For Jenna.

For me, what started out as a really shitty day ended up pretty damn amazing with the music of the ocean in harmony with Emily's voice.

Mugsy lets out little excited yips while he's slipped back into his puppy dreams as if in agreement.

18

EMILY

Jake and I seem to have declared a detente. He insisted on having Jenna come over to help me with Mugsy so I didn't need to tackle the stairs. He even offered to make a run for groceries, which I politely declined. I stocked up enough on my bike ride from hell to last me until the Rover arrives in a few days.

I spend my days trying to find inspiration in the riveting view before me. The ocean is everything I need it to be: beautiful, magnificent, wild, stimulating. So, why I can't feel anything beyond my own oppression is beginning to terrify me.

I'm frightened. I'm afraid if I look too closely at what's been handed to me, I'm going to see I should have sacrificed more, worked harder, dedicated myself more.

I'm finding no solace in my solitude. I'm spending hour after hour sitting on the back deck staring out over the water, trying to find some inspiration. The vastness of the water just reflects what I already know. I'm all alone. And I'm beginning to lose faith I'll ever find my way back to my soul—that is, if I ever knew where to locate it to begin with.

Then I feel a cold nuzzle against my hand, and tears well in my eyes.

"Sorry, Mugs. I know I'm never truly alone with you around, baby." Seemingly satisfied, he finds a patch of sunlight and plops down into it.

I let out a long sigh. I've flipped through all the original drawings of my dresses trying to feel that tingle in my mind and in my hands. So far, the first few days have produced nothing but frustration.

Why did I come here if it was only for this? I pick up the pencil to begin drawing when a flash of Jake's long-lashed brown eyes comes into my mind. My heartbeat accelerates. Without thinking, I press the tip of my pencil down so hard, it snaps.

No. Just no.

I refuse. I'm not going to give myself time to think about a man when I'm only here for a few months. I need to find me again. I need to recover from what was so I can find out what my future holds.

The problem is, I can't not think of him. Each night I heat up some of the pasta he thoughtfully brought over, I smile. Such a small thing, but it shows the caring man beneath the hard-ass. That, combined with what I know from Dani's chattering during our fittings, make him fascinating as hell.

And holy hell, I'd have to be inhuman to not say that I didn't feel the spark between us when we were so close petting Mugsy the other night. I could smell his fresh, marine scent that complemented the ocean air. It stirred something I haven't felt in longer than I'm ashamed to admit considering I was engaged.

I can't do this. I came here for a reason.

Dismissing Jake from my thoughts, I discard the pencil in my hand. Picking up another, I begin to draw. Minutes later, I let out a growl of frustration.

Because what I've drawn is Jake's eyes as they bore into mine over Mugsy's head.

Disgusted with myself, I toss away the sketchbook. I walk to the railing, chastising myself the whole way.

There's no way I'll act on this attraction. Too many people could get hurt.

And I'm the last person I'm concerned about.

19

EMILY

I'm unsurprised to find Jenna at my door the next morning. What I am surprised by is her hair being back to the natural color shared by her father and her cousin. She's a stunningly pretty girl with her father's warm brown eyes and Dani's more dramatic features. Calling out a greeting, she walks in through the open balcony door. "Hey, Em! I brought breakfast."

I groan from my position on the couch. Mugsy thumps his tail in anxious welcome. I swear, this dog understands most food terms and other important words like "treat," "walk," and "rub." "Sweetheart, after the amount of pasta your father brought over the other night, the last thing I need is more food. I'll be eating off that for a week."

She trips on her own two feet on her way to my kitchen. "Wait, Dad brought over food?"

I raise a brow. "He didn't tell you about his peace offering?"

"He's a jerk, Em," she says bitterly. I'm disturbed by the animosity in her voice.

"Why?" I challenge her. Jake Madison doesn't give off that vibe, but if this girl tells me he is, I'll be calling my family so fast to get us out of here...wait, us?

"He moved me away from everyone I know right before my senior year! Just because I got into a little trouble," she wails.

I let out a sigh of relief. "Honey, that sounds like him trying to be a good parent," I start when she whirls on me.

"What do you know about it?" she fires off at me. Her eyes are angry and bitter.

My eyes narrow. "You think that's the worst thing that can happen to you, Jenna? You think your life is ruined?"

"Isn't it?" she cries dramatically.

Pushing to my feet, I wince over the soreness in my leg, even four days later. I'm going to have to call Jason to see if I need to visit a doctor, damnit. I make my way to where she's standing. "No, sweetheart. Not even close. Try having your parents die in front of you. That's one way of changing the course of your life in a big way. What you're dealing with is a mere inconvenience in comparison to that." Hobbling away, I call out, "Don't worry about Mugsy; I need to exercise my leg."

"Em?" I hear her call anxiously out right before I slam my bedroom door.

Feelings rip through me, driving an incredible urge to sit on the beach and sketch.

"What the hell did you say to my daughter this morning?"

I close my eyes behind my sunglasses. Just like I thought, Jake is a concerned father, and if Jenna would open up her eyes, she might see that.

"Should I assume whatever truce we had is over?" Closing my sketchbook, I start to stand, but Jake scrambles down the beach a few feet ahead of me. Mugsy takes exception to not being acknowledged and bounds after him.

He stops to pet Mugs before he begins laying into me. My heart tingles. Damnit.

"All I know is Jenna came back from your place in tears, ran over, and gave me a huge hug."

"And that's a problem, why?" I ask, bewildered. If I could hug my mother or Aunt Dee one more time...

"Listen, lady, my daughter hasn't hugged me since I moved her away from her friends to this island. She was blabbing on about how I could be dead. So again, what did you say to her?" His fiery temper sparks my own.

And God, does it feel good to let it out.

Struggling to my feet, I say bitterly. "*Your* daughter was complaining about what a dick you were this morning. I tried to steer her from that line of thinking—God knows what I was thinking." I shake my head. I ignore the crushed look on Jake's face. "Instead, I let her know there could be worse things that could happen to her life than being here."

"By telling her I could be dead."

"No, by telling her she could have had to watch her parents be murdered in front of her," I shoot back. "That's the reality of the world, Jake. The world isn't perfect for every person growing up in it. And guess what, some of us have to get past hurdles like that to be the people we are. We don't want to hear about Daddy being an ass because maybe he is, but unless he's raping you or selling you into slavery or trying to buy his life with yours, then it just isn't that bad."

"Jesus." He freezes in place while I breathe hard. I can't believe I blurted all of that to this complete stranger, but damn him, there's something that makes me want to simultaneously shatter his illusions about me being heartless and take shelter in his strong arms all at the same time. Ignoring those feelings, I drop reality on his head instead.

"Life isn't a damn fairy tale. If you're so worried about your daughter being tainted by me, keep her away. Better yet, why don't you both stay away." Whistling, I call for Mugsy. We both slowly begin picking our way through the sand back up to the apartment.

MY ANGER LED me to design a tight-fitting bandage dress with three-quarter sleeves and a plunging back down to the tailbone. With the model's hair slicked back and left in loose curls, the design eerily reminds me of my relationship with Bryan, of trying to fit into a mold I didn't exactly fit into while being bound due to obligations only I felt. I'm trying to decide if the dress is finished, when there's a knock at my door. Lying my sketch pad down, I wander over to find a friendly but unfamiliar face. "Yes?" I ask cautiously.

"Ms. Freeman? I'm Dr. Fischer. I—"

I interrupt him. "May I see some identification, please?" I ask politely but firmly.

He blinks. "Obviously Jake didn't tell you I was coming."

"Even if he had, I'd still be asking for identification, Doctor," I drawl. I hold out my hand. He places his wallet into it. "I'll be right back." Closing the door in his face, I engage the locks. Loudly.

Pulling my cell from my shorts, I call Caleb. He answers on the second ring. "What's up, Em?"

"It appears my neighbor is showing a sense of remorse for the bike incident." I have little doubt Cassidy shared what happened with her husband. "A..." I flip open the wallet. "Dr. Robert Fischer has just landed on my doorstep. Do I have anything to be concerned about?"

"Address?" Caleb doesn't waste any time with frivolous questions.

Reading off the information, I glance out the window. The doctor has pulled out his cell phone. I suspect he's calling Jake. *Deal with it, buddy. I didn't ask for your help.* "Anything I need to worry about?"

"Nope. He's good. Tell him Jason will be requesting a copy of your report by the end of the day."

"Thank you." Disconnecting the call, I unlock the door. I catch the tail end of his conversation. "...never seen anything like it, Jake. Just took my ID and shut the door in my face."

"Dr. Fischer, please come in. Here's your identification."

Flustered, he turns around. The ruddy cast to his cheeks makes him look years younger than he is. "I won't apologize for the inconvenience," I say firmly. "As a single woman, I can't be too cautious with whom I let into my private space."

"Of course, I didn't mean..." he stammers.

"I assume you are here to check on my leg?" I lead him over to the dining room table. Mugsy comes over and sits next to me protectively.

"Well, yes. I've been treating Jake, Jenna, and Danielle for years if something ever happened while they were on the island. He asked if I could come by."

Before he starts giving me stories about the Madisons I really don't want to hear right now, I interrupt him. "Would it be possible for a copy of your report to be sent to my doctor by the end of the day? He's expecting it."

He blinks at me like a disturbed owl. "Of course. By the end of the day, you say? Certainly." Carefully he removes the bandage Jake applied last night. Suddenly, the jovial face takes on a different cast. One of anger.

"Ms. Freeman, you should have been in my office for stitches the day this happened."

I smile grimly. "If you could leave that out of the report, I'd be grateful."

Gently applying pressure to my bruised leg, I let out a hiss when he hits a tender spot. "Why's that?"

Through gritted teeth, I get out, "Because my doctor is my brother-in-law. I'll never hear the end of it."

Looking up at me, he smiles. "Then it looks like you'll be following my instructions to the letter to get this to heal properly, won't you?"

I groan in acceptance.

20

JAKE

"Daddy, Dr. Fischer just left. Should we go check on Em?" Jenna yells down from upstairs.

I don't respond because I honestly don't know. When Emily walked away from me on the beach this morning, I didn't know what to think about what she said to me. *Was she saying all of those things had happened to her?* My mind instantly shies away from that. But I keep remembering the ice-cold woman who threatened to call 911 on me the day we met. Now, I'm told by the doctor I asked to look in on her, that Emily essentially held him hostage on the front porch while she verified his ID?

What if Em has reason to be this scared? What am I doing by exposing my daughter to her?

"Give me a few minutes, Jenna," I call back. "I have to make a quick call." Heading down to the one place where I know I can get some peace and quiet—the music studio—I call Dani.

"Jesus, Jake. Tell me this isn't a complaint about Em. Brendan and I just got to sleep like four hours ago." Shit, I forgot they were on the West Coast this week.

Wincing, I run my hand across the back of my neck. "Not a complaint, per se..."

"Jake," she warns me.

"Dani, how much do you know about her background?" I blurt out the question.

There's murmuring on the other end of the line for a full minute. The next thing I know, Brendan's on the phone. "Why are you asking, Jake?"

I lay it all out on the line. "Jenna was complaining to her about me, and Em snapped, I think. She said something today that freaked Jenna. Something about life could be worse if you watched your parents being killed in front of you. Then when I tried to talk to her, she essentially told me to wake up because life is filled with all these nightmarish scenarios. Now, I have to wonder if I should let Jenna be around her."

Brendan sighs. "Listen, I can't break any trust—trust I only just gained, mind you. All I can say is talk with Em. If you're not certain about Jenna being around her, that's your decision. But personally, that woman—that whole family—is made up of the strongest people I've ever known."

"Not helping me much, man."

"That's all I can say. Talk to Em." Brendan hangs up in my ear.

"Talk to Em," I mimic. "Gee, thanks, buddy. Remind me to use infinite wisdom in your best-man speech."

"Daddy?" I close my eyes. I just can't win for trying today. But God, does it feel good to hear "Daddy" on her lips.

"Yes, Jen?"

"Why were you asking Dani and Brendan about Em?"

Nope. Not one thing. "Because she scared you," I answer honestly.

"Seriously?" Jenna's outraged.

I'm confused. "Well, yes."

"Dad, I was upset because Em was right. I was being immature, yet here I want you to take me seriously. I was blaming you for something you didn't do. Hell, you've been drilling it into me since Mom left that actions have consequences." Her voice is filled with bitter rage.

"Jenna." Holding out my hand, I'm actually surprised when she takes it.

"Listen, I was upset, because if I heard her right, Em lived through something truly awful, and I just wanted to hold on to you for a few minutes. Is that so wrong?"

I tug her toward me. "No, baby, it's not." I take a deep breath. "You weren't afraid?"

"Of Em?" She snorts. "Please. You're worse when you're upset. She gets all quiet and cold. You go all fire and brimstone."

I sigh over her head. "Okay, so maybe I had it wrong."

I feel Jenna shaking as she laughs. "So, now can we go see Em? I was going to take Mugsy out for her, but I ran out. I feel really bad."

Pulling back, I brush my lips against her head. "Yeah. Let's go see Em."

What I didn't count on was Emily not being there to see us.

21

EMILY

fter I escort Dr. Fischer to the door, I see magic in my driveway.

My Rover.

Three days early.

"Woohoo!" I leap into the air. Then yell, "Ow! Crap, stupid leg."

Dr. Fischer tsks me. "That's really not listening to doctor's orders, Ms. Freeman."

"Em," I say, almost absentmindedly. I watch as Chris, one of Caleb's analysts, gets out of the car. "Do you know what that is, Doc?"

Amused, he leans against the banister as he observes me watching Chris unload my bags. "No, what?"

"That's freedom. And freedom's a beautiful thing. Hey, Chris," I call down to the former Marine.

"Hey, Em. Where do you want these?"

I wave him in. "Anywhere inside is great. I can move them later."

He laughs. "Like hell. Caleb told me you managed to get injured up here. I'm supposed to give him a sit-rep after I've laid eyes on you. So, tell me where you want your bags so you can unpack."

"Let me guess, Caleb is your brother-in-law? The doctor?" Dr. Fischer asks.

"One of them, sir. She has a few of them. And no, he's not a doctor. Chris Henderson." Chris drops one of the bags to offer his hand to shake.

"Dr. Robert Fischer."

"Ah, Caleb wondered if you'd still be here. I'll be able to report in that Em's alive after her exam too. Maybe I can work in a few extra vacation days for all the intel," Chris muses.

I snort. "So happy to be good for something."

"Listen, Em, I'm just thrilled I get to go see my girlfriend a few days early. Then again, driving the Rover wasn't much of a hardship either," he admits.

Dr. Fischer laughs. "Em, stay off that leg more than you need to. Walk the dog if you must, grocery shopping, that kind of thing. No running, no swimming, no sightseeing for another week. If you continue to have any problems, come see me in my office now that you have a car."

I grin. "Will do, Dr. Fischer. Just send me the bill."

"Already been taken care of."

I shake my head adamantly. "No. I pay my own way. Send it to me."

He chuffs my chin. "Stubborn thing. I'll send it to you later." Chris is coming out of my apartment empty-handed. "Don't let her help you carry things up, young man."

"No, sir, I won't. It wouldn't just be you who would get angry."

I roll my eyes. Men.

It takes Chris less time to unpack the Rover than I thought it would, but then again, he's a former Marine who's used to carrying a hell of a lot more than my suitcases and sewing machine. "Can I take you out to lunch to say thanks?"

He looks at his watch. "Actually, Em, if you wouldn't mind just driving me back into town, there's a ferry I can catch back to the mainland. I have a car ready to rent tonight to head out to the Cape."

I grin. "Done. But we have to go by this amazing coffee shop on the way there. I'm buying."

He laughs. "You don't have to sell me on coffee twice."

AFTER I DROP Chris off at the ferry, I drive around the island to finally get my bearings. It feels so good to have the moon roof open and all the windows down. Since it's my left leg that's beat to shit, driving isn't hurting at all. I feel one of Aunt Dee's favorite expressions coming up through my soul. I just yell it out the moon roof: "Glory be!" Laughing, I turn up the music I've got pouring through the Meridian sound system.

It feels good to feel free for the first time in longer than I can remember.

I'm no longer tethered down by the weight of Bryan and all of his ensuing crap, egocentric brides who feel it's their life mission to drain me one snide argument at a time, or even the burden of love. Because as much as I love my family, and God knows I do, the unwritten obligation I placed on myself so long ago, I just can't handle right now.

I need to be Emily.

I need to find my way back to the girl who lost herself for hours inside of her head with nothing but her imagination to stop her. I have to find my own happiness again. With myself. If all I'm going to be left with in this world is me, I'd better know I like her a lot.

After hours of doing nothing but driving and absorbing the nuances of the island, I use my GPS to navigate back to the house. Parking in front of the garage door where I found the evil bike, I turn down the music before I roll up the windows. Hopefully Mugsy will be ready to go out so we can go for a quick walk and I can come back and drink a glass of wine. Humming completely off-key to Sara Bareilles, I'm reaching for my purse when there's a harsh knock on my window. Jumping, I turn and see Jake's infuriated face.

Exasperated, I open the car door. "What is your problem?"

"Where the hell have you been?"

"Nowhere." I shrug. It's the truth. I've been nowhere and everywhere. It's been glorious.

"Are you supposed to be driving on that leg?" he demands.

"Um, I use the right leg for the pedals. Can't see that it's a problem." Sliding out, I start to move by him, but he hooks my arm. My eyes widen at the intensity on his face. "I suggest letting me go."

"We were worried about you." I feel a warmth inside, a small glow, but I ruthlessly squash it.

"Why?"

"Because you're injured?"

I shake my head. "Your doctor cleared me."

"Yeah," he replies menacingly. "I called him earlier and he mentioned you had a friend drop off your car."

I cluck my tongue in mock annoyance. "Dr. Fischer is rather chatty, isn't he?"

Jake starts moving forward. I retreat in automatic response. "How about next time letting someone know where the hell you're going?"

I laugh in his face. "I'm accountable to exactly no one here."

"Really?" Brown eyes bore into mine incredulously.

"Yep. Now, if you'll excuse me." I start to move past him but find myself spun around and pressed into the rough cedar wood of the garage.

"No, I don't think I will." He glares down at me as his heaving chest moves up and down against my breasts, which are sensitized due to the heady combination of the sexiness of the man in front of me, the allure of the ocean air, and the crackling antagonism between us.

And before I can offer up even the slightest protest, out of nowhere Jake's lips cover mine. Whether it's out of a combination of fear, anger, or something else, I just don't know.

And my heart is pounding out of my chest at his bold maneuver.

I just got out of one relationship where I hated the man by the end, and suddenly I'm being kissed by a man I barely know but can barely get off my mind.

Abruptly, the freedom I experienced earlier is gone as I'm driven headlong into a vortex of confused emotions. Jake's mouth eats at mine in what may be the most overwhelming embrace I've ever experienced.

With a small sound, I wrap my arms around his neck and allow myself to be sucked under like a riptide takes everything in its path.

22

JAKE

What the hell am I doing? Hours ago, I was calling my cousin worried about this woman being a bad influence on my daughter, and now, hearing that she was joking and laughing with Dr. Fischer and seeing just how completely unburdened she is, I can't keep my hands off her. Her lips taste like caramel and coffee as they part under mine. Every stroke of our tongues against each other pulls me into the infinite world of possibilities.

Holy hell, what did I unleash?

My body molds into hers as I slide a hand into her hair, tugging her head back farther.

In the back of my mind, I hear a voice. I ignore it as I keep plundering Em's mouth.

Minutes pass. I forget where we are. Forget that I've known her for less time than it normally takes me to approach a woman, let alone kiss one. I feel like the universe is beginning to reveal some sort of secret to me through her kiss.

It takes me a minute to realize she's no longer responding. Standing within the confines of my arms, Em is holding herself stiffly. "Right, sorry about that."

Her spine relaxes marginally, before she says, "Hello, Jenna."

Crap.

"Well, I raced off to call work because I heard you were there with some guy, Em. I wanted to see if you were still there. Now, I come down to find you kissing Dad. Ew, just ew," my daughter says.

"Just to clarify, Jenna, your father was the one doing the kissing," Em argues. I flush a bright shade of red.

"Didn't look like you were protesting too much until you realized I was here," Jenna singsongs. My head snaps up. Suddenly, I'm not the only one who's turning a bright shade of pink. *Way to stick up for your old man, Jen,* I think to myself as Emily's and my eyes clash. "Anyway, don't let me interrupt. Dad, will you let Mugsy out? I'm heading back to the house."

"Sure, baby," I reply absentmindedly.

"There's no need..." Em begins, but I cut her off.

"I'd like to talk to you." She begins to protest, but I hold up a hand. "Just talk. We'll call this an aberration."

Scowling at me, Em agrees. "Fine." She begins to climb the stairs, leaning on the railing for support. Halfway up she turns. "Makes me wonder how you greet someone you haven't seen in a long time that you actually give a damn about."

After she makes it to the top of the stairs, I let out a long gust of air.

Because I'm not so sure how to respond. Normally, everyone but family is an intrusion.

What does it mean that Emily Freeman is sliding into the circle of people that isn't when I was ready to write her off just this morning?

AFTER I TAKE Mugsy for a quick walk, I gape at the amount of luggage that's been delivered since I was last in the apartment. "Are you planning on staying for a few months or for a few years?"

Em looks around and smirks. "This isn't even part of my wardrobe. Besides, what's in those bags"—she nods to the two near the dining room table—"isn't being unpacked. Not yet, at any rate."

"Why not?" Pulling out one of the barstools, I drop myself into it.

She shrugs. "It's filled with fabric, thread, beads, and other things I might need."

"Not ready to whip out a dress just yet?"

A despondent flash races over her face right before an indignant flame lights her eyes. "If I needed to," she says, her voice lethal, "I could have the hottest dress 'whipped out' in a matter of hours. And you can bet your ass it would be better than anything you'd see on this island."

"Only if you needed to, of course," I mock gently.

"What's it to you, Madison?" she hisses.

"I was just curious."

"You know what Albert Einstein said about curiosity," she throws out.

"That a brain that's curious never goes back to its original size?" I can tell she's impressed and trying to not show it.

"That wasn't the quote I was thinking of. I was thinking of the one where he said something along the line of not having special talents but curiosity."

"Ah, but I do have talents, Em."

I feel my heart thump in a slow, steady rhythm in my chest as her eyes drop down to my lips. Turning her back to me, she reaches into her fridge for a bottle of water. "What kind of talents?"

Appreciating her effort to get the conversation back on neutral territory, I tell her, "I'm a musician. Slap an instrument in my hand and I'm a happy man."

Turning around, with water in her mouth, she nods. I see the liquid slide down her throat as she swallows. Just what every man wants to know—what a woman he finds infinitely attractive looks like swallowing. "Dani mentioned you're a music teacher?"

It's a question, so I pull myself back to our conversation. "I am." I'm a little more than that, but I don't reveal that to anyone.

Not even my daughter. Not yet at any rate.

"Do you enjoy it?" Her genuine curiosity makes me relax. A little.

"Now, I do. When I first started out, I felt like I was giving up on every dream I ever had," I admit.

Something dark flashes behind her eyes. Something completely unreadable. "I can appreciate that."

"You mean there was something you wanted to do other than design? From what I've seen, you've made a pretty big name for yourself."

She begins picking at the label of the bottle. "Something like that."

She doesn't offer any more insight, instead retreating inside herself as if I'm no longer in the room. "What was it?"

She shuts down. I literally witness her draw into herself. I want to walk around the counter and break through that facade. It's like there's two Emilys living inside her. One's so open and warm that I'm fighting everything inside myself from doing something infinitely stupid like kissing her again. The other's this closed-off cynic who looks like she's being submerged under the weight of the world.

It's the second Emily who responds. "I'll tell you the very day I let you see the journal you touched the other night," she vows with self-deprecating humor.

It shouldn't anger me, but it does. "Why can't you just give me a straight answer, Em? That it's none of my business?"

"It's none of your business, Jake," she says immediately.

"Why not? It's not like you have anyone else on the island to lean on."

"Maybe I want it that way."

"Do you really? You don't want anyone to care?"

She's crushing the bottle of water in her hand. "It'd be easier. That's for damn certain."

"You're full of shit," I challenge her.

Defenses fully in place, she goes on the attack. "What the hell is with you today? Hours ago you were confronting me on what I said to your daughter. Then you're kissing me. Is this some kind of test to break me? Believe me, a lot of men have tried."

"Now, see that? That's what concerns me." I shove away from the counter.

"What? That I've been involved with men who are assholes? News flash, Jake: I'm not a saint."

"No, I'm now concerned because you might teach my daughter that all men are," I say quietly.

"Bigger news flash: she already is beginning to think they are. You're doing a fine job of that all on your own without my help, apparently. Hey, where are you going?" Em yells after me as I walk out the door, closing it gently behind me.

It's time to have a serious conversation with my daughter. Because Emily's right.

Jenna's the one who matters.

First. Now. Always.

23

JAKE

"Give me a break, Dad. Aren't we past the point where you think we need to have this conversation? I realize not all men are jerks. And I'm not ready to talk about the other. If we have to have this talk"—Jenna buries herself deeper into the couch—"can't I have it with Dani?"

"Honey, it's my responsibility as your parent to sit down with you to talk about these things." I scrub a hand down my face because I'd rather talk to my daughter about boys, sex, and respecting herself as much as much as I want her to actually be having sex. In other words, not at all. But since Michelle decided that being a part of this family didn't matter to her and I booted her ass out years ago, the job falls to me.

Yet another thing to hold against my ex-wife.

"Dad, you know they teach this at school. I mean, you're a teacher!" Jenna exclaims, jumping up from the mounds of cushions she'd tried to bury herself under.

"I'm a music teacher, Jenna. Not a health teacher," I say exasperatedly. "How am I supposed to know what they teach and don't teach?"

"I don't know!" she cries. "Don't they talk about it in meetings at school?"

"I try to tune that part out," I mutter, much to my daughter's delight.

"This is seriously humiliating. Can't I just go search the internet or something? Maybe watch a video on YouTube?" My face must show how absolutely horrifying that thought is because Jenna cracks up laughing. "Calm down, Dad. I'm not that crazy. Knowing me, I'd find some sex tape between Dani and Brendan and I'd be scarred for life."

"Jen, stop. Please, I'm begging you." She's killing me, one word at a time. If I make it to my thirty-eighth birthday, it will be a miracle.

She giggles, the sound the purest music, lighting my soul even in the darkest corners. There are times when I might wonder, "What if?" about the music career I could have risked it all for. Especially when Dani comes to visit with Brendan. It brings up a whole host of doubt in my mind. Could I have been more than just a music teacher? Could I have had it all with Jenna at my side? Then I see the beautiful—if aggravating—young woman she's become and I realize it's no contest. No amount of awards on any mantel, no amount of money in the bank, could ever compete with the honor of being "Dad" or on the rare occasion these days, "Daddy."

Narrowing my eyes on her, I realize there's something different. It isn't the missing rainbow hues to her hair. I noticed that right away. There's a burden that's lifted that wasn't there a few days ago. Shit. Normally this means... "Jenna, did you meet someone?" I demand.

It must be an art they teach to all females in the womb, that perfect condescending eye roll. "Not in the way you think, Dad. But..." Her voice trails off.

Reaching behind me, I grab another throw pillow and toss it at her. "Come on. You know you can talk to me." Until the last year, when she started hanging out with kids who spent more time in trouble than out of it, Jenna knew she could always come to me with whatever was on her mind.

"Lynne's awesome, Dad. I don't know how to explain her." Jenna's contemplative. Suddenly a different thought crosses my mind.

"Jen, are you and Lynne together?" My voice is completely

neutral. I have plenty of acquaintances who are happily married to their longtime partners. It wasn't an easy path, and if this is the road my daughter's choosing to take...

I don't have to worry long. Jenna's eyes get comically wide. She sputters when she starts to talk before she falls back into the pillows laughing. When she lifts her head, there are tears of laughter streaming down her face. "No, but thank you for asking me versus lecturing me." Her face looks sad for a minute. "A lot of my friends aren't so fortunate."

Seriously, I look at her. "Jenna, if that's the path your life takes you on, you know I'll always support you, right?"

Her face softens. "Yeah, I know. I'm really lucky like that." Her face gets sad. "Unlike Lynne."

Uh-oh. My parental alarm bells go clanging. "What's wrong with Lynne, Jen?"

Curling her legs under her, she explains, "You've actually met her."

"I have?" I honestly don't remember.

Nodding, Jenna confirms, "At Sacred Grinds. We share hours."

The light dawns. "The pretty dark-haired girl with the blue eyes."

Jenna nods soberly. "See, Dad, that's the thing. Her parents berate her for being a little overweight. All the time. She's got such low self-esteem, she can't see how pretty she is. I was hoping at first Dani might be able to talk to her, but that might be the wrong person. I just don't know." Jenna's hurting and frustrated for all the right reasons.

The pride I have in my daughter at this moment wants to burst out of me. I know I was instrumental in how she sees people, but I didn't do it alone. My parents and Dani's had a huge part, especially in the early days after I threw Michelle out. I don't know what I would have done if I couldn't have called one of them up when she was running a high temperature or throwing up or having a temper tantrum. I remember texting all of them photos of outfits when we couldn't settle disputes in a store shopping, and on my salary—well before things changed—they helped make sure Christmases and vacations were never wanting.

In between, I've been able to exercise my creative juices in the best way I know how—teaching kids to find that burning love of music. For me, the ability to teach—while having the time to keep playing—has been my refuge all these years. I've burned out hours of anger at my ex on a drum set. I've strummed away frustration on my guitar. I've sang when I've felt particularly joyous. And on rare occasions I've picked up the gleaming restored sax that stands proudly in the corner. But my sax is special, and it takes the right set of emotions to get me to pick it up these days.

Back in college, I wrote a paper about the rights of musicians and the protection of their work. I remember using a quote from Plato where he stated that music is moral law that gives soul to the universe. I remember being thunderstruck but finally feeling someone understood how I felt, even if he died about sixteen hundred years ago. And yet, that too is insane. That a man who sat and looked at the stars and dreamed could feel the same way then about something that I do today.

I am so fortunate. Which is why I think on some level it bothers me that Emily...

A lightbulb goes off. "What about Emily?" I say slowly.

Jenna frowns. "What about her?"

I hold up a hand. "I don't know Lynne. And we barely know Emily. But it seems to me she's willing to take on your old man on more than one occasion," I say ruefully. "And she's a designer."

The look on Jenna's face when the idea takes root is more satisfying then when a student can tell the difference between Mozart, Bach, and Beethoven. "That's...inspired, Dad." Jenna's wheels are turning at a mile a minute. Then her face falls. "I just can't see Lynne going for it."

I shrug. "Why don't you invite her over for dinner? Get her used to being around here. Then you can go do girl things while I disappear and play for a while. When you're ready for me to drive her home, I will."

Jenna bounces up and down like a kangaroo on steroids. "Can I ask her to sleep over?"

I groan, knowing that despite the distance between our rooms I'll still be woken up by shrieks at dawn. But I won't deny my daughter any happiness after she's been so miserable since we moved here. "Yes," I agree with a father's inbred reluctance.

But it's all worth it when she jumps up from her blanket of pillows—which go flying everywhere—and dives into my arms. "Thanks, Daddy." Dashing off, she calls out, "I'm going to call her right now. Can we have pizza for dinner?"

"Suckering me into a sleepover and pizza, Jen? That's pushing it!" I call out to her retreating form. But I immediately give in to such an innocuous request. "Find out what Lynne likes on her pie."

"I will!"

Left alone in the family room, I begin to pick up the mounds of pillows Jenna was nested under. Unconsciously, my eyes travel over to the garage apartment through the windows. Em's sitting on the back deck—a solitary figure sketching in a notebook with Mugsy at her feet. I'm pulled toward the window to be closer to it, to her.

Leaning against the sill, I'm absorbed in her. She continues sketching for a while. Picking up the phone next to her, her smile shines brighter than the sun blanketing the island as she slips it to her ear. It's like the infinite promise of summer, warm and seductive.

Ripping myself away, I yell out to Jenna, "Text me when you're ready to get Lynne!"

"Okay, Dad!"

Hurrying down the hall to the music room, I stop by the bar. Turning on the tap, I fill a glass with some water. I refuse to give too much thought to what I'm about to do.

I haven't played it in forever. When I hit the music room, I pull out a few reeds, drop them into the glass, and set it on the floor carefully. Letting them soak, I walk over to my sax. Lifting my neckpiece from the back of the stand, I slip it over my head and clip it to the back of the beautiful horn. My breath shudders out.

It feels so wrong and so right.

After I polish and seal the first reed, I scrape off the rough ends. Maybe that's why playing the sax is so personal to me; even preparing to play it reminds me so much of life. Attaching it to the mouthpiece, I take a deep breath and let the smooth jazz spin me into another world as I work through the crazy emotions that only it can rip from me.

For hours, until Jenna texts me, I play. My lips are swollen from the brutal pressure I've put them under. And still, I can't get my new neighbor—or her words—off my mind.

24

EMILY

It's been a few days since I've seen Jake. Thank God. After that kiss he laid on me before walking out, I'm not sure if I'd jump him to grab his face for more or pummel him. It's a close toss-up.

Jenna, on the other hand, still comes over each day to make certain I don't need any help before dashing off to work. After I carefully talked with her the second day, she waved off my worry with a huge hug. Telling me I was right, she quickly became my right hand —well, actually, my left leg. Because my leg is still bruised, I'm trying to avoid the stairs down to the beach more than once a day. With Jenna's invaluable help in the morning, I'm able to take Mugsy for his nightly walks. I sent Jason pictures of my leg yesterday. He warned me I might be looking at a month before I feel up to running the way I was before the bike chain decided to attack.

Each morning, after sleeping to the sounds of the ocean crashing against the sand, I'm beginning to find everything easier: waking, walking, eating, even sketching. The tingle that flows through me when I hold the charcoal in my hands is returning as I sit on the back deck overlooking the ocean. I'm in the middle of playing around with a design cut on the bias with a fluted hem when I hear a familiar screech of "Oh my God!" behind me.

Grinning, I don't move from the lounger I'm stretched out on. "Hi, Jenna. Come on over."

"Um, Em? Are you dressed? I brought a friend by to meet you," Jenna asks hesitantly.

I laugh. Even though I have a bikini on underneath one of Phil's old shirts in the breezy morning air, to the casual observer it might look like I'm only wearing the shirt. Phil's fairly broad-chested, so even though I'm the tallest of the women in our family, his clothes still dwarf me. "I'm wearing a swimsuit."

Two sets of feet come walking along the outer deck. Mugsy lifts his salt-and-pepper head and thumps his tail before resting his head back on his paws. I frown. Normally, he'd be all over company, begging for a treat. I might have to call my veterinarian in Collyer to see what the chances are that Mugs picked up a bug. But I'm distracted from my thoughts as Jenna bounces in front of me. "Hey, Em!"

I grin at her exuberance. "Hey." I smile at the girl behind her who reminds me a lot of Corinna when she was that age. Tall and lushly built, she's hiding behind her clothes. *Likely she's going through the same torment Cori went through*, I think bitterly. "Emily Freeman." I hold out my hand and start to stand.

"No, Ms. Freeman. There's no need to stand!" The young woman races over. "I'm Lynne. Jenna mentioned you got hurt that day you came into Sacred Grinds."

My mind spins before her name clicks into place. "You relieved her shift," I remember. She smiles, and just like Cori, it lights up her face. *This girl is beautiful*, I think admiringly. Flipping the page, I start a new sketch while talking.

"Yes, ma'am."

I snort. "Please, call me Em."

Both girls giggle. "I owe you coffee, Jen," Lynne says.

"Why?" I ask.

"Jenna bet it would take you less than ten minutes to invite me to use your given name," Lynne says shyly.

Jenna winks at me. "Em's cool like that."

"Ah, another life goal met." Both girls look at me in confusion. "Being cool again."

They laugh.

"Did you both just come to hang out?" I draw in the dimple that appears in Lynne's cheek when she smiles. Lynne's smile disappears while Jenna's gets determined.

"Em, I wanted you to meet one of the main reasons I wanted to go into fashion. I want to design a plus-size line for my new best friend." Jenna's voice is filled with determination.

I stop drawing. Every once in a while, human nature still manages to surprise me. I never thought I'd come to Nantucket and find such tenacity as inspiration.

I certainly didn't think I'd find it in the heart of a sixteen-year-old girl.

"Oh, sweetheart. Come here." Placing my sketch pad aside, I stand up. Opening my arms, I embrace this fearless girl who in just a few short days has wormed her way past the barricade I keep around my heart. "I wish half the world had your nobility, but I think if you were to ask Lynne what she wants, she'd probably tell you that more than anything, she wants to fit in. Right, Lynne?" But when I hazard a glance at the other girl to see if my fashion instincts are still firing on the right cylinders, I see awe on her face.

"Is that how you see me, Em?" she gapes.

Crap, my sketch pad was face up.

"Yes, but I normally don't let people see my drawings until they're finished," I say gently. Tears fill Lynne's blue eyes. "Oh, honey, I'm sorry. I can stop drawing you if you want. I didn't mean to upset you!" I cry out.

"Nobody has ever seen me like that before. I look...pretty."

Reaching over gently to cup Lynne's shoulder, I say simply, "That's because you are."

She shakes her head. "Not in comparison to you, Em. Or Jenna. Or anyone else for that matter."

Sitting back on the lounger, I pat the spot next to me. "Lynne, come sit down." After she does, I curl my good leg beneath me. "Part of being a designer is designing beautiful things. But more importantly, it's bringing the natural beauty to the surface. Not everyone is built the same. I mean, look at an Olympic athlete. Did you know that a number of them are considered obese by most medical charts?" I state matter-of-factly.

Lynne gasps. "I had no idea."

I nod. "Body mass, and body shape, are unique to each individual. The important thing is to find your style and play to that strength." Both Lynne and Jenna look thoughtful. Then Lynne's face crumbles.

"But you should hear the girls at school, Em. They're cruel."

Mentally cursing the narrow-minded view of vicious teens, I simply say, "I know someone who could tell you a thing or two on how to deal with that."

"Who?" both girls ask simultaneously.

I grin. "My sister, Corinna. She is probably one of the most gorgeous women I've ever met. She's also built with curves I would kill for, oh, say anytime I wear a strapless dress," I snort.

"Do you think it might be possible for me to contact her?" Lynne asks, subdued.

Reaching for my iPad, I pull up FaceTime. "Why not now?"

"Seriously? She won't mind?" Jenna says, jumping up and running around the lounger.

"There is nothing, and I do mean nothing, my family won't do for me." Feeling the warmth of that steal through me, I switch out of my sunglasses so I can see the screen. Pressing FaceTime video on Corinna's number on my list of favorites, I'm surprised when a shirtless Colby answers. Both girls gasp. "Colby! Put a damn shirt on! I have two teenagers with me, for Christ's sake!" I yell.

"Not on my account," Jenna says dreamily.

"Dibs," Lynne calls. Jenna elbows her, in mock exasperation.

Colby's deep laugh crinkles his eyes in the corner. "Sorry, girls, I'm already taken. Hey, princess, Em's on FaceTime!"

"Ohh! I'll be right there!" my sister yells from offscreen.

"How's life in Nantucket, Em?" Colby tries to keep the phone above his chin but fails abysmally when he slides into one of the stools surrounding Cori's kitchen counter. I slap my forehead as the duo behind me let loose with another round of giggles. "Oops, sorry." His wry grin tells me he knows the effect he's having.

"What are you doing home anyway?" I ask curiously. "Aren't you normally at the office by this time?"

He nods. "Except Caleb, Keene, and I had a meeting with the other department heads that went really late. So, the guys and I decided we'd sleep in and go for a run this morning instead."

I let out a loud snort. "I can just picture the three of you out on a run. Who had to come in first?" My brothers-in-law are seriously competitive with one another. To make it worse, they're all military veterans who all work together. Competitive is an understatement.

Laughing, my sister pulls the phone away from her fiancé. "Ali. That's because she dropped off Kalie and decided to join them. She then decided to race them all to...hey! I didn't know you had company!" Corinna's musical drawl lights up in excitement. "Hi, girls!"

"Hi!" Jenna leans over my shoulder in excitement. Lynne leans closer and waves.

"Cori, the blonde hanging over me like a new appendage is Jenna, Dani's niece. The brunette sitting next to me is her best friend, Lynne." I gesture to each girl in turn.

"Hi, Miss Corinna," Lynne says shyly.

"Hey, Miss Corinna." Jenna waves.

"Oh, please. Drop the 'Miss.' I don't need to feel older than I am." Corinna laughs.

"Princess, you look about twenty again in that getup," Colby says from offscreen.

"Do I want to know you're wearing, Cori?" She has the phone so close, I can only see the edges of her trademark tank. I lament my sister's choice of clothing. Then again, as she often points out, she works long hours in a too-hot kitchen, so style isn't a concern.

"Hold on." The image jostles as Cori starts walking. "Here you go." Using the flip function, Cori turns the screen around so I can see her outfit in the mirror.

I burst out laughing. Colby's right. Corinna does look about twenty in her cutoff jean shorts and hot-pink sneakers. I narrow my eyes. "Is that Colby's ratty-ass Army tank you're wearing, missy?" I demand.

"Hooyah," she chants. Smacking my forehead into the iPad, everyone starts laughing at me. "Listen, you try baking in a kitchen that's hotter than my man without a shirt on... Um, Em? Did I send them into shock?" Corinna looks worried.

I look at the girls who are both in a dreamlike state. Grinning, I tell my sister, "Nope. That would be your man who did that when he answered your phone a few minutes ago. Shirtless," I add when Corinna's confused expression doesn't clear.

"Colby! You didn't!"

"It was Em, babe. How was I to know she'd have two girls with her?"

Corinna rolls her eyes.

"I feel for the parents of those girls though. They're both knockouts. If we ever have girls, I swear, I'm getting another gun."

"Then I get another knife," Corinna replies sweetly.

"Hold on. How is that fair?" Colby argues. "Your knives cost more than my guns."

"Exactly. Now let me talk to my sister and we can argue the protection of our future children later."

"I'm sorry," Lynne interrupts. "But did that man just call me a knockout?" Wonderment fills her voice.

Corinna and I exchange a look while Jenna yells, "I told you that those girls at school were just bitches."

"Jenna, language," I correct quietly.

"Sorry, Em," she says sheepishly. Lynne's still in a daze.

"Lynne?" Corinna calls out. The girls redirect their focus to her. "I need a favor, and I think you might be the one to help me. I'm supposed to go to some dinner with Colby's grandfather. It's kind of a big deal, and I don't have time to listen to Em blather on about what I should wear because I have to get to the kitchen at the office. Can you take notes for me and shoot me an email?"

"Me?" she says incredulously.

"Girl, if you're like me, you're constantly being bombarded with fashion advice. Em's is the best," Corinna says simply. "What she's going to talk to you about is likely what she plans on telling me. It saves her work if you could pass it along. She's supposed to be working on her designs." Corinna throws in an eye roll for effect.

God, I love my sister. I hope the smile I'm giving her conveys all my gratitude. I'm pretty certain it does when she winks at me before beseeching Lynne. "Please, can you help me out?"

Lynne nods, still somewhat in a daze. "Thanks, sweets. I really appreciate it. Now, Em." Corinna's focus turns to me. "I am glad you called. There's a surprise coming for you soon."

"Does it involve you working extra hours?" I keep my voice stern. Corinna has a tendency to work too many hours as it is. I don't need her working overtime to send me a care package.

"Not at all," she assures me. "It does, however, involve Jenna."

Now I'm confused. "Huh?"

"You're getting some visitors up your way for Miss Thing's birthday next week," Corinna tells me smugly.

I turn around to the weight on my back. "Jenna? It's your birthday?"

She blushes. "I'm just turning seventeen. Dani and Brendan always come spend my birthday with me."

Lynne lets out another sigh. "I'm going to meet Brendan Blake." Corinna and I burst into simultaneous laughter. Lynne looks at us both and blushes bright pink.

"Don't feel bad, sweets. Our brother, Phil, was the exact same way when he first met Brendan," Corinna tells the girl.

"Was there any of us who weren't?" I add drolly.

"Smith certainly doesn't think so." Corinna names the head of

Brendan's road crew. We both crack up as she tells the girls about the night all of our siblings descended upon Brendan's country show in Connecticut en masse. Jenna and Lynne are in awe when they realize Corinna got called up on stage. And both girls squeal when they hear about Corinna's proposal from Colby.

It truly is the stuff of teenage dreams.

A half hour later, a reluctant Corinna ends the call, reminding Lynne she has to listen to my advice. After Cori's gorgeous face disappears from the screen, Lynne turns to me and says, "Tell me everything I need to know, Em. I want to go back to school feeling as confident as Corinna is."

Smiling, I start to talk about colors, A-lines, V-necks. The girls listen enraptured while I pick up my sketch pad and begin to fill in the details of Lynne's face. When I'm done, there's a bright laughing young woman in front of me with her best friend, the beach in the background. Signing the bottom with just my initials, EDF, I tear it out of the pad.

Solemnly, I hand it to Lynne and wait for her reaction. "You are that beautiful. Remember that. Fashion doesn't change that."

"I happen to agree, Lynne," a deep voice says from behind us.

We all turn as one to find Jake walking toward us, an unreadable expression on his face.

My stomach flips around as I take in his broad chest in a tight-fitting tee and jeans, his eyes shadowed by sunglasses.

Damn. I did not need this.

25

JAKE

Somehow, I knew the cool facade Emily Freeman presents to the world was just that—something for her to hide behind. She smiles, she laughs. She's warm and caring. And apparently has a heart she shields with enough armor it might take a weapon of mass destruction to blow a hole to get through. And I thought Jenna was hiding her emotions? Emily could teach a course on it. Despite the tension thrumming through my veins, I keep a relaxed pose while taking in the startled women in front of me.

Until these past two weeks, pulling a smile from my daughter since the last time Michelle attempted to visit has been next to impossible. If memory serves me correctly, that was over two years ago. In between the door closing behind my ex, and my spinning around with the latest explanation to my daughter, she grew up and realized that Mommy just didn't want to be there.

And Daddy's excuses didn't quite cut it anymore.

Since Emily moved in, I've seen the Jenna I knew was hiding inside come out. Between silly laughter with Lynne—who's become a permanent fixture at our home the last couple of days—to random shared laughter when I'll be driving her to Sacred Grinds for a late shift and a particularly awful song comes on the radio, the Jenna I know has been coming back to me. She hasn't needed to be prompted—or yelled at—to clean her room, help around the house, or get ready for work. Before this week, I could barely remember a time when my daughter wasn't disrespecting or arguing with me.

But right now, I'm beginning to understand why there's a new glow about her that has nothing to do with the tan she's acquiring from being in the sun so much. She's basking in the glow of a woman's attention. And that woman is stretched out on a lounger wearing an open men's shirt revealing a red bikini beneath that stirs my long dormant needs. Swallowing hard, I try to get this burning desire for my new neighbor under control before I do something stupid.

Like kiss her again.

Or rip the shirt from her and demand who it belonged to.

Because the more I'm around Emily Freeman, the more I'm convinced that she weaves more than just material together. Apparently, she can weave people's hearts back together too. As a result, my voice is harsher than usual when I bite out, "Jenna, time to go."

Emily drawls sarcastically, "Well, aren't you just the bright ray of sunshine." Jenna grins.

Clenching my teeth together, I try for some semblance of calm. "I've got things to do. Some of us actually have things to do beyond sunbathe." Like get over being incredibly turned on and irritated because of it.

The catalyst for my emotions curls her lip slightly, before she turns her back to me. I gape at her as she proceeds to ignore me in favor of the two teenage girls in front of me. "Think about what Cori and I were saying, okay? *Both* of you." She directs her comment to my wayward daughter.

Jenna nods eagerly. "I will, Em."

Em. Fucking Em. Who the hell is she to give advice to my daughter? And then my temper cools with the next comment out of her luscious mouth.

"Jenna, sweetheart." Emily directs an open smile at my child, and inside my chest, my heart stops. I swear the earth didn't move; the moon collided into the sun. "You've been such a huge help to me with Mugsy this week and generally keeping my spirits up because of my leg, and if it's all right with your father, I'd like to talk to you about a birthday present." Her head tips toward mine, but she keeps her focus on Jenna.

As much as I don't want to give her credit, I'm both surprised and impressed she didn't ignore me and give it to her anyway. "What are you thinking of?" I ask.

Turning just her head, her curls bounce from the ocean breeze. She bites her lower lip in concern, not out of seduction. Though, damnit, it still riles my body up in the same way. Hoping my voice is still under control, I prompt her, "Em?"

"If she doesn't have a dress for her birthday, maybe I could make her one?" The words are rushed out.

Jenna gasps in surprise. Then she jumps up and down.

"And Lynne too," Em tacks on.

The girls look at each other in wonder before screaming, "Yes!"

"I just thought, they're going to be going to college soon," Emily hurriedly explains. "This could be something they could take with them."

I'm astounded. Emily's actually anxious I'll say no. Even without the fact I've seen her work on a woman I consider more of a sister than cousin, I would never, could never, break my daughter's heart by saying no. Softly, so only Emily can hear, I say, "Her birthday is next Friday. Does that give you enough time to do both dresses?"

"Bet your ass it does," she says back just as softly. "You can tell her yes, and I'll get started."

Jenna and Lynne are clutching each other hopefully, waiting on pins and needles. "All right, Em. If it won't be too much trouble..." I can't finish the sentence, because my daughter is running across the deck and slamming into my body with such force, I'm knocked back a foot.

"Thank you, Daddy. Thank you." Her heartfelt whisper ricochets between my head and my heart. Before I can recover from that, another more hesitant set of arms wrap around me. Lynne leans in and whispers, "This is too amazing."

Squeezing the girls tighter, especially my daughter, I say, "Now, let's give Emily some space. We have to get Lynne home and"—my eyes meet those the color of the moon hitting the ocean at midnight, and I force my body not to shudder in reaction—"Em has some work to do."

"Give me just one second, Daddy." Jenna breaks away and runs to Em. She takes her by surprise when she throws herself against her. With an "Oomph," Emily practically falls to her back on the lounger, unable to counterbalance Jenna's exuberance. Jenna says something muffled. Emily's face softens. Lowering her head to rest on my daughter's, their blonde hair mingling, I'm slapped in the face with what I could have had if my ex hadn't been such a self-centered bitch.

I hurt for Jenna living on the scraps of a woman's love.

I ache for everything I couldn't give her.

I yearn for the need to step forward and wrap my arms around them both.

Clearing my throat, I get out, "Sorry, Emily. Now, Jenna."

Her head lifts from Emily's. She steps back reluctantly. "Right. Thanks, Em."

Emily's lips tip up. "Go, before everyone gets in trouble and I don't get to design anyone any dresses." Then she tacks on with a wild burst of humor that unless I missed my guess, she shows very few people, "Unless it's for you, Jake. I'm sure your legs would look great in one."

After I snort out my response, I wrap my arms around both laughing girls in order to lead them away. After I've guided them partway down the deck, I look over my shoulder. Emily's pressing her lips tightly together. I catch her eye and mouth, "Thank you." She just smiles and shrugs her shoulders as if it's nothing.

It's more than nothing, but what it is I have no idea.

26

EMILY

I can't get the fabric I want for Jenna and Lynne's dresses anywhere near Nantucket. I frown as I put down the phone the next day. I know I have bolts of fabric in my closet at the farm that would work perfectly. The question is, how do I get them here in time?

Tapping a pen on a pad next to me, I pick up the phone and call the one person who I know can figure out any problem. One ring...two...

"Amaryllis Events. This is Cassidy. How may I help you while you're supposed to be relaxing, Em?"

"I'm impressed. You actually checked the caller ID this time," I drawl.

"I know, right? If Ali hadn't just walked out of my office, I probably would have been engrossed in the new system she put into place."

I frown. While I'm not completely inept, I can't say I'm a computer genius. "What new system?" I demand.

"Brace yourself, sister." Cassidy's smooth voice turns wildly amused. "She put in an intake form that is virtually mistake-proof."

"I'm certain Phil will manage to find a way around that, Cass." My voice holds a wealth of sarcasm. But it's true. If there's a way for Phil to skip over the details he doesn't care about to get to the things he does, he will. We've all felt the pain of his mistakes, but recently none so badly as Corinna and Ali.

"I thought the same thing. But Ali had the software team design the form so that Phil can't even get to the flower-ordering screens unless he's gone through a series of questions with the client that explicitly rule out additional work. And, get this: they'll have to sign an acknowledgment of it when they sign the contract so big brother doesn't get blamed for their mistakes."

The sheer genius behind this design may—I'm still wary until I see it in action—make this Phil-proof. "If this works, how big is Ali's bonus?" I wonder aloud.

"Big. And she might earn some extra time off after your show," Cassidy assures me.

"No kidding. How long did she work on this?"

"Apparently, she's been designing it on the side for years. Since she and Keene were first dating."

I blink and pull the phone away from my ear. "That's almost three years, Cass!" I screech.

"I know. Then again, trying to figure out all the ways Phil can manage to trip up an order..." Her voice trails off.

"And it integrates with scheduling?"

"The only two people who can override it are Ali and me," Cassidy assures me.

"Wow." We both sit in silence, absorbing the shock of what Ali did. "I have no words."

"Just think, Em. No more screaming at Phil because he quadruple booked Corinna."

"No more double bookings of bridal appointments." After a moment of shared harmony, I ruin it by asking, "Then what are we going to yell at him for?"

"Ali already thought of that. She figures he'll still do something stupid, you know like open his mouth. She had a tracking sheet built in for all of us where we can track what an annoying pain in the ass he is." While I use every force of will to not spew the iced tea I'm drinking on the sketches I just finished, Cass says dreamily, "Did I mention it was going to be a big bonus?"

I lose the fight. Fortunately, I manage to turn my head at the last minute and save the designs. The tea lands harmlessly on the floor.

"You sound better." Cassidy's still feeling mellow.

I chuckle. "Even if I wasn't, that news is certainly enough to get me to a whole new plane, sweets."

"True. Phil's out with Jason today. When he comes in tomorrow, it's going to be holy hell. I can't wait."

"Make sure Holly gets it on video," I beg, rubbing a hand over my heart. It's moments like this I wish I was home so I could be with my family.

"I will. Now, what's up? While I'm thrilled beyond all words I got to share this news with you"—her grin lights up her voice—"I know that's not why you called."

"I hate to ask for a favor and ruin your mood."

"Em, we're putting an electronic leash on Phil. My mood can't be ruined."

Just wait. "I need you to go into the fabric room at my house."

"Except that." Hearing her chair wheels, I can only imagine she's now on her feet. I confirm that when I hear the back-and-forth click of her heels. "Jesus, Em. That room looks like someone blew up the nearest Calico Corners store and air-dropped it in there!"

"Cass," I soothe her, "I promise you'll be able to find this one."

"The last time I went into your fabric room, I was in there three times over three hours. Three hours, Em. I thought Caleb was going to send in a rescue team for me," she snaps.

"It won't be that bad..." I'm cut off before I can continue.

. "Em, how many different fabrics are in there?"

I ask unthinkingly, "Which season?"

"See? See? This just proves my point!" She proceeds to moan in my ear, much to my amusement.

"Cass, honey, you'll have no problem finding them, because the fabric is still in a box on the floor. The box is bright green. I had it shipped from Ireland. You can't miss it."

There's dead silence on the other end of the line. "Really? You don't need me to go on FaceTime with a flashlight so you can see the embossed print of black on black?"

Knowing she'd do it for me even if I needed her to, I am happy to tell her, "Nope. I just need that box." My voice fills with frustration. "I just don't know how to get it to me before the weekend, and I really need it."

"Oh, that's easy. Hold on a second." Hearing the soothing hold music we chose, I wait.

And wait.

A few minutes later, Cassidy comes back on the line. "Is Friday too late?" She sounds worried.

I blink. Two days? "Cass, it's not business. I won't charge it to our account."

"It's not being shipped. I had to make a phone call. I know someone who's headed to Nantucket. I just asked if they could bring your box to you."

"That's..."

"Yes?"

"That's freaking amazing!" I jump out of my seat to dance without remembering to take care of my bad leg. "Ow, shit!" Dropping back into the chair, I rub the fading bruises.

"Did you go to a doctor? Ugh, I wish I could just send Jason up to you as easily as I'm sending your fabric," she frets.

"I saw a doctor, Cass," I say exasperatedly.

"He's not Jason."

"True." Our brother-in-law is an amazing doctor who specializes in trauma care at NYU. "If it's not better in the next week, I promise, I'll go back."

"Deal. Now, is there anything else you need?"

I say the first thing that comes to mind. "Just your arms wrapped around me."

"Just as soon as I can, my Em. That's a promise." I hear the other line ring. "I have to go."

"I know. I love you."

"Same here. Call later."

"Will do." I disconnect the call on my end. Picking up the sketch pad, I think about the bolts of chestnut brown and purple *doupion* silk I received in the mail from Roisin Cross in Ireland. Pulling my iPad toward me, I look up my last order. It's too bad I have nowhere to go, I think with some regret. There's a bolt of the black silk in the box as well.

TWO DAYS LATER, my box arrives on the arms of one of the best-looking delivery guys I've ever seen.

I mean, I think most of the known universe wouldn't mind having Brendan Blake as a delivery boy. Brendan, being led by Jenna around the side of the deck carrying my box, would cause most women and quite a few men to faint. Especially when he drops the box and sweeps me into a hug that lifts me off my feet. Laughing, I can't catch my breath. "Well, this is a surprise!" Hell of an understatement, if there is one.

"That box and the hug are from Cassidy," he tells me as he lowers me back down. "I have something special for you from Corinna that almost didn't make it here because I wanted to eat it. But this is from me." He kisses me gently on the cheek, then looks down to my bare legs. Letting out a long, slow whistle, he mutters, "Jesus, now I know why Corinna was all up my ass about making sure you were okay."

"It isn't so bad anymore, Brendan," I assure him. "Really."

"She's right," Jenna chirps. "Em's been able to take walks with me and everything."

"And you got your medical degree from where, munchkin?" Brendan shoots back.

As Jenna pouts, I gently rebuke Brendan, "Jenna was instrumental in my recovery. She not only bandaged me up the first day, she's walked Mugsy every day since." Hearing his name called, Mugsy stretches and lifts his head.

"Hey, old man." Brendan crouches down. Mugsy slowly ambles to him and sniffs his hand, before gracing him with a lick. "Good boy. Sorry, Jen. I didn't mean that the way it sounded."

Jenna sniffs, ignoring her cousin's fiancé. "Em, is that the fabric? Can I see it?"

"Absolutely!" I say enthusiastically.

Her face lights up. She runs for the box. Before she can make it, I dash her hopes. "In about two days once I've pieced the dress together."

"Mean, Em. Just mean." Jenna pouts.

"Hell, Em. I didn't know the dress was for Jenna." Rubbing the back of his neck, he smiles. "Gonna make Dani jealous though."

Thinking about the black fabric, I smile. "There might be enough in the box to make her something as well."

"I almost regret bringing one of your other dresses to wear if you're in that kind of mood." We all turn in time to see Dani Madison skip down the deck. Dressed in a baseball cap, cutoff jeans, and sneakers, she looks like a college cheerleader, not like the world-famous model who drops men to their knees.

Since I'm closest, I'm the one who receives the first of the exuberant hugs she's doling out. "Hey, babe. Been too long."

Pulling back, Dani looks down at me. Studying my face for a few minutes, she breaks out in a wide smile. "I knew this place would be good for you."

"A lot of things have been good for me."

"Just not biking," Jenna pipes up. I roll my eyes as Dani growls.

"I am killing Jake the moment I see him. I asked him to throw out that piece of junk years ago." Giving me a once-over, Dani winces when she spots the bruises I suspect I'll be sporting for a while. "That chain could have fractured your calf, Em."

"I'm fine." I wave off the concern. "It's over. Move on."

"Yeah, let's talk about where we're all going for Jenna's birthday." Rubbing his stomach, Brendan says, "I'm hungry."

"Seriously, is all you do think about food?" Dani gripes.

"Now that we're done with this part of the tour, babe, I'm indulging. Besides—" Giving her a wolfish smile and a wink that causes her to blush, he continues. "It's not all I think about."

"I'm sure you all will have a great time," I interrupt before Jenna makes herself dizzy by continuing to roll her eyes. I love the fact that her whole family is going to such an effort to make a big deal about her birthday.

Dani frowns. "What do you mean 'you all,' Em? You're coming too."

I shake my head. "It's a family thing." I, more than most people, get that.

Jenna's irritation with her family ends. Her lips tremble. "But you have to come, Em. I called the restaurant and told them six. I want everyone important to me to be there."

Stepping up to Jenna, I cup her face. "Sweetheart, I wasn't invited. It isn't right for me to crash your party," I say gently, though my heart warms at her words.

Then I hear him. And the hair on the back of my neck raises. It's a good thing I left it down this morning so it covers my reaction to just his voice. Despite my best efforts, I can't get that damn kiss out of my head. I'm even starting to dream about it, which really sucks because I'm no longer waking up refreshed first thing in the morning.

I'm waking up frustrated.

"Actually, Em, that's what I was coming to talk with you about." Jake comes up behind me. Laying a hand on my shoulder, he looks around. "It seems my family beat me to it."

"Beat you to what?" Turning around slowly, I try to prepare myself for the impact of seeing Jake.

Really, I do.

But there's something inside me that clenches when I see his tender smile directed at his daughter. And it isn't in my stomach.

Shit.

27

JAKE

Standing back, I'd been watching Em interact with my family for a while before I made my presence known. Her complete lack of awe in Brendan's presence as well as her obvious affection for Dani and Jenna make her even more appealing to me than she simply is for being a knockout with a smart mouth that kicks me in the gut.

But there's something else that I just can't quite put my finger on.

Whatever it is, I know I'm not feeling it alone. Despite her cool facade, I feel the tremble ripple down her slight frame when I lay my hand on her shoulder, the most innocent of touches. I address Brendan. "We're going to Cru. Remember the last time Dani took us there?" I give my future cousin-in-law a rakish grin. The two of us had to escape out through the kitchen to avoid the hordes of people who descended on the restaurant after the two of them were recognized. She hadn't been too happy.

"Seriously? We're going back there?" Dani's frustration is evident.

I chuckle, knowing I'd get a rise out of her. "Relax, brat. I reserved the private room for us. The only fans you two will have to deal with will be the waitstaff and Jenna's new bestie." I tack on the last as a warning in Brendan's direction. He waves his hand, dismissing my concern. He's used to handling adoring fans after shows. And the one or two that are welcome into our private circle he'll gladly take on for an occasion like this.

Emily's held herself stiffly without saying a word. Deliberately, I jostle her. That gets me an elbow to the gut I do my best to hide my reaction to. "What? You don't like seafood? It has some of the best on the island," I ask innocently.

"I shouldn't intrude. It's a family thing," she repeats softly. There's a note in her voice I can't comprehend. Lowering my head, I try to read her face, but it's closed off.

I wonder what I'd have to do in order to rip it off permanently. Since the thought of that is now more tantalizing than worrisome, I ask, "Did I do something to offend you?"

Her brows winging up immediately cause me to laugh uproariously. Clarifying, I add, "I mean recently."

"No," she says begrudgingly.

"Then come with us," I coax her. "More than anything I could give my daughter, you sitting around the dinner table yakking on about fashion will likely make her birthday." I wait for the explosion.

It doesn't take between one heartbeat and the next.

Pulling herself from the curve of my arm, she stands in front of me. Her fists are clenched at her side. "I do not sound like a boorish animal when I talk about design, Mr. Madison."

She rips off her sunglasses, and I'm treated to the whipping fury in her eyes. In some ways, I almost wish I could paint instead of playing every instrument I've ever touched. I'd love to capture her eyes right now. The dark blue is swimming with nature's untapped fury after a storm has been unleashed. I should know. I've memorized what the sea looks like at those hours. That's when I most ache for a woman in my arms. And knowing I can find that look in Emily Freeman's eyes, I don't know which one of us in more trouble.

"I know. I'm teasing. Please, come with us," I say softly. "Not because you're being pressured, but because you want to. Because you feel something for my daughter. And maybe you're starting to

understand that I have no idea what's happening between us either."
I'm probably going to scare the hell out of her with that.

The war is visible on her magnificent face. She's fighting something within herself. I'm anticipating her denial since I can see she's
fighting something even though it's in complete conflict with the
longing I read in her eyes. So, it's a shock when I hear the whispered
"Yes" come from her lips.

Stepping farther away, she bunches her hands and mutters,
"Shit," before ignoring me. Turning toward my family with a smile,
she says, "I guess I'm coming."

Jenna lets out a whoop I think they can hear in Madaket. Dani
leans back and throws her hands in the air. Brendan just gives me a
knowing look even as he stands and applauds. Emily shakes her
head. "Jesus, it's just dinner, y'all."

Fed up with the antics, Mugsy trots over and sticks his snout in
my hands. Stroking his silky ears, I watch a woman who's fighting an
internal war bring smiles to everyone's face around her—including
mine—simply by being who she is.

And in my head, I hear the notes of John Coltrane. My fingers are
suddenly itching to grab my sax and start playing. Again.

BRENDAN and I left Dani and Jenna over at Emily's while we hauled
all their shit out of their rented Lexus. Lifting another behemoth suit-
case out of the car, I wheeze. "Jesus, she's packed like this since she
was a kid."

Brendan manages to laugh as he struggles with Dani's garment
bag, makeup bag, and duffle that likely contains her shoes. "Normally, I give my road crew tickets to some sporting event to make up
for when Dani travels with us."

Struggling to make our way inside the front door, we finally get
through and drop the bags. Both of us breathing heavily, we look at
each other and burst out laughing. "You know, Emily's sister didn't
just send a box up for her," Brendan tells me conspiratorially.

"Wait, this is Corinna. The woman who actually managed to have you create edible food that didn't poison people on TV?" I demand.

Brendan slaps a hand on my shoulder. "One and the same. What do you say we get the boxes out of the sun and we take the one earmarked for this house down to the studio?"

Throwing my arm around his shoulder, I readily agree. "You ready to listen to the new song I wrote for you?"

"Bet your ass I am. I need to pay for a wedding to a woman who packs like she's moving." We both laugh, but mine has an underlying tinge of gratitude.

When Brendan first came into Dani's life, he wandered outside when I was playing one day and sat down and joined me. From blues, to jazz, to country, to rock, our musical tastes just clicked. Soon the two of us just started jamming. Before we knew what was happening, we'd cowritten two songs for Brendan's album. That was five years ago.

I expected an acknowledgment in the album jacket, sure. What I'd never expected was a royalty check.

I tried to give it back.

Brendan schooled me on how music publishing worked. He explained every single time he sang the song live, every time it was played on the radio, every time someone bought the album, I would get a percentage of the composition fee. "So shut up, put it in a college account for your daughter, and deal with it."

I did.

Brendan and I work well together. When he's looking for something a little less country, a little smoother, we collaborate to make it happen. I have little doubt that by the time he and Dani leave the island, we'll have another couple of songs for him to bring back to his band. And I'll have more money to add to Jenna's growing trust fund she knows nothing about.

We walk back to the car for the most precious of all our cargo: bakery boxes. Carefully, he hands me the first box before picking up two himself. He warns, "The one with a *J* isn't to be touched until Friday. I've got to get that out of sight, stat."

Incredibly touched, I verify, "It's for Jenna?"

Brendan nods. "Corinna baked a hell of a cake for her. Dani and I watched her do it while we were in Connecticut last night."

"Does it need to be refrigerated?"

With a wry smile, Brendan shows me the box. In a bright blue marker, it says, "Refrigerate, B, and DIE! Love, Cori" I read it out loud, chortling. "She knows you well."

"Remember, she had to coach me through cooking on national TV. This was pretty much how she got me through it."

Leaving Emily's box on the kitchen counter—it's hard to mistake when there's a love note from her sister on it—Brendan and I make our way to the basement where he slides the cake onto the far side of the bar. "Cori's the only woman I know who can make fondant taste like something other than chalk," he declares as we make our way to the music room. "I swore I was going to get sick last night eating the hell out of the scraps."

"You suck," I say without heat. In answer, he just points to the box in my hands. "Do you know what it is?"

"No idea. But let me assure you, it's going to be amazing."

We cross into the studio before I think to ask, "Think we'll need forks?"

"Pop open the top and let's see," he urges me. "Especially before the girls get back."

Looking down, I see a few notes. There's a message to Jenna, one to Dani, another one to Brendan, and one to me that shocks me. "'Jake, take better care of my sister or the next baked goods you'll see will be thrown in your face. CF.' I guess I know where I stand with your friend."

Brendan just laughs as he reaches for my guitar. Quickly making sure it's in tune, he slings the strap over his shoulder. "Cori's not shy about her emotions, man. Never piss her off though," he warns.

"Why's that?" I pop the top and find it filled with every kind of brownie there could be. Chocolate upon chocolate, oatmeal with chocolate chips, something that smells like—I take a long whiff—

cinnamon. "God, did I die somewhere between the car and here?" I ask aloud.

"No, that's when you taste the cake she made. She does this kind of baking for fun."

I reach for a cinnamon square. Upon taking a bite, I'm assaulted by a burst of brown sugar that melts on my tongue. Swallowing down the miracle on my tongue, I'm hit with an inspiration. "If you don't know what you want to play, I do."

"You taking lead?" Brendan grins. It's so rare for him to not be in front of a stage singing in front of tens of thousands of people, he's happy to pass the mic off when he's not on stage.

Swinging an electric bass over my shoulder, I turn on the mic in front of me. "Why the hell not?" I begin playing a familiar bass line.

Soon he's strumming away. Together, we lose ourselves in Jagger and the Stones. Until we hear Jenna's feminine screech of "They have the other box down here, Dani!"

Busted.

But when I look toward the door and expect to see the lanky frame of my cousin or my daughter, I'm shocked to see Emily's amused face staring at the box of baked goods. "Jesus, Corinna said she was sending up a surprise. She should have known better than to entrust it with two men."

I defend Brendan and myself before he can speak. "Yours is on the kitchen island."

Leaning out the door, she yells, "Protect the box in the kitchen too, Dani. Those are apparently mine." The squealing that can be heard from the upper floor assures me they found them. "Now, if you'll excuse me, we'll just take what's left of this box and be out of your hair."

"Come on, Em," Brendan teases her. "How long has it been since I sang to you?"

Sang to her? Why do I want to reach over and bash him with my bass? The husky laugh that prompts doesn't help. "You were singing to Cori, Brendan, not me."

"I could change that..." Brendan starts strumming on his guitar, but I cut him off.

"If anyone's going to be singing to our guest, I'll handle it, buddy."

Em's eyebrows shoot skyward. "You can sing?"

Hell yes, I can sing, but I simply shrug. "You?"

The laugher that bursts intrigues me. "Nor hardly. I'm often begged by my family to stop humming whenever I try." She continues laughing as she walks away, adding another layer of mystery to this complex woman. I've never known someone able to laugh at themselves so easily.

"Hey, Em," I call out. I unplug and quickly walk over.

She turns, and her eyes are still sparkling with mirth. "Yes?"

Hearing Jenna come down the stairs animatedly talking with Dani, I whisper a heartfelt "Thank you." There are no words to adequately explain what it means to have my daughter back.

"For what?" Confusion mars her perfect features.

"For helping fix something you saw immediately that was broken." Taking a step closer, I push a wayward curl away from her face. I don't miss the hitch in her breath. Nor do I miss her struggle to slam down the mask. It's too bad I've seen beneath it.

Now, I'll keep trying to get to the woman I know who hides behind it.

"I didn't do anything special," she protests. Putting distance between the two of us, she insists, "You're a good father, Jake. I have no doubt about that."

"Then what is it you doubt?" I'm talking about more than Jenna, and we both know it.

"Me," she says simply. "I doubt I'm worth the effort. No." Shaking her head, she continues. "I know it." Turning away, she calls out, "Did you two abscond with my box? I don't even know what Cori sent me."

Darting away from me—probably swifter than she should on her leg—she races away toward the stairs.

I wet my lips. Suddenly, I'm in the mood for a whole different kind of music.

28

EMILY

"Can sing a little, my ass," I mutter a half hour later. Jake Madison is too damn sexy for his own good. An insane girl could fall a little bit in love while sitting in this room. Between him and Brendan singing Imagine Dragons' hottest new single as Brendan strums away at the guitar and Jake thumbs the bass, I can't tear my eyes away.

Someone have mercy on me and just drop a hurricane on the house or something before I spontaneously combust. Leaning closer to Dani, I whisper, "How do you handle going backstage?"

With a low laugh, she glances around for the girls. She needn't have worried; they're off in their own bubble of excitement. "Why do you think I visit Brendan on tour so much, Em? By the time we make it back to the hotel..." Her voice trails off, and I grin. Lucky bitch.

"Ladies, we're going to go back a few decades," Brendan calls out. Dani perks up.

"How far back, baby?"

"Your favorite decade." The words are barely out of his mouth before Dani jumps up and starts shaking her million-dollar ass. I fall onto her spot on the couch laughing.

"You are such a goofball." The funny part is she's just like this on a set too.

"Em, they're about to start singing '80s music." Dani's eyes are flashing wildly. "Think ballads. Think Jack Wagner. Think saxophones!" Giving me a once-over, she says, "I have no idea what kind of spell you've managed to cast on this family, but keep at it, will you?" before she flops back down next to me.

Gaping at her, I stutter out, "I haven't done a thing."

Lifting a hand, she ticks off on her hand. "One, you healed whatever was broken in Jenna. Two, you helped her friend..."

I interrupt. "That was Cori talking to her."

"Who you put her in contact with," Dani steamrolls over me. Lowering her voice, she murmurs the last one quietly. "And three, that sax hasn't been played in years, Em. Years. So, whatever is going on with you and Jake? Let. It. Happen."

"Not going there, Dani," I warn her.

"Why not?" she challenges me.

"Didn't I just get out of an engagement?" I should be offended when she just flaps her hand at me. And what does it say about me when I'm not? That Bryan was a douchebag and I should have dumped his ass earlier? Probably.

"Is your heart broken?"

I snort. "Hardly."

"Then I was told to remind you that you're not dead and you weren't sent with batteries," Dani says calmly.

I flush horribly. "I'm killing Corinna the minute I get home."

"No, you're not. Listen, he's my cousin and I don't want him hurt, but you're both consenting adults..." Her voice trails off.

"Gee, thanks for the advice, Danielle," I bite out sarcastically. "Remind me to add that bit of wisdom to the price of the next dress I design for you."

She grips my hand tightly as Jake steps up to the mic. His eyes find mine across the room as his sexy-as-fuck voice belts out another song. Brendan's wailing away on an electric guitar. Jake lifts his hand from the bass as he sings the last notes of the ballad just as Brendan walks over to the electric keyboard to finger in the last notes. Jake's singing about true love and being what someone needs. My stomach does a nosedive down to my clit which is now throbbing insanely.

This can't happen.

Not now. Not ever.

Standing, I tell Dani, "I'll be right back." Quickly crossing the room to the doors that lead to the lower porch wrapped around the main house, I shove them open. Desperately needing air, I race as fast as my leg can take me toward the end of the deck away from the music room. Bracing my arms on the ledge, I watch the power of the waves crashing against the beach.

Kicking off my shoes, I step down the few steps until my toes hit the sand. I move quickly away from the house so I can lose myself in the sound of the ocean. "What am I doing?" I whisper.

I can't, just can't, be feeling things for Jake Madison. *Jenna's father,* I tell myself firmly. *Keep it on that level, Em. Yes, he's a good-looking man...okay, stop lying to yourself.* He's sexy as hell. But he has a personality that borderlines on bi-, no, tripolar. One minute, he's a pain in the ass. The next, he's the stern father who's lecturing his almost grown daughter. Finally, he's the...the...

He's the man who pushes every single one of my buttons, I admit. *Stop lying to yourself. He's sexy, dominant, and full of heart. He cares for his family as much as you care for yours. He's arrogant and protective.*

"So, what's the problem?" I say out loud.

"That's what I'd like to know. Is everything okay?" Jake's concerned voice comes from behind me. Closing my eyes at his nearness, I try to pull down my mask before facing him.

I can't give in to what I'm feeling. It would be an enormous mistake. I feel that deep in my soul. If he touches me, I might as well drown myself in the enormous ocean in front of me, because I won't be the same when I walk away.

And I have to. I'll have to walk away.

That thought is what finally gives me the strength to answer, "Yes," but instead of it coming out with my usual determination, something else leaches through.

My need.

His footsteps are muffled between the softly lapping waves and the sand. The next thing I know, Jake's standing in front of me. He opens his mouth before a smirk twists his lips. "Was it the '80s that finally broke through to you?"

"I don't know what you're talking about," I state haughtily. I move to turn and head back to the house, but he captures my wrist and tugs. Flying back, I land sideways into his arms.

He stands there holding me for endless minutes under the starlit sky. "You need to let me go," I say softly.

"Why?"

"This isn't part of why I came here," I tell him honestly.

His bark of laughter both reassures and unsettles me. "Me neither, lady. But I can't seem to escape the fact that the more I see you, the more I want to do this."

"Jake," I offer up as a token protest as his head lowers. Pulling me more flush against him, our bodies align under the vast sky while he steals what little there is of my breath in a kiss so perfect, I know I'm in worse trouble than I thought. Because if I thought I was enchanted by his daughter and helpless to his voice, I'm drunk on his kiss. It floods my blood like the most potent of wine. It echoes in my heart like the fiercest of storms. It scares me down to the soles of my feet.

It warms me deep in my heart.

Pulling me closer against his muscled body, one of his hands cups the back of my head while the other smooths up and down my back. Sliding my arms up around his neck, I hold him closer. Feeling my acquiescence, Jake molds me against him. His head angles slightly, pulling me deeper into the vortex of the storm.

When we finally break apart for air, our lips seem unwilling to part. Jake peppers my face with a few tender kisses even as he's easing me back. "Em?"

He expects me to talk? After a kiss like that? "What?" I'm barely able to get the gritty word out past my swollen lips.

Here it comes, I think cynically. The brush-off.

"I know why you can't sing."

Flabbergasted, I gape at him. He wants to talk about music? "Excuse me?"

His voice has risen to be heard over the crashing waves. "It's because all the music is trapped inside your soul. You just sing where most people aren't allowed to see it, so they can't hear it." With a lopsided smile, Jake touches my cheek before he backs away. "I'll see you back at the house." Turning, he jogs through the sand back toward the stairs, leaving me immobile as I watch after him.

Facing the ocean again, I try to get my heart's rhythm back under control.

I am so completely screwed.

29

JAKE

It took me a few minutes to cool down after a kiss so scorching, I nearly tumbled Emily to the beach to taste the softness of her smooth skin I saw on display the other day. I was of half a mind to, but the vulnerable look on her face stopped me.

I want her to want me, not be uncertain about it. So, I walked away from the singularly hottest moment in my adult life to come back and reassure Dani and Brendan that "Em just needs a moment."

Fortunately, Jenna and Lynne had run upstairs to get everyone a refill on drinks because otherwise I'm certain there would be no end to the questions. When I left her on the beach, her delicate lips were still a bit puffed up...

I endure their knowing looks by ignoring them and tossing a reed into a glass of water well before Em slips back in through the door she escaped through earlier.

Preparing it through rote motions, I turn back to Brendan, whose face is filled with thoughtful concern. "Are we still in an '80s mood?"

He nods, but his expression hasn't changed. "What do you have in mind?"

"Let's lighten things up," I suggest. I walk over to the sax in the corner and pull out a reed. Popping it into my mouth to wet the already broken-in reed, I use the lubrication from my tongue to ensure it feels right before I attach it to my mouthpiece.

"No freaking way!" Jenna exclaims, bouncing up and down. I grin at my daughter.

"Em, are you in for a treat," Dani drawls. I see Em kick her and shoot her a death glare. I can't help the snicker of laugh that escapes. Feral eyes turn on me. They shouldn't turn me on, but after having her wrapped in my arms, it seems anything she does will do that. Provoking the beast I already awoke even further, I wink at her.

Jenna and Lynne are giggling in the corner. Em looks at me and mouths, "I hate you."

My lips twitch before I turn my back to her. I lean over to Brendan and murmur a song we haven't played in forever. He rolls his lips together tightly. "Are you sure you know what you're doing?"

I admit, "I haven't got a damn clue."

He sighs. "I didn't think so." Walking over to the keyboard, he starts playing the opening notes to a late '80s song that is happiness and seduction wrapped into one.

Perfect.

Even Jenna and Lynne are singing along—I guess '80s music is popular again. Em's eyes widen when I step up to the mic again. But it isn't until I swing the sax up and start blowing that I watch her mouth the words "I'm fucked" to no one in particular.

It fuels me.

Em's mouth is agape. Seeing that tears the music from my soul. Just the way any good sax playing should. The need to pick up this instrument again started when she opened her heart to my daughter with her smiles. She drove the urge higher when I heard her laughter. But the minute my lips touched hers with intent, I have to admit to myself that I was fighting a losing battle.

How can you fight this kind of insane attraction? It'd be like trying to stop a freight train with a bunny rabbit.

Instead, I'm letting it flow through me. I'm letting the music speak for me as I reach for notes I forgot I could play just to seduce her. Judging by the look on her face, it seems to be working. When I drop the sax from my lips, she exhales, as if it was my lips that captured hers during that run of notes.

And maybe it was.

I finish the song not taking my eyes from her. She's laced her fingers tightly together—whether that's to avoid pummeling me or not I'll never know because she jumps up right after and announces, "That was...incredible, but I have to go." Turning apologetically to Jenna, she explains, "I have to let Mugsy out."

"I could—" Jenna starts to offer, but Emily cuts her off.

"There's no need, sweetheart. I have a lot to do tomorrow on both of your dresses to get them ready for Friday." Her smile encompasses Lynne.

"You have something for yourself to wear. Right, Emily?" I feign concern. I really just want to force her to look at me.

I can practically hear her gritting her teeth before she offers me a facsimile of a smile. "Since Dani doesn't need a dress, I'm whipping up something for myself."

"How...practical of you. It's not yellow, is it? I've heard chickens wear that a lot," I taunt lightly after what happened between us on the beach.

If I could die from a look alone, I have little doubt I'd be a writhing mess on the floor. "No, it's black. As in *little black dress*. We'll just leave it at that." Tossing her hair over her shoulder, she quickly hugs the girls, tosses a wave at Brendan and Dani, and ignores me.

I grin. Best night I've had in a long time.

"Hey, Jenna, can you and Lynne go grab another round of drinks?"

"Sure, Dani. We'll be right back." Both girls scramble up the stairs eager to help out. I'm so distracted by thoughts of Em I don't realize Dani's untangled herself from the couch to come stand next to me. That is until she hauls off and pounds me in the shoulder. "Shit, what the hell was that for?" I curse her silently in my head even as I rotate my arm.

"It's for whatever you did on the beach to put that wild-eyed look in Em's eyes, jackass. Don't play around with her, Jake," Dani warns me.

I want to tell her this gravitational pull is just as frightening for me, a man who has shut himself off from all but the basest of female needs since Michelle left. I have no clue what I'm doing or what's happening between us. But I'm intrigued. Em has shifted something deep inside of me. And I have to explore it. Instead, all I tell her is "What happens—or doesn't happen—is between Emily and me."

"Then you're more of a fool than I originally thought. Everything you're thinking of is about to have repercussions on every aspect of your life. Including Jenna." Her words cool off my ardor like nothing else would. "Think on that before you do anything stupid like kiss her senseless in the moonlight."

"Did she say something?" I'm in shock she opened up to say anything.

"She didn't have to, moron. The signs were all over her face." Dani stares at me before reaching up and wiping something near my lips. "And yours. This shade of color really isn't good on you."

Flushing, I realize I walked in with Emily's lipstick all over my face. I realize I don't give a damn. I'm not hiding from anything. Choosing to stay quiet is probably smarter, because I don't know what I *should* say.

"Just...be careful. Okay? For all of your sakes." Just that quickly, my irritation evaporates when I recognize the very real concern in her eyes.

Cupping her shoulder, I pull her as close as I can with the sax still in the way. Brushing a kiss on her temple, I murmur, "I appreciate it, Dani. But there are some things that are just inevitable."

"The last time you said that, you wound up involved with Michelle." I cringe knowing she's right.

"Should I stay locked in the past, or should I try to move forward?" I ask quietly. Dani stiffens under my arm as my aim strikes true.

"I know this is a family thing..." Brendan interrupts.

I glare at him. "You are family."

"Then I'm going to add in my two cents' worth. Before tonight, I would have never seen you together with Em. Now"—he shrugs—"I get it." I begin to smile before his next words wipe that from my face. "It's just...I know more than I can say. She has this enormous heart she keeps locked behind a barricade for reasons I can't share, Jake. She's only here for such a short time. You could be starting something that ultimately hurts both of you."

"Is that what you thought when you and Dani first got together?" I demand.

He smiles over at my cousin—the woman who I know damn well aligns the stars in his sky. "No. And it wasn't easy. But every moment of heartache we went through was worth it."

Leaving my side and crossing over to Brendan, Dani slips her arms around him. "It was. But..."

Laying a finger on his lips, he shushes her before gently brushing his lips across hers. "But nothing, Dani. Jake needs to find his own path. All I will say is be careful, Jake. I know the Freemans. What you see with them isn't what's beneath the surface."

I let that sink in. "It rarely is."

LATER THAT NIGHT, I'm standing beneath the rain shower trying to find some way to relax before I sleep. Water sluices over the back of my neck as I bow my head. Brendan's words are echoing through my head, but they're a distant warning in comparison to the replay of the kiss I stole from Emily in the moonlight.

When Michelle and I ended, I found discreet ways to take care of my needs when Jenna would be with my parents or Dani. I haven't been a monk, but neither have I formed any kind of an emotional bond with a woman. Hell, half the time I walked away from the experience feeling just as empty as when I walked in.

It's been two weeks and I already feel twisted up by Emily. Closing my eyes against the dripping water, I conjure up an image of her face. I never thought there'd be such fire buried beneath the ice. In the short time I've known her, I know she's, brilliant, dedicated, warm-hearted, fierce, independent, and a ball of flames in my arms.

Christ, I don't know that there's anything that could keep me from walking away.

Tipping my head back, my hand drops down my body until it circles my rock-hard cock. Bringing images of the woman consuming my thoughts to the forefront of my mind, I begin slowly stroking. Faster and faster, I can't help it. The need, the want, the flash of desire she brings out in me. I can't explain it. All I know is that it's more. Bracing my legs apart, I throw my arm up against the tile in front of me as the tingle begins at the base of my spine.

When I explode, it's Emily's name that falls from my lips hoarsely.

30

EMILY

With my leg almost completely healed, I've dragged my sewing machine out to the deck to finish the final topstitching on Jenna's dress. She'll be by in a little while to try it on, and all I can think is serenity. Now.

After last night, I need to be near the calming influence of the ocean as much as possible. What started out as a quick errand to pick up my sister's box of goodies ended up as a barely veiled seduction. Lifting my foot from the pedal, I rub my hand over my tired eyes. It does me no good to take out my frustration on the dress. I'll just end up ripping out stitches. That time-consuming task on the delicate fabric will make me more pissed than I already am.

Almost as irritated with myself as I am for imagining Jake's face as I came on my own fingers last night.

I was so stimulated between the sound of his voice, the feel of his lips, and his hard body pressed against mine, I was drenched after I made my way back to the apartment. I didn't even make it to the bed before I had slid my shorts to the floor. Sprawled out on the couch, I imagined how husky his voice would get as his mouth traveled down my body.

I'm still resentful of his effect over me. It lasted well beyond his lips tasting me, my own hands being on me, and well into my dreams where I imagined all the things I'd do to him if he was spread out before me like a buffet.

Unlike some of my family members, the traumas of my past didn't inhibit my sexual desires. I appreciate a man's sexuality—especially when it sparks my own. *Which I must have put into severe hibernation while I was with Bryan*, I think derisively. That man had absolutely no creativity in the bedroom. I hope his next conquest enjoys the missionary position because dominance to that man involves him being on top. I can't help but giggle.

"I really hope you're not laughing about last night. It'd kill my ego," Jake says from behind me. Spinning around, I see him holding two cups from Sacred Grinds. One's decorated with "Em" and a bunch of flowers and smiley faces.

Going for a cool facade, I ask, "Did you have to pay extra for the artwork?"

One side of his lips cocks into a smile so hot, I really have to control the urge to cross my legs to stop my clit from throbbing as hard as it is. "Nope. That would be Lynne. She picked up Jenna's shift this morning since Jenna was up half the night jabbering with Dani." Stepping closer, I can smell the spice of his aftershave. "Here you go, lady. If you slept half as good as I did, I figured you might need this."

"I slept fine." For the three hours I managed to squeeze in right before the sun came up, I slept great. Then the vivid dreams of Jake started up again and I soon found myself rolling around my bed searching for something that wasn't there.

He shakes his head—silently calling my bluff—even as he steps forward to rest his arms against the balcony. "Before the dress fitting begins, I wanted to talk with you."

Lifting the lid to make certain I wasn't about to scald my mouth, I take a careful sip. Recapping the drink around, I ask, "About?"

"Dani pointed out a few things to me. I haven't been able to sleep all night thinking about them." His voice is grim.

Fear clutches my chest. How much does Dani know? Through her relationship with Brendan, it's entirely possible the two of them have been brought more firmly into our family circle and know our secrets. Covering up my reaction by taking a drink, I wordlessly gesture for him to continue.

"How long are you here for?"

That wasn't what I was expecting at all. Cautiously, I respond, "Till the end of the summer. At the latest. I have responsibilities to get back to." Including a trip to France and oh, that small matter of Fashion Week. God, the weight of the responsibilities bearing down on me curdles the sickeningly sweet caramel. I now want to throw up. Putting the cup to the side, I ask, "Why?"

"Because in another life, I'd be chasing after you with everything in my arsenal, Emily."

"Em," I correct him quietly. He shakes his head.

"I can't, Emily. I have to keep you at a distance. Don't you see? If I allow myself to be around you the way I want to, I'm going to do something stupid around you again."

"Stupid?" I parrot. Suddenly my anger rises to the surface. "Well, isn't that the finest of compliments I've ever received, Mr. Madison. I swear, I can't recall when I've ever received one so well articulated." Stomping into the living room, I find my purse tucked into the stool next to the counter. Grabbing out a ten, I storm back outside.

Jake's eyeing me warily. Spotting the money, he says, "No way, lady. Coffee was on me this morning. I just want to talk so we know where we stand."

"I think you've said quite enough. Obviously, you think I'm some sort of idiot. Let me get something through your egotistical skull." I slap the money into his chest so hard, he has no choice but to grab it. It's either that or bleed from the nail I'm digging in right behind it. "*I* decide who I'm going to become involved with. *I* decide who I let into my life *and* my bed. And *you* can go to hell if you're too stupid to figure that out. You think I want to feel this—thing—happening?" I yell. God, sliding back into my own skin feels so damn good. "You are so wrong."

"Tell me why."

"Why what?"

"Why don't you want to feel it?"

"Because," I say stubbornly.

"Because why?" He's such a damn pest. I give him a version of the truth.

"Because there's nothing at the end of it. I've traveled down this road. It's empty. If you're lucky, you find respect. Other than that, there's nothing but a few nights in bed."

I've shocked him. "I never would have suspected you don't believe in love."

"You do?"

He shrugs. "I believe in a lot of things."

I challenge him. "Like what?"

Turning his back to me without answering, he lifts his chin. "What do you believe in?"

Snorting derisively, I admit, "Not much, Jake. You should probably know that."

"Tell me," he demands.

I think for a few minutes. "I believe in truth. I believe in righting wrongs. I believe in paying back the blessings of the life I've been given. I believe in family."

"You don't believe in much."

"It's better than being let down. When you believe in too much, inevitably, you're going to be."

He crosses the boundary between us to brush a curl away from my face. "I wish..."

"What?" I muster all my strength from a heart that's suddenly aching to glare at him.

He shakes his head. "Nothing. Never mind. I just wish we'd met at a time when we both weren't so cynical, when we didn't have so much riding on us. Maybe then..." Leaning forward, he presses a kiss on my forehead. "Thank you for befriending my daughter, Emily." When he steps back, I don't know why I feel this pang of loss.

But I do.

So, it makes my voice cool when I say, "Maybe I shouldn't join you all for dinner Friday." He's already shaking his head even as he backs away.

"Do you believe in promises?"

Damn him. "Yes."

"Then I'll see you Friday." He turns and walks away.

31

EMILY

L ater that afternoon, Jenna's final fitting in the long-sleeve, empire-waist, chestnut-brown silk dress is complete. Even if she gets a little taller, or grows a little more, this dress should last her for years. Lined in the same material, its rich decadence is pure luxury. I grin as she twirls barefoot on the deck in front of Dani and me.

"You know, Jen, if you take care of that dress it will last you for years." Dani's being particularly serious with her niece. "Em's brilliant. That style, in that color, will last if you want to wear it with any color heels, jewelry, or hairstyle. Well done, my friend."

I shrug, slightly embarrassed by the praise.

"Come closer for a second," Dani encourages her niece. She begins inspecting the dress. Running her hand over the back, she stills. Leaning around her niece, she gapes at me. "No way."

"Stop, Dani."

"I can't believe...stay still, Jenna!" Knowing me too well to know I wouldn't put my signature trademarks on just any dress, she locates them all within seconds. I bite my lip. I wasn't going to say anything but just let Jenna enjoy having a beautiful dress. "Sweet Jesus, Em. I'll add her to my policy to protect it."

I shake my head. "Ali started one for her and one for Lynne. They'll be held by Amaryllis Events until the girls are twenty-one or graduate college."

Jenna freezes and demands, "What are you both talking about?"

I shrug helplessly. Dani is quick to explain. "Any new design Em does is copyrighted, Jen. The owner of that first dress has certain markings on it. Your dress has them. You're wearing a one-of-a-kind original."

Even as Jenna's mouth falls open, I whisper, "Happy Birthday, sweetheart."

"Really?" Tears fill her eyes.

"Well," I joke, "I'll hold the design until the fall and likely sell it as a casual bridesmaid dress, but yes. The dress will be known as 'The Jenna.' Lynne's will be the same way."

"I don't know what to say." A single tear starts to fall down her cheek.

"I do. Don't tell your father you're wearing a dress I'd estimate costs five thousand dollars," Dani drawls. I could smack her. Hard.

"Five...five thousand dollars?" Jenna screeches. "Holy crap! What kind of policy was Dani referring to?"

Hesitantly, I reach up and run my hand over her hair. "Insurance, baby. All of my original designs have it on them. Since the dress is a gift, my company will pay for the insurance until you decide to sell the dress..."

"I'll never sell this, Em," Jenna vows. Dani grins behind her.

"Or if something were to happen to it. Who knows?" I shrug. "After October it might be worth more than it is now."

There's a pregnant pause. "Is there something you haven't told me?" Dani asks silkily.

Oh crap. "Umm, I'm showing in Bridal Fashion Week?" I barely manage to get the words out before I'm engulfed by two screaming Madison women. "Jesus, Jenna, don't rip your dress!" I yell.

"Right. Jenna, go change. After I smack Em for not saying anything before now, let's take her out to celebrate. I doubt she's done much of that. Knowing her, she's probably been freaking out about the designs she has to get ready."

"I hate you know me this well," I grumble. Jenna flies off the deck and inside to change.

Dani uses the opportunity to corner me. "It wasn't just ending the engagement, was it? You needed to get away from everything."

"I was drowning in Connecticut." It feels so good to just say it. "I needed to go somewhere where I could try to find me."

"Has it worked?"

I tilt my head back and forth. "Somewhat. Some days, the designs flow out of me with no problem. I already have a few dresses I'm finalizing. Others..." My voice trails off.

"And Jake isn't helping." I laugh bitterly when she brings up her cousin.

"You don't have to worry about that."

"Oh? Last night there seemed to be something for me to be concerned with."

"Well, apparently, my not believing in happily ever after, admitting I won't be here longer than the summer, and thinking he's a jackass because I'd just fall at his feet seemed to change his mind."

Dani chortles as if I've just told her the funniest joke in a while. "Oh, God, Em. I loved you before. But this?" She slaps her leg and howls.

"You're weird, you know that?" I ask her.

"Yep. It's why you adore me. I'm not some prima donna bitch." Very true. "But Jake is likely in shock, Em. Women gag over themselves about him, and he's turning himself stupid over the one who isn't?" Dani can't control her glee. "Once he processes everything you said, I guarantee you he's going to be back. I almost wish I could have a front-row seat with some popcorn to witness how he digs himself out of this one, but I don't think you'll want anyone to watch during that kind of action."

"Want to watch what, Dani?" Jenna's changed and has come up behind us. "I left the dress inside, Em. Is that okay?" She wraps her arms around my waist and squeezes hard.

"That's fine, sweetheart." I glare at Dani while Jenna waits for her answer.

"What can't you watch, Dani?" Jenna persists.

"Watching an overgrown boy learn how to become a man. It can get awfully messy. Sloppy even." I make a choked noise in the back of my throat. "Now, let's go get lunch and then go shopping. I want to find shoes for you that go with that dress, Jen."

Knowing there's no way I'm getting out of this, I say, "I'm not driving. I need a glass of wine."

Dani grins. "Drinking won't help."

"Neither will your commentary, but the wine might numb both."

Dani just throws her head back and laughs.

"I'll take Mugsy for a quick walk," Jenna exclaims. "Come on, Mugs. Come on, boy!"

The minute Jenna's out of earshot, I turn on Dani. "It's not happening."

"I'm pretty certain it is."

"What makes you so confident?" I demand.

Throwing an arm around my shoulders, we watch Jenna walk a slow-moving Mugsy down the beach. "Do you hear that?" Coming like a whisper on the wind, I hear the mournful wail of a saxophone. "As annoying as it was growing up, I prayed I'd hear that sound again, Em. You do that to him."

"It's going to end."

Dani nods sagely. "It might."

"I don't want anyone hurt. I can't deal with Jenna being hurt." *Or anyone else*, I add silently.

"Then go into it with your eyes open, Em."

"I'm not the one who walked away, Dani." And why that's like a beach burr stinging me, I can't explain.

"He'll be back," she says confidently.

"And I care about this why?" I ask sarcastically.

"Because you're the opposite of what he thinks he needs, but you're everything he dreams of."

I snort. "Yeah, right."

Jenna's making her way back with Mugsy. "Trust me, Em. Come shopping. But I guarantee you that by the time dinner's over Friday, Jake's over here begging for a second chance or I'll model one of your dresses for free."

I think about my upcoming Fashion Week. "You've got yourself a deal."

We shake on it.

AFTER A QUICK LUNCH, Dani, Jenna, and I hit up an amazing shop called Serenella. I immediately gravitate toward the accessories where I nab a Roksanda belt to go with my yet-to-be-made dress for Friday night. Its pink color perfectly matches the Jimmy Choo sandals I threw in my bag at the last minute before I set off for the island.

Dani picked up a few odds and ends for herself, as well as a pair of cute turquoise leather wedges to complement Jenna's dress. After calling Lynne to get her shoe size, she convinced the shop owner to hold a black pair with the promise that Lynne could exchange them. I think the store owner was salivating over Dani being in her store at all, let alone buying as much as she did.

"That was fun," Dani says cheerfully as we make our way back to her car.

"It was," I agree.

"You didn't buy much." She frowns.

"My dress doesn't need much. This"—I shake the bag—"is exactly what it needs."

Dani's silently laughing. Jenna's head is ping-ponging back and forth between the two of us. "What am I missing now?"

"It's just I've known Em for years, sweetheart. If she says her dress doesn't need much, it's likely because her dress is going to make one hell of a statement on its own." Dani's outright cackling.

"All I said was it was going to be a little black dress." My voice is innocence.

"Shouldn't that be Little Black Dress, capitalized?" she asks me pointedly.

I shrug. "Maybe."

"Can't I be told anything?" Jenna grumbles from the back seat.

Dani and I burst out laughing. "It's nothing really, sweetheart," I assure her.

"Just Em's way of dealing with a problem that's—popped up." Dani is laughing herself sick at her own double entendre. I could smack her.

Instead, I carefully switch my glasses for my shades. "I'll enjoy having you work for me for free."

"Lord help me, Em. If I end up having to work for you for free, we're both going to be miserable," Dani warns.

Even as I grin, there's a part of me that knows she's likely right.

32

EMILY

Friday's come around far too quickly, but if anything, the work I've completed on Jenna and Lynne's dresses has certainly put me in the right frame of mind to design. I've shot off three more sketches to Ali, not including the two bridesmaid dresses. When she called me screaming in delight, she demanded, "Now, where the hell are the rest of them? I hate to be a pain, but you only have a few months, Em."

"I'm well aware of that," I bite back. The collection is half-done, and while I feel some relief, I'm just not there yet. I know it, Ali knows it, and my frustration is palpable.

"Then do what you have to do," she says softly. Tears spring to my eyes. Damn, it's a good thing I don't have mascara on yet. "What you've sent over is incredible. I think it's the best work you've done."

"What I'll do next is going to be better," I say with a confidence I'm not entirely sure where it's coming from.

"I don't doubt that. You going out tonight?" Since I asked Cassidy for the fabric and Corinna's no doubt been in touch with Brendan, I have little doubt my family knows of my plans even from hundreds of miles away.

Soon, Dani, Jenna, and Lynne are going to descend on the apartment so I can do their hair and makeup. I need to have mine complete before I get started. Sighing, I reach for my foundation brush. "Yes. It's Jenna's seventeenth birthday. We're going to a restaurant by the wharf."

"And Jenna's Dani's niece? One of the two girls now on the corporate policy?"

I roll my eyes. For all she's a smooth interrogator in the courtroom, Ali sucks when she's trying to pull information out of one of us. "Yes, Ali."

There's silence on the other end of the line. "That's great, Em. I think you're giving her some really special memories." When nothing else follows, I become immediately suspicious.

"Really?"

"Yes, really. I'm not digging for information on her hot dad. If I want that kind of news, I'll just ask Corinna." When I growl, she starts to laugh.

"Aren't you married?" I challenge.

"Yeah, but I'm not dead, sister dear. And don't tell me you're marrying Holly. Jesus, the legal and PR nightmare that would cause is enough to give me hives."

Remembering the night Holly, Corinna, and I drunkenly vowed we were going to have a triad ceremony and become sister wives, I say innocently, "Listen, now that Cori's engaged, at least you're not dealing with the triad part."

"Gee, such a heart, Em." Ali snickers. "Other than that, how's the leg?"

I look down at my only slightly mottled leg. The cuts healed up quite nicely. "Not bad," I tell her. "I finally got to shave."

"Always a plus," she responds dryly. "And since Keene just walked in and you've managed to traumatize him since you're on speaker, I'll let you go now. Love you."

"Kiss Kalie. Hug your man," I tell her.

"Always do. Bye, babe."

"Bye!" I call out right before she disconnects.

I grin into the mirror as I apply blush and quickly apply smoky eye makeup to draw out my eyes. Setting the whole thing with finishing powder, I debate whether or not to slide into my dress. Nah, better not risk it. Leaving my hair down, I walk into the family room just in time to see everyone arrive. "Good, you're all here."

"Em! Look what Daddy bought us." Jenna and Lynne each hold out their wrists. Jake did good, I admit grudgingly. He bought the girls each rose-covered wrist corsages to make the night even more special. Score one for Jake. That was very, very, sweet. "Listen, *ladies*"—I emphasize the word—"my job is to finish getting you ready for your date. Apparently, he's being charming this evening bringing you flowers. If my brother was here, he could tell you what those meant. Did you know every flower has a meaning?"

"No. Do they?" Lynne asks.

"Absolutely. Phil could tell you stories about flowers and never stop talking—well, he has a problem with that some days anyway." Everyone laughs.

"Em, while you're starting with them, do you want me to go apply my foundation?" Dani asks as she strolls in the door. She's holding a white box in her hand. On her wrist is a beautiful orchid corsage. "Here." She holds out the box.

"What the hell is that?" I demand, shoving my hands behind my back.

The girls giggle while Dani just smirks at me. "All I have to say is I hope what he bought matches your dress since you haven't let me see it." Shoving the box in my hands, she makes her way into the bathroom.

Damn you, Jake, I think to myself. *You were doing what most men do. You were backing away.* Carefully taking it from her, I open the lid like it's about to bite me. Inside is a perfect calla lily corsage. It's beautiful.

And it gives me an idea.

"You know," I say slowly. "I was wondering how to wear my hair. Think I could use this"—I hold up the corsage—"to tie it to the side?"

"I think," Dani says as she walks out of my bathroom with her foundation on, "having seen your dress that it should be renamed to a little black vest."

Giving her a beatific smile, I innocently respond, "Why do you think I wanted the belt so badly?"

We both start to smirk. Then we laugh. And soon our laughter becomes contagious to two confused teenagers who I hope never understand the nuances of our conversation.

A FEW HOURS LATER, I've finished transforming three already exquisite women into something pretty damn special. "You know, each of you could be walking the runway tonight." Just as Lynne's about to roll her eyes, I capture her chin in my hands. "Including you, missy, so stop making those eyes spin in your head."

"Yes, Em," she says meekly.

I soften my smile remembering how long it took Cori to realize just how beautiful she is. "You know, the most important person who has to believe in you is right in this room."

Confused, she looks around. "Jenna?"

I turn Lynne so she faces the full-length mirror in the living room. Seeing her transformation for the first time, she gapes at her own image. "No, you."

While the girls are occupied, I slip into the bedroom and close the door. Sliding my shirt off my shoulders, I slip the backless black silk vest over my shoulder. Cinching it closed with the pink belt, I smile slowly. Well, this is certainly one of my more intriguing designs.

The front is demure. A spread collar leads to a thin slit open all the way down the front until the material overlaps. Held tightly by the belt, the skirt falls about four and a half inches past indecent. But it's the sides and back that make this little black dress a showstopper.

Where the front completely covers me, the back is only held together by a strip of silk across my shoulders. As a result, the sides of the dress are nonexistent. Bending down, I quickly strap on my almost four-inch pencil-thin pink heels. As I straighten, I catch sight of my amaryllis tattoo on full display. So—I frown—is my panty line.

Reaching my thumbs beneath the skirt, I slide the thin wisp of silk off and toss it into my hamper. Turning once again, I nod.

Almost ready.

Using the elastic on the corsage, I pull my hair over one shoulder and lay the calla lilies flat. With a couple of quick flicks of my wrist, the sloppy side ponytail helps to tame my curls. Putting in the sparkling diamonds my family bought me after my first dress was published in *Brides* magazine, I give myself a final once-over.

I'll do.

Opening the door to my room, I take one step out before the whistles start. Dani stands up in a violet strapless dress I made for her earlier in the year. Doing a walk-around, she mutters, "You're going to start a riot in that dress."

I shrug. "I have no one to answer to but myself, Dani. It's just a dress."

"It's a declaration of war."

"Fashion always is. Haven't we both learned that by now?

JUST AS WE'RE about to walk out, we realize we can't all fit into one car to get to Cru. Dani calls Brendan to say even if we take their Lexus, we still need two cars. Lynne generously offers to stay behind and ride with me, but I encourage her to ride along with her best friend. The Lexus will seat five comfortably. Waving the girls off, I close the door behind them and lean against it with a small sigh.

Now, not only do I have a few minutes' peace before I have to see Jake at the restaurant, this way I can call my family on the way there.

Right before I head out, I snap a few photos of my outfit, which I send to our family chat, and check Mugsy's food and water. I frown. He hasn't eaten much today. Squatting down next to where he's been sleeping, I feel his nose. It's cool and moist. "Maybe you just have an upset tummy, my love?" I reach over and scratch his tummy. He rolls over to his back and kicks his back legs in the air. "Oh, you love that, don't you, baby?" I croon. "How about tomorrow, we spend the whole day doing this?"

His lick to my hand is my answer. *Yes, please.* I laugh as I stand. "Be a good boy. I'll be home later."

I navigate the stairs in my stilettos carefully. Once I'm safely inside the Rover and on the main road, I call out, "Call-Holly-Cell," knowing my youngest sister is most likely to have her phone in her hands during a family dinner.

The phone barely gets through one ring when I hear, "Hello there, sexy. How can we help you this evening?" Holly's smooth voice comes through the phone.

I grin. "I take it you got the pictures."

"Got them? Phil still wants to know what you're wearing on top of that. Since I tried to explain that was the dress, he's been screeching that Caleb and Keene had better get someone up to Nantucket ASAP to guard your body." Holly pauses. "Needless to say, Keene's laughing for once over Phil's antics. I'll send you the pictures later."

"Please, Hols. Oh my God." I'm grinning so hard, my face is beginning to hurt. There's an ongoing battle between Phil and Keene that has lasted for years. Keene's staid, overprotective personality clashes with our often mouthy, fly-by-the-seat-of-his-pants brother. Normally, Phil manages to one-up him, but this time it seems Keene is holding all the cards.

And Phil obviously doesn't like it.

"It just isn't big brother's week, is it?" I muse.

"You mean between Ali emasculating him at work and now Keene trampling down on his fun here at the farm? Nope. He just can't catch a break." Holly's voice is full of humor. "It's been *fabulous.*"

We both crack up. "I don't have much time before someone steals the phone away, but I just want to say something important." Holly's voice turns serious.

Uh-oh. "What's that?" I ask cautiously.

"In all the pictures you've sent, it's been great to see the light come back in your eyes. It's good to have *you* back, Em." In the middle of what she's saying, which grabs my heart and twists it, Phil takes her phone.

"Jesus, where the hell is the rest of your dress?"

Nothing like big brother to wipe away the emotional sentiment of the moment. "Well, if you saw my original design, this would seem almost chaste," I drawl.

I'm now obviously on speaker because the choking noises Phil's emitting are echoed by the raucous laughter of my entire family. Cassidy shouts from across the room, "You tell him, Em!"

"What I really want to know is who's taking up my job of spitting things in Phil's face while I'm away," I demand.

That sets off another round of laughter.

Suddenly I'm taken off speaker. Phil's voice is the only one I hear when he says, "Welcome back, baby. We've missed you," right before he hangs up on me.

Grinning, I pull onto Straight Wharf. Eyeing a spot and realizing it's about a block and a half from the restaurant, I decide to not push my luck. Turning on my signal, I slide the Rover in smoothly. I disconnect my phone and toss it in my purse, then swing my legs out of the car before striding down the street. Not oblivious to the admiration in the stares I'm getting, I smile when a gentleman holds the door to Cru open for me. "Thank you," I murmur, stepping into the elegant restaurant.

An attractive host makes his way over. "Can I help you?"

Keeping my voice low, I murmur, "I'm with the Madison party."

"Certainly. This way please." Guiding me away from the bar closer to the spectacular view, he moves swiftly to set of double doors. "Your party's inside already, Ms. Freeman." Moving one door open slightly, he allows me to pass without exposing a view of our entire party to the dining room. I make a mental note of the excellent customer service, knowing Dani was so worried about it.

"Thank you."

"Thank you for choosing Cru for your celebration. We hope you enjoy your evening." Closing the doors swiftly behind me, I realize the noise behind me has been cut off.

Then again, so has the noise in front of me until Jenna breaks it.

"Hey, Em! There's a seat open next to Daddy."

Of course there is. "Thank you, sweetheart. I apologize for being late."

When I work up enough nerve to see where Jake's sitting, he's not there. That's because his fingers are slipping beneath my elbow. "Let me escort you to your seat, Emily."

"Thank you," I murmur quietly. *Remember, Em, you're here for Jenna. Once you're done, you're free of any obligation that includes Jake Madison.*

But when I get a good look at Jake, the room starts to spin. Making my feet move in any capacity seems an impossible feat. His already gorgeous face is covered in a five-o'clock shadow. His jaw tightens as he takes me in from the top of my head to the strappy sandals that put me close to eye level with him. His eyes drift over to the calla lilies tucked under one ear down to the slit between my breasts. My nipples harden under his perusal.

Damn me for reacting this way.

It doesn't help when he leans in and his breath mingles with mine when he says, "I was a fucking idiot."

Somehow, those words unlock me from the spell I was temporarily under. I feel my lips tip up even as I whisper back, "You're still an idiot. And I still make my own decisions."

I pull my arm away and glide gracefully to my seat. But I swear I could feel half the air being sucked out of the room once Jake got a good look at the back of my dress.

33

JAKE

Emily's dress is pure wickedness, carefully crafted to tease a man senseless without quite displaying anything but the long length of her legs and the skin of her back. Following her to the table, I have an overwhelming desire to run my hands over every inch of her smooth skin.

I'd be touching a hell of a lot and still not everything I want to be.

The silk slides against her body like the ocean waves against the sand with each step she takes. And just like the ocean, it beckons the nearest fool to become her victim. I feel like a shipwrecked sailor of old, under siege. She's a siren, a witch, a goddess, and I know I'm drowning.

Holding out her chair with the hope she'll sit down quickly, I push her up to the table and take my own seat. But as I'm quickly coming to learn, nothing is easy with Emily Freeman. Instead, she torments my senses further by crossing one magnificent leg over the other. Slowly. Tanned from the summer sun, they're showcased in heels so high, I know they'd leave marks down my back if I ever I managed to get them wrapped around me.

And I managed to offend her by making her feel stupid? I was more than an idiot. I was what idiots trampled on in order to kneel at her feet.

Tuning into the conversation around me, I hear Emily laugh at something Brendan's saying. My fist clenches as she reaches past me for the bread basket. "Here," I snap, snagging the basket to slap it into her hand. I don't think my overloaded senses can take too much more.

Eyes widening behind her glasses in amusement, she coolly says, "Thank you," before turning back to Brendan to ask where the next stop on his tour is.

For Christ's sake, is she planning on ignoring me all night? Well, the most important thing is she's here for Jenna's birthday. Clenching my teeth hard, I stay silent while the conversation flows around me.

That might have continued until a waiter walks up to begin taking our drink order. Emily flashes him a welcoming smile. The young, good-looking fucker seems to take that as an invitation. When he brushes his thumb over her shoulder the first time, she stiffens. The second time, she struggles to move forward. The third, and I grip his wrist. And not lightly. "Touch my date one more time and I'll not only take off your wrist, I'll see to it you never work on the island again," I growl menacingly.

Just as the words fly out of my mouth, the manager of Cru steps in to see how we're faring. His face turns a mottled shade of red. "Troy, out," he barks.

Scurrying off, the waiter shoots me a filthy look. Even as the manager is offering us his profuse apologies, I lean over to her. "You're not walking back to your car alone. Brendan or I walk with you. Do you understand?"

Nodding, she reaches for a drink of water. "Your date?" Her eyebrows are practically in her hairline.

"It was the first thing I could think of." And I want it to be true so badly, I can taste it.

Emily shrugs. "Fine." She turns her attention back to her menu.

Hooking an arm over the back of her chair, I ask, "Are you okay? Do you need a drink?"

"Yes. That was...annoying." Her lip curls in a mild sneer.

Happy to be on speaking terms with her, I ask, "Wine?"

"What can you tell me about the Garden of Elyx?" She taps the cocktail list. "Will it quench my thirst?"

"I can guarantee you, you'll leave here never forgetting the taste."

"Is that so?" Her finger rubbing her lower lip, she shakes her head.

I inhale deeply and smell mint, something I know I will forever always associate with her. "Yes."

Turning away from me, she picks up her napkin and lays it gently in her lap. "Is there any way to get a taste to see if I like it?"

"You'll love the taste."

"Hmm, if that's the case..."

My eyes bore into hers. "You'll love it. Don't even try to convince me otherwise."

She shrugs. "It was kind of a letdown. New things tend to be."

"Or it could surprise you. Maybe you should try again."

"Or maybe I should just leave well enough alone. Go for something safe. Like white wine. There are some perfectly acceptable wines on the list. Like the *En Remilly*."

"Take a chance."

"Why?" The word is barely a breath on her perfect lips.

"Because..." Suddenly I'm sick of playing word games. Suddenly I just want to say the words pounding through my head. "Because when I'm with you, I'm willing to believe that any amount of time might be enough. Because I want to be your choice for however long you choose. However much of yourself you're willing to give."

Her lips part of their own accord. Her breath comes out jaggedly. "I can't promise anything."

"I know."

"Then where does this leave us?"

"Right now? With you ordering a drink." I raise my hand to the manager to call him over. The manager is at our side in a moment. "What can I get for you, miss?" Holding my breath, I wait while she places her order, knowing that she's doing more than just that. She's at a flash point—making a decision on whether or not to give me another chance. Because if I go at her with everything I've got, I know I have a good shot at breaching the walls she has to keep out sadness and pain.

But what she doesn't realize is they're also the same walls that keep out joy and love.

Her eyes holding mine, she says, "I'll take the Elyx."

The manager turns to me and says, "And for you, sir?"

I run a finger along her cheek unobtrusively. "I'll have the same."

JENNA'S BIRTHDAY goes off without another hitch. Emily and Dani proceed to gross out the girls with their oyster shooting. Amid the squeals of "Gross!" and "How can you swallow *that*?" Brendan and I exchange sardonic smiles. These women alone are trouble. Together they're a keg of dynamite. In a huge way.

The whole room is roaring at stories Brendan, Dani, and Em have been sharing. At some point, the girls started asking questions about which was worse: crazy fans, cocky models, or bridezillas. The three exchanged glances and answered simultaneously, "Yes."

This set off another story. And then another. Em's presently telling one where she's waving her hands back and forth. Each time she does, my cock jumps eagerly against the zipper of my dress slacks.

Sweet merciful God in heaven, if I look just right, I can just catch a glimpse of her full breast from the side.

My torment is brought to a swift end when a knock comes on the door. In a flash, members of the Cru front and back of the house staff come sailing into the room holding a cake made by Corinna Freeman just for my little girl. Jenna's eyes get super wide when she sees the almost too beautiful to eat dessert heading her way.

Emily whips out her phone and immediately begins taking pictures—no doubt to send to her sister. Brendan has out his phone, and he yells, "Hey, birthday girl, thank Corinna for your cake!"

"Ohmygod! Em, your sister made this?"

Em's laugh is pure beauty. Even knowing her such a short time, I know it's reserved for those who have found their way into the inner sanctum of her heart. "While I'm sure she did, why don't you ask her?" She gestures to Brendan's phone. "I'd bet my earrings that's her on the phone."

"Like I'd miss this?" comes a voice like dark honey. "Jenna, Lynne, let me see the dresses Em ended up making for you."

I'm laughing when Jenna and Lynne get up and do a fair job mimicking Dani on a runway. But damn if tears aren't burning the back of my eyes when Lynne says, "I feel beautiful, Cori. You were so right about everything you said."

Corinna's smile can be heard. "Remember it was really what Em said. If you listen to her, you'll never go wrong."

Em chortles. "I'm writing down the date and time to remind you that you said that."

We all laugh. Corinna takes her lumps with good humor. "I didn't want to intrude, but I wanted to share with y'all that tonight's dessert is a vanilla bean cake with cookie dough chunks, chocolate ganache, and Italian buttercream filling. It's topped with chocolate ganache and a vanilla bean–flavored fondant." We all groan in delight. "Jenna?"

"Yes, Corinna?"

"One of the best parts about any birthday is blowing out the candles and making a wish. But to make sure your cake lasts the longest, let Em place them for you. She'll know where they go on so the cake won't spoil as fast, okay?"

"Thank you so much!" Jenna gushes.

"Corinna?" I speak up. Brendan turns the camera on me. I smile. "Thank you."

"Trust me when I say it was my pleasure," she drawls. "And since there's no random bikes lying around, you can have your piece sliced and served, not smashed in your face."

"Beat it, brat." Emily stands to her full height. Corinna lets out a low whistle when she gets a load of her sister.

"Damn, Em. Your pictures didn't do it justice. That *is* one hell of a dress. I think *you* need to take a walk on the 'runway' so I can lord it over the family."

"I think not, sister dear." Em plops back into her seat.

Within seconds, Jenna and Lynne are egging her on. Brendan's keeping the phone steady, and Corinna's laughter grows stronger as the girls pantomime how Em should walk. Even Dani gets into the act, using the length of the room to take a turn. "See, now I even have a picture of Dani wearing the dress you made for her," Corinna calls out.

Leaning close to Emily, I murmur, "Dani's wearing you as well?"

With a devilish smirk, she leans close. "You're the only one who's not. I made Brendan's tie when I made Dani's dress."

Irrational jealousy steals over me even as she gives in. "Fine, fine! I'll do it. When I land on my rear, you all know why."

Standing, she carefully removes the calla lilies from her hair. Her curls go wild, much like I imagine the woman inside is. Moving into the corner, she lets out a sigh. "Cori, I swear to God..."

"I won't tell Phil. Lord only knows what he'd say," her sister promises. "Now, walk."

I've seen dozens of fashion shows. I've seen the edgy walks models use to work an outfit. What I've never appreciated is the simple seductiveness of a woman's body accentuated by the fluid grace of her walk. Each step she takes is stripping me of another excuse, another reason, to throw out my caution. I've ran. I've fought and been fought. I tried to walk away to avoid the messy entanglement I know being involved with her will be.

She'll leave. She has to. And I have to stay.

We have nowhere to go.

Maybe Emily was right. Maybe there's nothing to hope for—to believe in.

Except, when I see her laughing at herself as she says goodbye to her sister with her arm slung around my daughter, there's a tiny impossibility that wishes there is.

34

EMILY

Hearing footsteps behind me, I look over my shoulder. Should I be surprised to find him making his way toward me? I guess not. Not after the way he stared at me as I tipped back oysters at dinner. Not after the way his mouth gaped open when he saw my dress. What I am surprised at is the way my heartbeat races at the sight of him. Since I drove back from Jenna's birthday dinner alone, I've done nothing but replay the way his eyes heated when I walked into the restaurant, the way his lips parted in surprise as I slid into the available seat next to him.

The puff of air that passed his lips when I crossed my legs before sliding them under the table.

The rational side of me tells me it's too soon. For Christ's sake, I just met him weeks ago. He has a daughter, I have a business to run—and eventually return to. We're the perfect definition of temporary. This has nowhere to go.

So why do I know it's about to happen?

Because, when I lie in bed at night, it's his face I imagine as I slide my hand down to my wetness. It's his hands I imagine coasting over my skin. I already know his fingers strum a guitar like it's a lover's skin. It's his lips—those fucking lips that play the saxophone better than anyone I've ever heard—that make me wonder what he can do to my body as my clit reaches the point of no return.

Right before my body surrenders. Alone.

Jake's shirt is unbuttoned, untucked, with the sleeves rolled up. Sometime between the time dinner ended and now, he's lost his shoes and jacket. He's prowling toward me on bare feet with only a crystal tumbler filled with clear amber liquid in his hands. Trying to regain some semblance of calm, I lift my chin in challenge.

I haven't felt such an urgency to be with someone in what seems like forever. The lovers I've had before have never made me want with the sheer need he does. From Jake, all it takes is him coating his lips with his tongue as he licks off some of the liquid that clings to them as he lifts the tumbler to his lips. Or when I caught his hand clench by his plate as I leaned past him for the bread basket tonight at dinner right before he grabbed it and slammed it into my hand. Or any of the many times when he's just turned his head and pinned me with those penetrating eyes.

But I'm not alone in what I'm feeling. He wouldn't be here tonight if I were.

Judging by the glare he's giving me, it's as if he's trying to cast a spell to ward off this inane attraction between us. Instead, all it makes me want to do is ignore him, prodding the beast that I know lives inside him further, and spread my legs wider to see what he'll do next.

I'm not given a chance to decide as his scent penetrates my space.

Jake traps my body against the railing, one hand placing the tumbler on the smooth teak in my line of sight. His other is pushing my hair off my shoulder. "This fucking dress..." His voice trails off as his lips graze my exposed neck. I can feel him fighting our combustible urge fearlessly and losing. Just as I did.

"What's wrong with my dress?" I ask breathlessly. Tipping my head back to give him easier access, I acquiesce to the need catching fire inside of me.

"Nothing that taking it off your body won't fix." He pushes his hips into mine, and I can feel the evidence of his desire against the thin silk clinging to my skin in the beach air. My nipples pebble hard in reaction.

"I spent a few hours yesterday making it." My head drops forward as his hand shoves my curls away from my neck.

His lips skimming across my bare skin stop moving. "Seriously?"

I wiggle around until I'm facing him. The position has our bodies straining against each other, every crevice and hollow fitting together from shoulders to knees because of the heels I'm wearing. The breeze flutters his sun-kissed hair. "It wasn't meant to make you stop."

Caging me in between his muscular arms, he ducks his head and captures my lower lip between his teeth. Sucking on it for just a moment, he releases it. I feel like he's warming my body up the way he warms up his sax—for a night of hard play, slow blues, and pounding rhythm. "I wasn't planning on stopping."

"Then why did you ask?" I breathe the question as I lean closer into him.

"Because if I rip this dress off of you, it's good to know you can fix it." His mouth crashes down onto mine.

I can still taste the Garden of Elyx on his lips that we both drank at the restaurant earlier. The sweet raspberries and apricots mixed with the brandy he just swallowed add another layer of aphrodisiac to my already overwhelmed senses. The wind blowing what hair Jake doesn't have tangled in his fingers, the tang of the salt air in my nose, combined with the taste on my mouth knock me under like a tsunami.

I'm going under with nothing to cling to except the force of nature in front of me.

Raking my nails up his chest, the light hair of his chest is damp with the heat coming off his body. I hear the hiss of breath escape his lips as I catch his flat nipples between my fingers and squeeze. Wrenching my mouth away from his, I begin to trail my own lips across his skin. "God, Emily," he moans. Pulling my head back, he searches my eyes in the purple dusk of the sunset. "I shouldn't cross this line."

Able to duck my head down to bite him, I elicit another moan, even as I agree with him. "I know."

"You should tell me to go," he says even as his hands slide down to my ass to pull me closer to his erection.

"I should," I agree.

"We're not going to last."

I know. I have less than two months before I have to leave.

"We're going to be each other's worst mistake," he warns me. His hand begins to slide under the hem of my dress. Sliding it upward, he discovers the reason I've had no panty line all night. It's because I've had none on.

He lets out a painful groan. "All night? You've been sitting next to me like this all night?"

I nod, my face in his shoulder. "I'm surprised I didn't leave a wet spot on my dress. Why do you think I kept crossing my legs so much?"

"I hoped," he growls, reaching past me for his drink, "it was because you were as turned on as I was. I thought you were tempting me to come to you." Before he can lower the glass, I reach out and snag it from his fingers.

I turn the glass so my lips touch the same spot his were before I ask, "Is that going to stop you from wanting to fuck me?"

"God no."

"Good. But first I want to taste you. I can't tell you the number of times I've gotten off thinking about it." His eyes wildly dilate at my blunt comment.

Removing the glass from my hands, he carefully puts it down before stepping back. His chest is moving up and down frantically. Arms akimbo, he braces himself like a sailor on the deck of a ship that's about to face the storm of his life. "Then get on your knees," he dares me.

One step forward. Two. I lay my hand in the center of his chest before I walk around him in a circle, stripping off the unbuttoned shirt as I go. Dragging my nails across his back as I make my way around, I whisper in his ear, "I get on my knees for no man."

The smirk that crosses his face is a sexual challenge unto itself. "Then tell me, lady, how do you plan on doing it?"

I spin Jake around, taking him by surprise. Pushing him up against the deck railing, I take a step back and drop my hands. Going to work on his dress slacks before I slowly bend at the waist, I brace my hands on his thighs. Tipping my face up to his, I run my tongue over my lips before I lean forward. Sliding my hands upward, I yank all the material blocking his thick cock from my view out of my way. As it springs toward me, I grasp it tightly. His head tips back, and his eyes close on an escaped breath.

Challenge accepted.

"You want to know how? Watch me." I lower my head to the tip of his cock and begin to swallow him against the backdrop of the darkening sky where the crash of the waves mix with his hoarse groans.

35

JAKE

Madness.

My legs begin to shake as Em brings me closer and closer to the edge. Even though I can feel some cum leak out, I refuse to fall over unless I'm driving hard into her pussy while I'm doing it. She isn't the only one who's spent her nights fantasizing. And I might lose what's left of my sanity if I don't end tonight with her long legs wrapped around my back, her heels digging into my spine as I find release.

Fucking Christ, her mouth is destroying me. I'd be a puddle on the deck floor if it wasn't for the railing I'm almost desperately holding on to.

She trails her nails up and down my thighs, causing the hair on my legs to rise in the wake. Every inch of my body is on fire for this woman. If I'm not careful, she's going to brand me in the process. Then what will I do when another woman I let in walks away?

Em chooses that moment to let my cock pop out. I'm torn between whimpering and relief. Until she shifts her weight forward and pulls first one of my balls into her mouth and then the other, lavishing them with the same attention she gave my cock.

Fuck. Me.

My eyes roll back in my head as my hips involuntarily thrust in the air, desperately seeking release. The coolness that's dropped down on us is all that's saving me from completely blowing my load. It sure as hell isn't the diabolical Emily Freeman. Between the silk of her dress, the wet heat of her mouth, her firm grip, and the unspoken forbidden of doing this where anyone could come out on the porch next door, I need to take over before I lose control.

Now.

I thread my fingers into her soft, golden curls. Pulling her away from my tormented cock, I yank her into a deep kiss that leaves no question about how she affects me. Tasting myself on her lips just causes my balls to pull up tighter.

It's time to see if she likes being on the other end of the scale. And fortunately for her, I have absolutely no problem being on my knees to play this particular instrument.

Sliding my pants up only far enough to cover my ass, I turn her so it's her back to the ocean but with the moonlight finally down around us. Emily will now be able to look into the reflective doors behind us and see herself as I make her come.

"I wasn't quite done," she protests after I finally let her lips go. I can't help but smile. I've never met a woman who stimulates me on every level quite the way she does.

"What didn't you have a chance to do?" I was going to die if she kept going.

Looking like the cat who didn't get a chance to swallow any cream, she pouts. "I wanted to feel you hit the back of my throat so I could swallow you down. Boys," she says in mock disgust, her blue eyes taunting, "seem to think a woman has to be properly on her knees to get them to come. Men know better." Leaning into my body, she whispers, "And you didn't even let me prove it to you."

That's it. My control snaps. If some part of me isn't inside of her, feeling those tiny muscles clench around me, I'm going to explode all over the deck. Probably rougher than I should be, one hand grips her ass so I can grind my still-exposed cock against her core, even if it is covered by silk. The other moves up her sides to where her exposed arms so generously give me access to her perfectly shaped breasts.

Her nipple stabs against my fingers as I pluck at it, playing with it like I would a bass. Her stomach tightens and undulates against me, and her soft moans fill the night air. I laugh, knowing when I sink down and slide the material of her dress to her waist, the only thing that will stop her juices from flowing down her legs is my mouth.

God, yes.

The breeze picks up one of Em's curls, slapping it against my cheek. Almost as if the lady herself is daring me to get on with the night's proclivities. I don't have to be reminded twice. Brushing the barest of kisses across her mouth in complete contrast to the rhythm I'm still grinding against her mound, I begin the journey southward. Her hands, which had been clutching my shoulders before, grasp my head. As our mouths align, she presses a hard kiss against me before murmuring, "Didn't you stop me for a reason?"

I grin. "Yes, ma'am." This bundle of seductive fire and joy is everything at this moment. Who am I to deny what she wants? What I'm so desperate to give her?

When my mouth is on an even level with her tits, I latch onto first one nipple and then the next with a fervor that has her crying out. Pressing each against the roof of my mouth, I suck hard. The tight bud elongates farther as my tongue lashes against it back and forth. The combination of Em's whimpers and nails gouging my back tell me I could probably get her off just like this.

But I want more.

Unleashing her second nipple with a pop, I leave them exposed—much like she did with my cock. Capturing her gaze, I drop to one knee and then the other as I slide her excuse of a skirt up her long legs. Just as I suspected, the insides of her thighs are glistening with her desire. But what causes me to sit back and my cock to start leaking more fluid without her touching it is her perfectly bare mound. Tracing it gently with one finger, I smear some of her juices around her outer lips. "Em?"

"Yes?"

"Don't plan on sleeping tonight." Pushing her outer lips apart, I lean forward and flick my tongue over her clit, short, quick strokes that have her lifting her leg and wrapping it around my shoulder.

I just hope she can balance on those heels for as long as I plan to feast. Clenching my hands on her exposed ass, I pull her forward and begin eating the dessert I've been craving instead of the cake I only nibbled on earlier at the restaurant.

And it's fucking amazing.

36

EMILY

I moan loudly into the night air the minute Jake's wicked mouth touches my bare pussy. And damn him, he just settles back to prolong my—our—agony.

I want him to slide his thick cock up into me while I hear the ocean waves crash against the beach. I want to feel his fingertips—rough from the hours spent playing—slide over my nipples as he takes me. I just...want.

"Please," I plead. His head moves away from me—damn him. He smiles against the inside of my thigh.

"Give me something, Emily. Since you won't go onto your knees for me," he mocks me.

"Or any man," I return. I'm willing to give him just about anything else.

Just not my nightmares.

"Then take your dress off so I can see all this smooth skin." Fingering the silk, the material catches against the calluses on his fingers. "It won't take much to rip it from you, but if you made it, you might want to keep it."

Holding his gaze, I undo the thick elastic belt I bought at Serenella. It falls to the floor of the deck with a clank. Without a whisper of sound, the vest that makes up my dress parts. Jake's jaw unhinges. "Sometimes, fashion is knowing all about how to accessorize."

"That's it? That's all you've been wearing all damn night?"

Letting the whisper of silk slide off my shoulders, it falls to the deck, leaving me standing only in the pink Jimmy Choo sandals that match the belt on the deck floor. "Aren't you glad you didn't know at dinner?" Raising my eyebrow, I wait for his reaction.

"Might have embarrassed everyone if I laid you on the table and did this," he mutters as he pulls me back toward his face and buries his nose and mouth against me. One of his hands slides up my stomach to pull at my nipple while the other squeezes under his chin to dip inside my dripping hole.

"God, Jake. Stop teasing me!" I pant. I grab onto his thick hair and yank his head up.

Satisfaction flashes briefly before something darker, more intense chases it away. "You mean you want something like this?" Two fingers thrust into me.

"Yes," I hiss, my hips undulating against the wicked smile playing on his mouth.

"Maybe I can speed up the tune a bit," he muses, right before he lowers his mouth back to my clit and sucks. Hard.

Jake's shaping one of my breasts with one talented set of fingers while the other is picking up pace thrusting in and out of me. I can hear how wet I'm getting, and it's just turning me on more. A high-pitched squeak comes out of my mouth. I'm so close to coming. "Jake," I moan his name as I sway on unsteady legs.

"Fucking come, Emily. I want to drown in your scent before I slam so deep into you neither of us forgets this." Jake pinches my nipple on an upward thrust of his fingers. When he lightly bites down on my clit, I lose all sense of reality and do just that.

The tension in my body snaps, and I scream. It's been so long—too long—since a man made me feel like this. I don't understand why now, but I keep thrusting my hips forward, seeing stars beyond those over the ocean. Jake keeps working my clit between his lips until the aftershocks have me staggering on my feet. "No..." I push his head away. I can't.

Surging to his feet, he slides his hand into his pocket before shoving his pants down and off. I have mere seconds to appreciate the thickness between his legs before he hoists mine around his waist. "You fucking well can," he bites out between gritted teeth. "I haven't held off coming not to feel you rippling around my cock as tight as you just did around my fingers."

Tightening my arms and legs around him, I rub up against him. "Then what are you waiting for?"

His head darts from left to right. I can tell the instant he spies the lounger I was sunbathing on the other day. Walking over to it, he uses his foot to kick out the back so it's supine without letting me down. "After I come down on top of you, put your legs as high as you can on my back."

I shiver in response but nod anyway.

Jake lowers me to the lounger and tears open the condom he palmed from his pants with his teeth. As he's rolling it on, I can't help but touch myself. Even my very fertile imagination couldn't have imagined the darkness of the hair coating his chest and balls compared to his head, the strength in his legs as he stands at my side, the look of his hand as he strokes his cock next to me...

My eyes fly upward and clash with his. "I was waiting to see if you were going to come again without me. It was so fucking hot watching you. It was better than any fantasy I've had lately." His words mirror my own.

Lifting my hands from my drenched pussy, I hold both my arms and legs open for him. He straddles the chair before lowering himself on top of me. Wrapping my legs around him as tight as I can, I feel the thick brush of his cock against my clit before he lines up. He brushes against my hole a few times. I gasp, then whimper, "Please. Now."

Pulling my fingers that I had been using to touch myself while he watched toward his mouth, he licks them thoroughly before sliding them back down to my clit. "Play us a melody, Em," he says, right before he thrusts deep inside me.

My back arches as his mouth crashes down. Thrust after thrust, Jake gives me the beat, the ocean gives us the tempo, and I play the melody to the hottest sex I've ever had. His hips are pistoning away at me when suddenly I feel all of my inner muscles grip him tightly. I come all over his cock.

Just the way he demanded.

"That's what I wanted to feel," he mutters. Dropping his head, he pushes hard once, twice, and on the third hit of his hips against my inner thighs, I feel his heat burst inside me before he lowers his body onto mine.

As we lie there panting, I can hardly breathe. It has nothing—and everything—to do with the weight of the man lying on top of me.

What have I done? I think in a panic.

Jake was right.

We're going to be each other's worst mistake.

I just hope we have enough sense not to take anyone out with us when it's all over.

37

EMILY

Late the next morning, I sit up in bed alone. I'm not surprised. Jake left sometime around sunrise, brushing a kiss across my shoulder with a muttered "I need to get going." I'm pretty sure I waved a hand in his direction before I buried my head back into the pillow. His deep chuckle told me how amusing he found me before I heard the door close.

The man took me under so many times last night, he should do me a kindness and drop me off at the Shipwreck and Lifesaving Museum to have me restored. Sweet Jesus, I'm sore in ways—and in places—I never imagined I could be.

Groaning, I think even my fingertips hurt from clutching Jake tighter to my body as he spread me across the bed and licked me from the top of my head to my toes, spending special attention everywhere in between. By the time he flipped me over onto my stomach to take me on my knees, I was clawing anything within reach: the sheets, the bedpost, him.

If last night was a moment out of time, then I need to immortalize it. Immediately.

Sliding out of bed, I debate showering until I realize I want all of the feeling of Jake on me while I sketch. I want the lingering scent of his body on my skin. I need the soreness of my muscles to truly do justice to the body that captured mine under his as his weight lay over mine. Stepping over to the dresser, I grab a Collyer Wildcats T-shirt and slip it over my head. After pulling on a pair of panties, I wander into the kitchen.

And stop dead in my tracks.

Sitting in a vase on the counter are some of the hydrangea that grow rampant around the yard. There's a folded piece of paper beneath them. Trembling, I walk directly to it.

I want to see you again. PS - I locked the door using the master after I took out Mugsy.

I know that Jake meant the gesture to be sweet; he could have no idea behind the dual meaning of hydrangea and how eerily perfect they are in this moment in time. When I broke up with a long-ago boyfriend, I was sent them. After throwing them out, Phil told me they stood for two things: heartfelt emotions and heart-lessness.

Which one are we going to wind up being, Jake? I think wearily as I reach out to touch the delicate blooms. Some of the petals fall to the table. But even as I turn away, I know I'm going to be with him again. Because for the first time in forever, I feel alive inside. I don't feel trapped inside walls of my own making.

Flopping on the sectional, I grab my journal. When the last page is open, waiting, I stare blankly out at the ocean view before a cool wet nose nuzzles against my hand. "Hey, old man. I'm glad Jake took you out."

Mugsy just thumps his tail in response before leaping up onto the couch and curling next to me.

Closing my eyes, I stroke his silky fur. I frown when I feel a bump near his head. "Seems like you're getting another one of those cysts, baby."

He lets out a sigh under my tender ministrations. We sit like that for a few minutes before I hear his soft snore. Opening my eyes, I smile softly. He's completely out. Shifting, I reach for the charcoals on the coffee table. Picking one up, I begin capturing the erotic memories of last night, beginning with the look on Jake's face as he walked toward me.

A FEW HOURS LATER, an impromptu nap is disturbed by the landline in the apartment ringing. Groggily, I reach over for the receiver. "Hello?"

"Don't tell me you've been asleep since I left you this morning." Jake's voice, deep and amused, is on the other end.

Yawning in his ear, I know he can't see my body's reaction to just his voice. *You're in control, Em*, I tell myself. "No, Mugsy and I just were taking a little puppy nap."

"That sounds like fun," he says wistfully.

"Hmm, it was. I suppose I should shower though."

There's a pregnant pause on the other end of the line. "You haven't showered yet?"

My curls dance crazily around my head as I shake it. "No, I've been very lazy."

"Hold on a sec."

I hear him tell people he'll be right back. "Unlock your door, Em." Confused, I ask, "Why?"

"Just do it." I can hear his footsteps on the decking that connects our two decks.

I jump up from the couch, leaving the phone where it is. Running into the bathroom, I slather a toothbrush with paste and run it over my teeth. Looking in the mirror, I cringe seeing the aftereffects of last night's makeup over my face. Grabbing a couple of wipes, I run back out just in time to see Jake at the bottom of the stairs. Quickly, I unlock the back slider before racing over to the full-length mirror. There's nothing I can do about the corkscrew curls dancing around my head, but the raccoon eyes... I'm frantically scrubbing at my face in the mirror when the door slides open on the track behind me. And I freeze.

If I thought my desire for him was an aberration, a quench that could be satisfied by a night, seeing him shatters that illusion. I'm almost resentful of the fact that Jake just standing in my space causes a flood of heat in between my legs. My hand holding the wipe drops from my face as our eyes meet in the mirror. "What are you doing here?"

"Did you really think I could know that your body was still marked by us and I wouldn't do anything to find out if it was true?" He makes his way around the furniture until he's standing behind me.

His hands slide off my shoulders and down my arms until they reach my fingertips. In the mirror, I watch him gather them together until they're both behind my back. While my breasts are displayed more prominently, I also have access to the ridge of his cock that was pressed up against me.

"I love the idea that your body holds our scent." He drops his head and nuzzles his way past my hair to my skin. "I love that you didn't immediately race to wash away our night together."

Our breathing is harsh in the quiet room. His free hand roams over my T-shirt and my upper thighs while his lips sear the side of my face and my throat. I let out a low moan in response.

"I want to find your soft opening and fill it with my fingers, my tongue, and my cock. Tell me you want that too."

I don't even hesitate. "I do," I whisper. Slowly, he releases my hands and cups my face.

"Let me come back to you, Em. Tonight— every night—as long as we have them."

Saying yes will put a massive chink in the armor of my defenses. But in the midst of feeling weakened by the madness we shared, there's a part of me that recognizes this may never be enough. I may need these moments in the days when I'm living in solitude to protect those I love beyond reason.

Knowing I will somehow pay for this weakness, I pull my hand free and touch his lips. "Yes."

His lips curve in a bow that wraps his face in masculine arrogance and relief. I expect him to crush his lips against mine. Instead, he surprises me when he merely nuzzles against me. "Now, go get dressed. We're cooking out tonight." His eyes are alight with something I haven't truly seen since I arrived.

I think it might be happiness.

"Do I have time to clean up?" I ask wryly.

"For the sake of the two teenagers who are eagerly anticipating your arrival? Yes. If you want, I'll take Mugsy out when I walk back." The sweetness of the gesture causes me to melt inside.

"I'd appreciate that." I smile. I run my fingers through his hair before I brush a kiss on his lips. "Is there anything I can bring?"

"You forget, I've seen your fridge. So, the answer is no. Just throw on something casual and come on over when you're ready. We'll be on the back deck." Dropping one more kiss on my lips, he whistles for Mugsy and they're out the door.

Soon, I'm drying off from a shower with a glow to my skin the sun had nothing to do with. And when I work up the courage to meet my own eyes in the mirror, I feel the first tinges of fear.

Fear that I won't escape this summer without feeling my heart break for the first time since Aunt Dee passed away.

And knowing I'll pay for it.

I always do.

38

JAKE

The weeks pass by too quickly. The more I'm with Emily, the more it feels right. The more we feel right. And how can that be when we've known each other for such a short period of time?

And it scares me, because the more I become attached, the more I want to be with her, the less I feel I think she feels the same way. I still know as little about her as I did on the day I met her. If she'll only trust herself with me in the here and now, then I'll smash every clock, destroy every calendar, ruin every metric of time so there's only the present, no past and no future.

Each day the nights become shorter, and every night when I hold her close in bed, I curse the moon glowing over the crashing waves. I know in my mind that each day we have together is the same length of time, but I've learned that when the heart is involved, time is subjective.

Each day as the sky changes from the depth of midnight to a hazy shade of purple, I go back to my cold bed alone. I want to say the hell with this separation of our hearts, our minds, our lives. Be with me.

But I can't.

I can't watch another woman walk away with my heart.

I slide away from her warm body. She murmurs a protest. I quickly dress by her bedside so I can stay with her as long as I can.

Because I know better.

Time is moving too fast.

Just as I'm about to slip out the door, Em rolls over in her sleep. In the glow from the light in the hallway, I can see she's still asleep from the hard loving I gave her earlier.

But I don't know which one of us is dreaming when I hear her whisper almost silently, "Don't go. Stay."

It takes everything in me to put one foot in front of the other and walk past Mugsy out the door.

39

EMILY

Designs are flowing out of me. They're just not *it*. I can't pinpoint why, but I just know something's off. Scrubbing my charcoal-coated fingers over my face, I must look like I did when Phil, Cassidy, and I would come running back to Aunt Dee's from playing in the pluff mud down by the marshes near our trailer in South Carolina.

Frustrated, I put down my sketchbook and pick up my journal. Flipping back through the worn pages, I study the detailed sketch I drew of my mother's face as she promised me everything would be okay. *I know you suffered because of me too, Mama*, I think to myself. Would my father have ever fallen prey to the need for more money if I hadn't been born?

It's funny what you remember. As a child who was supposed to be asleep in the quiet, I heard angry footsteps on the stairs. I heard heated whispers between people who were supposed to love each other. I heard words that made a lie of the perfect fairy tale they were supposed to be living.

None of this would have happened if you had never been born.

Flipping ahead of the drawings of my parents' murderer—I still to this day don't know who the killers were—I land on a recreation of the first drawing I did of Aunt Dee. It had been the third anniversary of my parents' death. Cassidy and Phil had been out playing in the yard. I was hurling anything I could throw in my silent agony: books, magazines, pillows. If it was able to be picked up, I was trying to hurl it in my fury at the injustice of the world where my parents were gone, and I was left in this world alone.

Finally, Aunt Dee had enough. She demanded I clean up the mess I caused. Refusing to speak to her, I spit at her—the vilest thing I could think of. It landed between us, a barrier unable to be crossed by either of us. Although my horror was as great as hers, I'll never forget the look on her face at what loving me cost her.

Pride.

Staring at the sketch now, I realize I managed to capture the pain and the agony of what loving me causes.

A slow death.

I close my eyes in pain. Opening them, I stare blankly over the vast ocean. And I have words with the spirit that holds me captive every day my heart beats.

I made you a promise the day Dee died, you feckless bastard. If you left the rest of my family alone, I wouldn't fall in love again. Are Jake and Jenna your test to show I'm honoring my word so you don't hurt Phil, Cassidy, Ali, Cori, or Holly? Then I won't love them. I know love isn't mine to have.

Hearing Mugsy whimper in his sleep, I use my bare foot to rub him before I angrily flip to the back of my journal. Picking up the charcoal, I begin a new face. A new memory. Lance off a new wound so I can survive another day.

Even as I lose myself in the drawing, the lies I feed myself about not believing in love are the only thing keeping me back from admitting to myself I'm already drowning in it. There's no safe harbor for anyone who falls without knowing their love is returned. Only a riptide of emotion constantly dragging you away from shore.

And most of it's deadly.

40

EMILY

Mugsy and I are slowly making our way back up the stairs from a short walk on the beach when I spot Jake waiting for me on the deck. "What are you doing here during the day?"

His smirks. "I don't catch on fire in daylight, Em."

"I didn't think you did." Walking into his arms, I lay my head on his chest. "It's just a surprise."

"A good one I hope?" There's a note of uncertainty in his voice I hate is there. Jake and I have been together for close to two months. We keep things extremely casual around Jenna. We don't touch when we all hang out around town or at the beach, but just being with them centers me. I can sense his frustration. To be honest, it mirrors my own.

But how am I supposed to break a sworn vow and harm everyone in the process? I bury my head so the burn in the back of my eyes won't lead to tears. Holding him just a little tighter, I absorb everything about this moment: the salt air, the wind in my hair, his arms tight around me. When I'm alone in my bed in Collyer, I want to be able to pull this memory from my heart and think of it.

Then lock it away as tight as I can before something happens to it.

"How about we go get a beer?" Jake says casually.

I lift my head from his shoulder, my brow furrowed. "You mean at your place?"

His shoulders shakes. "I know Sconset is the best part of the island, but why don't I show you a part you haven't been to yet?"

"The island's not that big, Jake." I roll my eyes at him.

He swats my ass playfully. "Yeah, but I know for a fact you haven't been here. Otherwise you'd have already been shopping for members of your family. So, get one of your million pairs of shoes and let's go."

ON 5 AND 7 Bartlett Road, there's a triple threat to be had. The Triple Eight Distillery, Cisco Brewery, and Nantucket Vineyard—a locally conceptualized and run operation since the early '80s—serves up some of the most amazing wine, whiskey, and beer I've ever tasted. "How have I not had this since I got here?" I moan into my pale ale. We're sitting at one of many picnic tables on the vast property.

"I don't know. It's one of the best parts about being here on the island." Jake tips his head back to finish his lager. "Best part for me is they're open year-round too."

"So, when you're having a really bad day at school," I tease.

He jumps in. "Or when I want to flip because Jenna hasn't done her college applications."

"You can just stop by the local brewery for a pint?"

"Pretty much."

"Not a bad setup," I agree.

"Not at all. Only thing is they're only open till about seven."

"Why's that?" I'm curious.

"No idea," he admits. "But I'll take the trade-off since I get year-round. You up for sticking around for a while? There's a great band playing this afternoon."

I grin. "And we all know music's the way to your heart."

His eyes hold mine steady when he replies, "One of them, Em."

"Jake..." My voice is choked. I grab for my beer and take a long drink, but I can't let go of his eyes even over the rim of his glass.

He lets out a slow breath. "Anyway, this band has a female singer whose voice could blow the leaves off the trees."

Wow. "That's mighty high praise coming from you."

"I wanted Brendan to hear her sing, but he had to leave before they played here again." His frustration is evident.

"What about recording the event?"

He points to a sign tacked in the trees. *No recording of live performances without explicit permission of owners.*

I reach across the table. "Why don't you?"

His brow lowers. "That would mean giving up..."

"Any anonymity you get to enjoy on the island," I finish.

He nods. "Even though a few locals know, since it's been our haven for a long time, most don't connect us with Dani's success. It's not her permanent residence, and very few people know she owns it. But, now we're living here full time. I don't know what kind of impact that will have on Jenna..." His voice trails off.

"You're not sure what kind of effect it's going to have on her at school," I conclude.

"Exactly. Dani bought the house here when Jenna was just a baby."

"She was just starting out in the business then," I muse.

He nods. "And the first thing she did was buy this house. We used to come here as a family—her parents and mine—as kids. We've always loved it here."

"I love that you had that," I tell him softly.

His hand shoots across the table. "Will you ever tell me what your childhood was like?" His eyes are hidden behind his mirrored sunglasses, but I can feel their intense focus.

I can't stop the words from rising to my lips. And after they're out, I wonder how much they'll matter if he understands this small part of me. "I was an orphan. My parents were killed when I was seven."

His hand squeezes my hand so hard, I'm afraid he's going to break my fingers. "Jesus, Em. Accident?"

I pick up my drink and swallow a large drink before I choke out, "No. Murder."

Jake surges out of his chair. The next thing I know, I'm being pulled from mine into his strong arms. My face muffled against his chest, I whisper, "I can't...don't like to look back. It's...difficult."

"I can't even begin to imagine how the six of you survived." I don't correct his misconception that we're all biologically related. It's hard enough to share this monumental piece of myself. And I shouldn't even have done that.

"It wasn't easy." There's an understatement for the record books. "But we're family. We're strong and through whatever trials are tossed our way, we fight through them. For strength, for pride, and for love." Turning away, I grab my glass of beer and take another drink, needing the cool slide of liquid to release the tightness of my throat before sitting back down.

Jake's unusually quiet as he makes his way back to his seat. "So, you do believe."

My senses go on high alert. Warily, I ask, "In what?"

"In love."

"Believing in it isn't the same as accepting you're deserving of it."

He goes to open his mouth when the band fortuitously comes on stage. The crowd goes nuts. Leaning forward, he makes it so his voice is heard in my ear. "This conversation isn't over."

But it is, I think as I turn around in my stool to watch the lead singer step up to the mic.

It never should have started to begin with.

Because by even letting him in that much, I weakened myself and I damn well know it.

ANOTHER BEER AND HOURS LATER, I'm lost in the sweet summer air. I don't know the words to any of the songs, but my hips are swaying back and forth in my seat. I totally get why Jake wants Brendan to listen to this group. I'd pay a hell of a lot more than the price of a few beers to listen to them. And inspiration strikes.

"I'll be right back," I yell over the cheering crowd. Snagging a waitress, I ask if I can see the manager. She points out an attractive middle-aged gentleman standing back with his arm hooked around a woman. Weaving my way between people, I approach them.

"Hi. I'm sorry to intrude, but I understand you're the manager?"

The man grins. "Actually, my wife and I co-own Cisco with our partners."

Pay dirt. "Even better. My name is Emily Freeman." I hold out my hand, and we all shake. "My company is always looking for good products and good talent. You have both here. But since we're family owned and operated, I was wondering if you'd permit me to take a video of the band playing and maybe buy a case of each of your whiskey, wine, and a selection of your beers."

The owners exchange surprised glances. "What company do you work for, Ms. Freeman?" the woman asks warily.

I smile. All the times Ali's had us interviewed for industry magazines is about to pay off. And not just for us. "Amaryllis Events out of Collyer, Connecticut." I let that sink in before I add the coup de grace. "And I was just personally asked to do a show at Bridal Fashion Week in October. We're having an after-party that my sister is in charge of catering. If you think you might want to supply the liquor for that..." I let my voice trail off.

"Why don't you enjoy your day here at Cisco, Ms. Freeman? Drop by my office during the week and let's talk." Reaching into his back pocket, the owner pulls out a business card.

"In the meantime, we'll let our staff know you're allowed to video the live performance," his wife says breathlessly.

"Fantastic!" I exclaim. "I think once my siblings"—and Brendan, I think silently—"get a good understanding of your operation, Connecticut is going to be a huge fan of Cisco."

Out of the corner of my eye, I see Jake stand up trying to locate me. "I'd better go. My date has no idea where I've run off to," I admit sheepishly.

"Go, enjoy your afternoon. And I'll look forward to hearing from you during the week." We exchange handshakes all around before I return to Jake with a smug smile on my face.

Helping me into my chair, he growls into my ear, "What was that all about?"

I grin. I can't help it. Cassidy and Ali must be rubbing off on me. "That, Jacob, was killing two birds or more with one stone," I declare haughtily. "Not only did I just get you the rights to record the band, but I might have just secured Cisco to supply liquor for one of our catering events. I have to come back later this week to talk with the owners. Now, smile. They're looking our way." I wave over at them.

"Are you kidding?" Jake says incredulously. I shake my head, setting my curls dancing.

"You are incredible. Do you know what you just did?" he breathes, right before he lowers his head and kisses me softly in front of half of Nantucket.

A few moments later when we break apart, I ask dreamily, "Can I do it again?"

Jake laughs. Just then, our waitress comes up with a Reserved sign for our table and small glasses of whiskey. "Compliments of the owners, Ms. Freeman. Anytime you want to start recording, you're free to do so."

"Thanks." I expect Jake to pull out his phone immediately, but instead, he pulls me to my feet. "What are you doing?"

Without a word, he leads me into a throng of bodies crushed together on the dirt-packed dance floor. "This." Dragging me into his arms, we start swaying together just as one song ends.

"Oh." I'm filled with disappointment. I start to move away from him, but his arms close around me tighter.

"Not yet." Pulling off his sunglasses, he hooks them into his T-shirt collar. Reaching up, he moves to take off mine, but I catch his hand.

"I won't be able to see anything."

"The only thing you'll need to see is my face." Carefully, he hooks them on his shirt as well just as the singer says, "We're going to slow it down a bit," right before they sing a beautiful song about getting lost with a stranger on a crowded street.

There's nothing I can do but feel. The air is thick with the scent of malt and the freshness of summer. I can hear Jake's heart pounding against mine in a beautiful beat more intoxicating than the music around us. I can't see the band or the swirling people around us, but that doesn't matter. All that needs to fill my vision is the man dancing with me.

I'm overwhelmed with everything I want to say and never will. So, I do the only thing I can in this moment to let go of the pressure cooker of pain building up inside of me. Somehow, he's getting through the ice. And it hurts so badly.

I pull his mouth down to mine to show him without words what this day means to me.

When our lips break apart, he whispers directly in my ear, "Em," almost pleadingly.

I lay my fingers on his lips to stop the words.

I don't know if he wants to say what I think he does, but maybe I can still save him. Otherwise, I know I'll break. Because knowing the man he is—the strength, the humor, the father, the talent—is to halfway fall without ever having spent a moment wrapped in his arms. I might die if I ever hurt him.

Because that's what loving me does.

It kills.

41

JAKE

One step forward, twenty steps back. That's how I feel about my relationship with Emily. She's asleep in my arms, but I'm awake and frustrated. As I hold Em even tighter, the smell of mint and rosemary floods my senses. One night after we were lying together, our bodies still connected, I asked her what the scent in her hair was. Now, I'll never smell either without thinking of her.

I'll never be able to be in this apartment again without thinking of her.

Tonight, she cherished every inch of my body with her lips before taking me to places I've never been with a woman. But each time I try to talk, she stops me. Either with her delicate fingers, her mouth, or simply by falling asleep in my arms.

Cradling her close with one arm, I hook the other behind my head as I stare up at the vaulted ceiling. The day we had at Cisco turned into an incredible night. With Jenna at Lynne's, we grabbed a couple of burgers on the way home and just relaxed. Today ended up being one long, perfect date. Em opened up a little more about her family. She smiled as she explained their pecking order. When I told her trying to remember was giving me a headache, she let out her adorable giggle-snort before she said, "Now let me add in the in-laws and babies."

I want to ask her about her about her ex-fiancé to determine if she's hung up on the ass in any way, but I don't.

I suspect what brought her to Nantucket was a pure case of burnout, but she doesn't offer any information.

I can only dig to a certain level before she shuts down. But lately, I've noticed the mask she's been wearing isn't as strong as it was when she first came here. Take tonight for example: I sure as hell never expected her to say what she did about her parents. Pulling her a little tighter, I'm rewarded when she nuzzles closer in her sleep.

I have so many questions. Were the Freemans fostered? Were they wards of the state? I'm astounded this family managed to survive, but then again what did Jenna and I do? You shore up your defenses and survive, I surmise as I brush a soft kiss on the top of her head.

And Emily's still doing that.

"Are you ever going to let me in?" I whisper softly into the dark. I don't think I spoke loud enough for her to hear me.

My heart stops in my chest when she responds in her sleep. "It's safer for you not to."

What the hell is that supposed to mean?

Wrapping both arms around her, I pull her tight. Tomorrow, whether it means the beginning or the end, I'll find out more about the woman sharing her bed with me before my heart gets in too deep.

But as I manage to close my eyes and drift off to sleep, I already know that it's too late.

42

EMILY

J ake stayed over. Not once in the months we've been sleeping together have I ever woken up with his arms around me. When I braced myself for the usual note, I was shocked, thrilled, and horrified to find him looming over me. And that was before he leaned down and kissed me good morning with a simple "I didn't want to leave you."

After he made slow, tender love to me, he promised to be back after he grabbed clothes and "some real freaking food to eat. Jesus, Em. How do you survive on this crap?" He's holding up a container of greek yogurt.

"It's an acquired taste," I offer weakly.

"I'm not acquiring it. I'll be right back with real food. Go get showered, lady. After we eat, we'll take Mugs out." Brushing my wildly curling hair away from my face, he looks at me seriously. "Then, Em? We need to talk."

I try to dampen down the panic building inside me. "About what?"

He thinks about it for a moment before he asks me quietly, "Do you know you talk in your sleep?"

I literally feel the blood drain from my face. Stumbling away from him, I reach out for the island counter. I grip it to stay on my feet. *What did I say?*

"Em? Em, goddamnit, look at me!" Pulling my face toward him, Jake yanks me back into his arms. "Don't you see we're too far in? Don't you understand that letting me see who you really are isn't going to change how I'm beginning to feel?"

That's what scares the hell out of me. Because it might. Instead of responding verbally, I press my trembling lips together tightly.

That's the thing with silence: you can't argue back with it verbally.

Jake growls. Yanking me back toward him, he lowers his head and kisses me. Hard. Savaging my lips with his, he lifts his head only when the rest of my body is as shaking as my lips were. "Be back." He storms to the door. Throwing it open, he stomps out.

His footsteps echo in the stillness of the room.

I tried loving him less, I scream mentally. *It doesn't work that way. I love him and Jenna. If I never tell them, it hurts me, and that's what our deal was. Hurt me and no one else I love will die, right? Right, you bastard?*

Without waiting for an answer, I make my way to the bathroom so I can be dressed for when Jake comes back.

TWENTY MINUTES LATER, I've showered and thrown on a quick outfit. I'm running a pick through my curls when I realize Mugsy hasn't come in to see me yet this morning.

Frowning, I make my way to the laundry room where his bed is located. Standing at the door, I let out a sigh of relief. Poor old man, still sleeping? I walk over and crouch in front of him. Stroking his head that's more gray than black, I feel a chill whip through me.

"Mugs?" I rub his shoulder, but he doesn't stir. "Mugsy, it's time for breakfast. Jake's going to bring over something like bacon or some crap." My voice is shaking. "Come on, baby. It's time to wake up."

No.

Just no.

This can't be my punishment.

You bastard, you wouldn't do this, would you?

"Mugsy," I plead. "Mugsy, wake up!" I lay my head down on his chest and hear shallow breaths. I hear the door open and do something so instinctive, I never begin to question it. I scream.

"Jake!"

43

JAKE

I'm opening the door when I hear her scream my name. Everything stops: time, my heart, the world. Dropping the bag of groceries and other things I brought from the house, I race in the direction of her voice.

What I find shatters me.

Emily is lying next to Mugsy sobbing her heart out. Her face is buried in the scruff of his neck, and she's begging for him to wake up. "Jesus Christ," I whisper. "Baby, let me help."

"This is why," she's mumbling. "This is why."

"Em, get out of the way. I need to see what's wrong with him. We have to get him to the vet."

As she moves slowly away from Mugsy's body, I can see he's still breathing. Em's frantically pressing kisses to his face. "I love you, baby. I love you so much. I'm so sorry. It's all my fault."

And like pieces of a puzzle, her words from last night snap together with these.

Emily believes loving someone means they're going to get hurt. Fuck—I close my eyes briefly. This isn't her not wanting love; it's fear. And even with that, she's given so much of herself she's made me fall over the cliff with her.

"Let me take care of him, baby," I urge her.

"But..."

"I need you to get a blanket, call the nearest vet that's open. Let them know we're bringing him in." Even though I could get it done faster if I left her sitting right here, getting her out of the room and giving her a list of things to do will take her mind off the fact that Mugsy hasn't opened his eyes once since we've been here.

Emily scrambles to her feet. "Right. I'll be right back, baby. I promised you I'd always take care of you." Her voice breaks on the last word.

"Em," I say harshly. Her body snaps to attention. "Go. Now."

She dashes out the door, leaving me with her beloved pet.

I wait until I hear her on the phone before I lean down and whisper, "You're probably what saved her heart, Mugsy. I hope you know I love too, buddy, because I think I feel everything in the world for her."

Just as I finish, Em stumbles back in. "They're waiting for us." She rattles off the name and address of a vet near Cisco. "Do you know how to get there?"

Taking the blanket from her, I wrap it around Mugsy, before I heft him into my arms. "Yeah, baby, I do. Get my keys out of my pocket."

"I can..." she protests.

"There is no way in hell you're in any condition to drive, Em." Then I soften my tone. "Besides, you have to be in the back with him."

"Right." Reaching over to the bundle in my arms, she kisses his cheek again. "I have to be with my baby boy."

I close my eyes on the wave of pain emanating from her. "Let's go."

HOURS LATER, we're still at the vet. They started an IV on Mugsy as soon as we got there. Em's been curled into my side ever since.

I texted Jenna to see if she can stay at Lynne's. When she asked why, I told her. She immediately wanted to rush down to the vet. It took a good ten minutes of my fingers flying on the keyboard to convince her that Emily's in no state to have anyone else around. But there is something I need to ask. Jostling her lightly, I press my lips to her temple. She stirs.

"Baby?"

"Yes?"

"Do you want me to call your family?" I've spoken only with Corinna, and only briefly during Jenna's birthday at that, but if she needs them...

She shakes her head. "After, Jake. I'll call them..." Her voice breaks off when Dr. Hillman, the emergency veterinarian, comes out.

Too soon.

He squats down in front of Emily and takes her limp hand. My arm tightens around her shoulders.

"Ms. Freeman, I'm so sorry..." I can't hear the rest of what he's saying as Emily turns into my shoulder and begins sobbing so hard, I feel every piece of my heart break along with hers.

44

EMILY

Mugsy's gone.

The thought keeps playing over and over through my brain. Not as Jake drives us back to the apartment. Not when he cleans us both off in the shower. Not when I stare blankly at him as he cleans the broken eggs he dropped earlier to come to my rescue. And even when he pries my phone from my numb hands when I try to call my family to tell them, I can't let go of the thought.

Mugsy's gone. And it's my fault because I loved him.

He wasn't on my list, I think wearily as I lay my head back against the couch. I didn't bargain for him after Dee died. Therefore, he became a victim of being loved by me.

Or was he paying the price for me loving someone else?

Either way, he's gone. Tears just fall silently from my eyes. Removing my glasses, I toss them on the side table and let them flow.

"All right, Dani. I'll have her call when she's able to." After a brief pause, Jake continues. "Yeah, if you could contact her family, that would be great. If I were to hazard a guess, I'm going to bet that's not going to be tonight or tomorrow. She's wrecked. Yeah, I'll be with her."

The tears flow faster. Harder. I can't stop them. I don't even try.

"I'll let her know. Okay. Bye." My phone clattering to the tray on top of the ottoman in front of me lets me know how close Jake is. Within seconds, his warm body is heating my cold one as he wraps me up in his arms.

But do I deserve any warmth? I just killed yet another living thing simply by loving them.

I deserve nothing but the cold.

Shoving the heels of my hands into my eyes, I try to hold back the sobs. Jake allows my internal struggle for all of two seconds before he's lifting me onto his lap to hold me close. I try to struggle out of his arms, but he just tightens his arms around me. "I got you, Em. Let it all out."

I shake my head. Once again, I can't find my words to say what I want to—have to—to make him understand.

I have to let him go.

Tonight. Before he strikes again.

"What's going through your head?" he croons softly.

One word manages to come out. "*Theta*." And the viciousness with which I say that word shocks him.

45

JAKE

"I was seven when my parents died," she whispers. "It was eight days before my eighth birthday. Which is on August eighth. Do you know what the number eight means, Jacob? *Theta*. Death."

Shoving herself out of my lap she stalks over to the dining room table and turns, holding her journal. Hurling it at me, she says, "I only have myself to blame for Mugsy dying. I'm to blame for them all dying."

I don't open the book. Instead I look at her and whisper, "How could your parents' death be your fault?"

"I asked you if you ever studied history. You didn't. But I did. Quite a bit. Especially Greek mythology," she tells me oddly.

My brow lowers in confusion.

"Thanatos is the son of Nyx and the brother of Hypnos. He got his kicks by carrying off people to the underworld. He was represented by the Greek symbol theta. Theta means eight. Symbols are everything in my world, Jake. Do you think I'm a designer by accident? No, it was someone's grand plan for me. Symbols are everywhere in my brain. Everywhere. Designers use both visible and invisible ones to imprint feelings on a design." Wearily, she shoves a hand through her hair. "Why would the men who killed my parents spare me unless I was just as evil as they were? It has to be because they knew something worse was protecting me." Storming over to me, she flips open the journal.

And suddenly I'm looking into her private hell. She's opened up her world, and suddenly, I'm not certain I know how to comprehend the pain basting at me from carefully crafted sketches.

"My mother was dying—begging for my life. My father tried to use it to barter for his own. And the bastards who dragged me from my room to watch all this shot him in front of me. Then they released me. They just let me go, saying I was more precious than he was." Her breath is ragged. "Because of *theta*. I'm certain of it."

My gut churns. I want to silence her, to tell her she is wrong, but I let her continue. She needs to get all this pain out. "May I?" I gesture to the journal in front of me.

When she nods, I flip the page. I want to gag at the brutality she managed to capture, but I manage to control myself to a wince. I flip the page again and find a sketch of an older woman who looks remarkably like she will in forty years. "Who's this?"

Her face softens briefly before it crumbles further. "Aunt Dee. I chose my name after her."

That gives me pause. "Chose?"

Frightened eyes lift up to mine. She backs away slowly. "Shit."

I stand, carefully laying the book next to me. Who is this woman I've been sleeping with for the last few months? "Who are you?" It comes out harsher than I intend, but she's not the only one with someone to protect.

Swallowing convulsively, she doesn't answer. Instead, she whispers, "Flip the page."

Picking up the journal, I turn the page. While my mind absorbs what it can't possibly be seeing, I hear her whisper, "That's the day I first met my brother and first sister. They were beat to shit, huddling together at a park near my house. My Aunt Dee saved them, and I repaid that beautiful woman for all she did for me—for them—by not speaking. For a total of four years if you count the two before they arrived."

"Dear God." The book falls from my hand to the couch. I step forward to reach for her, but she holds up her hand.

"I've always been Emily. My mother chose that name, so I'll never change it. My middle name is Delores, because my Aunt Dee gave me love, gave me a home, and gave us everything even after she was gone. And we all agreed to become Freemans the very minute all six of us legally could. Because we were—are—finally free from the brutality that brought our lives together. But my siblings' stories aren't mine to tell." She lets out a deep breath. "Flip the page."

I do, and I see a scene of happiness. Warmth, laughter, love. "Flip it again." Emily's voice is empty.

From her mind's eye, Emily has drawn a slightly older version of her brother and sister as they stand in front of a casket. "Your aunt?" I don't know how much more I can bear, but I know I have to if I want to scale the walls she's been using to keep me at bay.

"Yes. And on that day I swore, *I swore*, I would never love anyone but family ever again." She rips the book from my hands, and I notice she's trembling. "Don't you see? I begged, and pleaded, and prayed no one else in my family would ever be taken again from me. Even if it meant I could never fall in love. Why do you think I agreed to marry a man I knew I would never fall in love with? I wanted a future—a family of my own—without harming them. And now?" Her face crumbles. "Mugsy's gone because I dared to push the boundaries too far. I'm being punished as a reminder of the consequences of believing."

How is it possible for a heart to break and soar all at the same time? Yanking her into my arms, the journal clatters to the floor in between us. I gasp for every breath as her burden becomes ours.

How do I convince her she's wrong?

I rack my brain for a way to make her understand there's no rhyme or reason to the losses she's experienced. Then her words tear into me leaving me just as broken as she is.

"This is why I tried not...it would have been a lot easier if you'd gone on not liking me."

And when her tears soak my shirt, all I can do is stand there and hold her.

46

EMILY

I 'm living with a time bomb over my head. Between knowing this and Mugsy's death, I'm almost afraid to sleep for wasting a minute of the day. I have less than a month left. And I need to store up the smallest of memories for random moments when it's cold and dark in Connecticut.

Laughing as Jenna and Lynne squeal when the tide comes rushing up on the beach.

Bumping my hip against Jake's when he teases me about making a perfectly edible salad.

Dancing on the deck after I get the Cisco Brewery contract signed for the company.

Curling up on Jake's lap as we watch the day end.

Randomly crying uncontrollably because of missing Mugsy.

Feeling either Jake or Jenna's arms wrap around me.

Because when after it's all said and done, this will be the summer I never forget for too many reasons.

Jake rolls over in his sleep. Jenna's alternating spending the night at Lynne's, so tonight he's with me. Pulling me close, the scruff of the hair on his chin sends chills down my spine. Silent tears fall down my face as I know even if I never say the words, it's too late.

My heart knows what it feels.

47

EMILY

"Ms. Freeman?"

"Yes?"

"This is Stacie at Offshore Animal Care. On behalf of everyone here, I want to offer our condolences again on your loss of Mugsy."

Tears burn behind my eyes before they slide down my face. It's been a little over two weeks since Mugsy died of a brain aneurysm. Dr. Hillman not only assured me this was common, but there was absolutely nothing I could have done to have saved him. "Thank you," I manage to get out.

The receptionist clears her throat. "Unfortunately, I also need to inform you that in order to release Mugsy's ashes to you, we need to have you come down and sign some additional paperwork. Either it was misplaced or not signed the night you came in."

While I want to spew outraged fury, all I feel is bone tired. "I understand. Mistakes happen."

Her relief is evident. "I am so incredibly sorry about this, Ms. Freeman. Truly. After this, we should have Mugsy's ashes back to you within a few days."

A shot through the heart might be less painful. "What time are you open until?"

"Five today. If we can't get the papers signed today, Ms. Freeman, it will mean more of a delay since we don't handle things on the island..." I cut her off.

"I'll be by." After hearing her thank me again, I disconnect the call. I'm buried under a pile of rejected sketches I've been working on since this morning. The emotions are so twisted inside me, I can't sort them out. Letting out a huge sigh, I close my eyes.

"Who was calling, baby?" Jake's voice startles me.

"The veterinarian," I reply wearily. His hands settle on my shoulders and begin rubbing. "God, that feels so good."

"What did they want?"

"Either I didn't sign papers, or they forgot to give me papers. I have to go down there to get them signed before they can..." My throat clogs on the words. "Anyway, I'm just going to head over there in a few."

Jake stops rubbing my shoulders and squats down next to me. "Em, I don't want you driving over there by yourself." He takes my hand between both of his.

"I'll be okay. I just have to fill out papers."

"The last time you were there, you were a wreck," he says bluntly. "Does it have to be done today?"

I nod. "Otherwise, I won't get him back for at least a week." Moisture begins gathering in the corner of my eyes.

"Damn," he bites out.

Taken aback, I jerk my hand away.

"No, it's not you, Em. I literally just agreed to have two guys come by for Dani to give estimates on the cost of painting the main house and the garage. They're due any minute. I came to let you know so you wouldn't be surprised when you see strangers walking around."

"Jake, I'll be fine. I'll drive carefully and I'll call you when I'm on my way back. It will take me less than an hour."

He bites his lower lip in that way that drives me crazy. "Stop that. You have painters coming," I whisper with a small smile.

A small smirk appears on his lips instead. He leans forward and presses his lips against mine. "I was thinking."

I raise a brow. He grins before reaching out and tapping a finger on my nose. "Not about that. How about Jenna drives you over? Then on the way back, you can drop her at work for me?"

Jake has been letting Jenna venture out with an adult in her car to gain more experience driving. He's still uncomfortable with the idea of her and Lynne driving themselves around during tourist season—something Lynne's parents wholeheartedly agree with. "That's awfully sweet, babe, but don't you think you should ask her?"

"Even if she didn't love you as much as I do, she'd jump at the chance to drive," he says wryly. He pulls out his phone and begins texting his daughter.

Oh. My. God.

He just said it.

"Jake..." My voice is a reflection of my heart: completely broken and utterly panicked.

His face takes on a shadow of my pain when he whispers, "Don't say anything. It doesn't change how I—we—feel." Leaning forward, he brushes his lips against mine. Seconds later, his phone pings with a response. "Jenna said she'll meet you here in thirty minutes. Better clean up your papers unless you want them scattered to the wind."

"Jake..." I can't say more than his name. If I do, I'm going to tell him I'm falling too.

And what kind of sick hell will that rain down on us?

"Later, Em. We'll talk later." Running a hand over my hair, he pushes to his feet before walking away.

I sit frozen, my eyes not seeing the ocean in front of me. Instead, I'm praying so hard this won't end up in disaster. All the pain I've lived through, all the ways I've managed to hold on to the recesses of my heart, and finally someone made me believe.

But now that I believe, am I strong enough to survive?

48

EMILY

"911. What's your emergency?"

"Help me, please," I whisper frantically.

"I can barely hear you, ma'am. Can you speak louder?"

"No. I...we've been in an accident. Jenna? Oh, God, Jenna!"

"Ma'am! Do you know where you are?"

My head is pounding, but I look around. "Polpis Road. Near Milk Street."

"Are there injuries, ma'am?"

"Yes. God, yes." I begin to cry.

Your fault, Emily. I know! I want to scream.

"We'll send ambulances, but we need you to stay on the line." I stop listening as I watch Jenna's chest stop rising and falling. "Jenna! Jenna, can you breathe? Can you hear me?"

There's no response.

"Noooo!" I scream. "No, Jenna!" Immediately ignoring my own bruised and battered body, I crawl closer to where I pulled her from the car. I try to feel for a pulse. I can't find one.

Your fault, Emily.

Maybe I shouldn't have moved her, but I thought I smelled gas, and I wasn't taking any chances. Fortunately, the air bags in the Rover cushioned the worst of the impact. Us rolling didn't.

"I'm beginning CPR. She's not breathing!" I scream. Praying the CPR classes Jason made us all get certified in actually work, I find her sternum and move the heel of my hand slightly below it. *Backwards from thirty, Em*, I can hear Jason's voice in my head. This way you won't lose count.

Thirty.

Twenty-nine.

Twenty-eight.

Twenty-seven.

You shouldn't have fallen in love, Emily. We had a deal.

Tears flow from my eyes and drip onto her bruised and beautiful face.

Fourteen.

Thirteen.

Twelve.

Eleven.

I have to make you keep up your end of the bargain.

"Then take me, you bastard," I hiss. "Then finally take me."

Five.

Four.

Three.

Two.

One.

I wait for her chest to resume its normal position. Putting my hand on Jenna's forehead, I put two fingers on her jaw and tip it back. Using the air from my heart, my body, what's left of my soul, I give her the first breath. I watch her chest rise.

It doesn't begin breathing on its own.

I drop my lips to hers and administer the second breath.

Nothing.

"*Fuck you!*" I scream out loud as I begin the chest compressions again. "Come on, Jenna. You didn't come to this damn island to die.

You just found happiness. You can't give up!" Less than a minute later, the second round of compressions are done.

I'm in the middle of the first breath when I hear the sirens.

The second is finished when the EMTs appear at my side.

"We've got it from here, ma'am." The two EMTs immediately begin picking up where I left off. Soon, they're sliding her lifeless body onto a board and loading her into an ambulance. I start to go after her, but a policeman stops me. "Ma'am, we need you to tell us what happened. First, can we have your name?"

I look at her blankly. My name? What does it matter who I am? Jenna's the only one who matters.

Oh, God. Jake! How the hell am I supposed to tell Jake?

I feel the blood leave my head, and I start to collapse. "Ma'am? Ma'am? Are you hurt? Are you okay?"

Following the policeman's pant leg up to his concerned eyes, I whisper, "I'll never be okay if Jenna dies."

And I burst into hysterical tears.

49

JAKE

It's been thirty-six hours since Jenna was brought into the emergency room of the Nantucket Cottage Hospital in a coma. I've been alone by her bedside the entire time, praying for a fucking miracle. I've barely managed to make two phone calls.

The first was to Dani, who I knew would take care of contacting our families. She swore to me she was on her way and to hold on. "That girl's a Madison, Jake. We were all born to drive you insane." But even from thousands of miles away, I could still hear the break in her voice. I went apeshit on a few doctors after that call.

The second wasn't any easier but way more surprising. Michelle's on her way to Nantucket. "There is no way I'm not coming, Jake. I haven't been the best mother, but damn you, I am still her mother!" She hung up on me at that point.

I still haven't been able to even look at Emily. Every time I walk out of Jenna's cubicle to talk to a doctor or nurse, I see her sitting through the double doors in the public waiting area curled into a ball. Her face is bruised, and her clothes are bloody.

I don't give a fuck.

My baby girl is dying because Emily couldn't wait a damn day to sign papers for her dog's ashes.

Mugsy was already gone and now Jenna...

Ruthlessly, I turn away and walk back into my daughter's room.

"Hey, baby. It's Daddy. I'm right here, and I'm not going anywhere until you open your eyes."

MICHELLE ARRIVES ABOUT five hours later. I asked the nurses to have her brought to a private room so the doctor can explain the extent of Jenna's injuries.

"None of Jenna's major organs were injured during the car accident. Her seat belt and the front and curtain air bags saw to that," the doctor repeats. I've heard this already, but hearing it again just infuriates me. I jump out of my chair and begin pacing.

Michelle looks at me nervously. "Then why isn't she waking up, Doctor?"

Sitting down, he takes my ex's hands. "Ms. Madison."

"Williams," we both say simultaneously.

The doctor falters before starting again. "Ms. Williams. As I explained to your ex-husband, Jenna's injuries likely happened due to the impact with the steering wheel. She has what we call a temporary traumatic brain injury. The coma is her brain's way of dealing with that trauma. We took tests yesterday, and we'll be sending her down for another round shortly." Standing, he says something I didn't catch on to yesterday. "Your daughter is extraordinarily lucky. Someone at the scene performed life-saving CPR on her. If it hadn't been for that, we'd be having a very different conversation."

"When can I see her?" Michelle asks.

"I'll take you to her now. Mr. Madison?"

I jerk my head in his direction. "Yes?"

"Only one person in with Jenna at a time. We can't have too much stimuli overwhelming her," the doctor warns me.

My breathing is harsh in the room even as Michelle says to the doctor, "I'll...I want to go see her."

"She's your daughter, Michelle. Go. Before they take her down for the tests," I rasp.

"Right." She starts to make her way out the door, but she pauses. "Jake?"

"Yeah?"

"This isn't your fault. It's God's will." She slips out the door without saying another word.

God's will...

Do you know what the number eight means, Jacob? Theta. Death. I'm to blame for them all dying.

Emily.

I need to have a few words with her before I focus on the only thing that matters.

Saving my daughter's life.

~

"Get out." My words are harsh. Not even letting her get a word in, I go on the attack. "This is your fault," I accuse.

"Jake, we were hit..." Emily begins, but I don't want to hear it.

Not now.

Not while Jenna's lying there.

"I was such a fucking fool. I should have listened to my first instincts about you and stayed far the hell away from you," I hiss.

Wounded blue eyes stare back at me in a face that's just as battered as my daughter's.

But Emily can walk. Emily can talk.

And Jenna can't.

"Jake, listen to me. Please."

"The very sight of you, Emily, is enough to send me into a rage. The idea that my daughter is probably dying because I made yet another stupid fucking decision about a woman..." My voice trails off. "Just get the hell out of my sight."

Then she does something she swore she'd never do, because as her pictures depicted, the last time she did there was a gun to her head. In the moment, it's probably the only thing she can think of to try to break through.

She gets down on her knees, her wet eyes beseeching me to listen. Too bad it's not enough.

"Jacob, please," she begs, tears flowing down her face. "Please, listen to me. I lo—"

I cut her off. "Don't you fucking say it. *If* you even feel what I think you were about to say, it's apparently bad enough to kill people. Haven't you done enough damage already?"

Turning, I push my way back through the double doors and toward Jenna's room. Emily's sobs ricochet down the hall behind me. I can't care, I just can't.

When I get there, Michelle tells me they've taken her down for more tests.

In an uncomfortable silence, we wait.

And wait.

50

EMILY

If the pounding in my head from the wreck wasn't causing me to be so sick, I'd have sworn I just died. I asked for it, but I didn't know it would hurt so badly. Isn't death supposed to be swift? Isn't there supposed to be an end where there's peace?

Obviously not for me. I'm meant to live a life in eternal hell where all I can do is live in a perpetual circle of love and death.

Is this what love is supposed to feel like? If so, I don't want it. If loving means feeling this kind of pain, I want to feel empty for the rest of my life. I hope I never smile, I hope I never laugh, I hope I never cry. I never want to believe again.

A security guard walking by comes over to me since I'm frozen in place on my knees. "Miss? Are you okay?" His reaches down to help me stand. I jerk away. The last thing I want is a man touching me.

Now or ever again.

Pressing my trembling lips together, I pull one shaking leg out from beneath me. Foot planted, I press my weight forward. Stumbling, he reaches out to catch me. "Please don't...touch me," I croak out in a haunted voice.

"Miss, I'd be remiss if I didn't recommend you get treatment. You look pretty banged up," he says, not unkindly.

Pulling what dignity I have left around me, I swipe at any lingering tears. Coolly, I ask, "Do you have a phone I can use? I was in an accident and have no means to leave the property."

Sympathy drops over his features. I don't want sympathy.

I want to go home.

"This way please." He holds out his arm and escorts me in the opposite direction from Jenna's room. At this point, even though I'll miss the child who wormed her way into my heart, I welcome every step it puts between myself and Jake Madison.

After a porter contacts a cab for me, the security guard waits with me—still obviously concerned—until I'm safely in the cab before turning and walking back into the building. I could have told him not to spend any more time worrying about me.

Pretty soon, I'll be just as dead to Nantucket Island as I already feel inside.

I'M VIOLENTLY ill by the end of the fifteen-minute ride back to Sconset. I don't remember much about paying the driver. I'm just grateful I remembered to grab the purse the police rescued from my crushed Rover before I slid out. Several times on my way up the stairs, I sat down to let the nausea pass. I almost certainly have a concussion. Since I refused to be checked out because I was waiting for news about Jenna, I don't know for certain. But I'd bet my life on it.

Unlocking the door, I grab the handset from the counter. Dialing one of the numbers I don't need to look up, I slide down against the wall and curl up as tight as I can.

"Amaryllis Events, this is Cassidy speaking. How may I help you?" Cassidy's voice comes through the line confident and happy.

Knowing I'm one step closer to home, I start to sob.

"Em? Em? What's wrong? Why are you crying? What happened? Phil, get in here, damnit!" Cassidy begins screaming in my ear.

"I need to come home. I have to come home. I can't get home." I begin to babble incoherently.

"We'll send Caleb's jet." Cassidy's voice is frightened and angry all at once.

"Can you tell us what happened, baby?" Phil must have hit Speaker.

They want me to talk, when all I want to do is fall into a cocoon of silence and never come out. It doesn't hurt so much when I'm locked away. But this is Phil and Cass, the ones who saved me the first time. I have to tell them what happened. "Went to sign papers...get Mugsy's ashes...Jenna...car crushed." I begin sobbing in earnest. "My fault. I love them."

"This is not your fault, Em." Cassidy's voice is cracking.

"Let's get our girl home first, Cass," Phil chides her gently.

"I'll have Caleb send the jet," she announces.

"Can't," I whisper. "I think I have a concussion."

"You think?" two voices say simultaneously. "Why the hell didn't you get checked out at the hospital? What did the EMTs say?" Phil demands.

This one sentence is going to let in all the pain again. I can't fortify my walls fast enough before I say it. I prepare to bleed. After all, don't I deserve it for daring to love? "The EMTs suspect a concussion. I...I didn't get checked out. I was waiting... Jenna was driving the Rover. Jake told me to go. He blames me." The sobs that rack my body hurt—God, do they hurt my head, my heart, and my soul. "I begged him on my knees to listen to me, but he refused."

I'm crying so hard, I miss out on the frantic yelling and scrambling on the other end of the phone. The next thing I'm cognizant of is Cassidy whispering in my ear, "Shhhh, Em. I'm right here. I'm not going anywhere. I'm staying right here on the phone with you."

Gasping, I whisper, "Promise?"

"I promise. Listen to me. Caleb, Keene, Jason, Phil, and Holly are on their way to you right now. They'll be there in four hours. I'm not hanging up until they get there, baby."

"Appointments?" I manage to get out.

"Fuck the business, Em! You're hurting. You are far more important than any client that walks in this door," Cassidy snaps.

My head is throbbing. I curl up on the floor of the kitchen in a ball.

"I love you, Em. I loved you from the moment you nodded for me to come home with you. I'll love you forever."

I swish my head back and forth. In my mind, I've twisted the deal I made. She can't say she loves me. Now, no one can. I can't have her die too. "Noo..." I moan.

"Yes, my Em. Yes, I do. I always will." There's a long silence where I just listen to her breathe.

"Cassy..." I use her dreaded nickname. One used only in the direst of situations.

"Yes, sweetheart."

"Don't leave me alone. Hurt so much."

And my older sister begins to talk about everything and nothing for the next four hours. Until there's a pounding at my door and she finally whispers in her shredded voice, "They're there. It's time to come home."

51

JAKE

It's the third day after the accident. Both Michelle and I have been taking shifts by Jenna's bedside. Although I should be surprised she came when I called her, I guess I'm not. For all her faults, she is Jenna's mother.

My anger has left me hollow and scared. I called Dani, who's still trying to make her way back to Nantucket as quickly as she can. Her flights have been delayed due to weather. Our parents haven't made it back from their vacation in Europe either. Connections from the Mediterranean aren't easy.

Neither of us have heard from Em. I'm freaking worried about her. Knowing the disaster of Em's Rover, I doubt her cell's in working order. After every text, my phone reads "Delivered," but since I'm almost certain her phone was caught inside her car, I'm positive the texts I'm sending aren't reaching her. Even then, I'm still trying.

I've also tried to call the apartment each time I'm away from Jenna's room. The phone rings and my heart frantically beats when it clicks, right before I hear Dani's voice repeat the number and asking the caller to leave a message. I've still been trying anyway.

What I did was completely wrong. I lashed out at Em because she was there, trying to offer her love and support. I lashed out because fifty percent of my heart was lying white-faced on a bed, immobile while the other was stumbling around...stumbling?

I groan out loud. How much more of an asshole could I have been? Em was in the car with Jenna. Did anyone check her for injuries? I was so focused on Jenna—on my baby—I never thought to ask. Then my panic sets in full force. What if she's at the apartment sick? She was in the accident with Jenna. Has she been checked out by a doctor? I spot a security guard and babble almost incoherently about what happened. After glaring at me furiously, all he would tell me is the lady in question was sent home in a taxi.

What if she's... No. She'd have come back to the hospital, I'm sure.

Temporarily relieved, I begin talking to Jenna again. "Come on, Jen. Come give your old man some hell. I need you to wake up so I can go find Em." It's a shot in the dark, but knowing how close the two have become, if she knows I completely fucked up, maybe she'll wake up. "I screwed up royally, Jenna. I did the same shit to Em that I do to you. I freaked out instead of listening. I yelled." I pause, thinking about everything I said. "Jesus, I'm such a bastard. But I can't leave you to go fix things."

"You must really be in love this time, Jake, if you're admitting all your faults to our daughter." Michelle's amused voice comes from behind me. Shit.

"I am." My voice is hoarse from the lack of sleep and overuse.

"And Jenna was with her in the wreck?"

I nod. "It was her car Jenna was driving."

"So, instead of finding out what I just found out, you went off on that poor injured woman?" Wait a second, is my ex actually sticking up for my girlfriend? Turning around to face Michelle, I'm shocked to see the extremely pissed-off look on her face. "It was *her*, Jake. She's the reason our daughter's even alive. She's the one who performed CPR on Jenna at the accident. The other driver was drunk, coming down the road from some brewery." Michelle waves her hand in the air.

I suck in a huge breath because I can't get any air. "Em saved Jenna?"

"According to the officer who came by yesterday, she apparently had to be dragged off our daughter. It was her quick thinking that got Jenna this far." Michelle stomps over to me and shoves me in the chest. "And it was *a drunk driver* who hit them, Jake. They *both* could be lying here."

Before I can respond, we hear rustling from the bed. Both of us turn. "Jen?" I whisper.

"Come on, Jenna. Snap out of it so your father can go fix his mistakes." Michelle's not done giving me crap obviously.

But what she says strikes something in our daughter, who begins to twist her head from side to side. "No...Em... Watch out!" she mutters. Jenna's eyes roll behind rapidly blinking eyelids. Her heart rate begins to accelerate.

"Michelle, call for the doctor!" I rasp. Not wasting a second, she hits the button for the nurse.

"We see the changes on the monitors. The doctor is on his way in."

A minute later, Jenna's doctor strides through the door. Lifting Jenna's eyelids, he uses a penlight before turning to us.

And smiles.

"She's going to be in this state for a while," he predicts. "But I suspect she'll wake up fully in a few hours."

Thank fucking Christ.

Michelle reaches over Jenna's bed and grabs my hand. "Almost there, Dad. Then you can go try to rectify your asinine behavior."

I breathe a little easier.

Just a few more hours.

Then I can try to figure out how to make the largest apology of my life.

∾

By NIGHTFALL, Jenna's eyes are open but drowsy. She smiles sleepily at me, before asking, "Em?"

I swallow convulsively. I reply as honestly as I can. "I don't know, Jen. I've been by your side the entire time, baby. The last time I saw her, her injuries mainly looked like bruises."

She nods slowly. "Okay. Check on her?"

She wants me to leave? I can't fathom the thought. Jenna's brown eyes have been welded shut for days. I can't just run off to check on Em even if something is pulling me to do just that. Her heart monitor starts going mad. A nurse pops her head in to ask, "Is everything okay in here? Mom, Dad, we need you to keep our patient calm. Otherwise, you're going to have to ask you to leave."

Michelle growls at me warningly, "Jake…"

"Do you want me to leave you with your mom? Do you want me to go check on Em?" I relent, albeit unwillingly. I'm so afraid if I leave, Jenna's going to close her eyes again and this time not wake up.

She nods slowly. Her brow furrows. "Careful?"

Leaning forward, I press a kiss to her still-bruised cheek. "I promise. I'll be back soon."

"Take all the time you need, Jake," Michelle drawls. As I pass her, she mutters, "I have a feeling you're going to need it."

"Is there anything you need?" I'm being polite and asking both occupants of the room, but really my question is for Jenna.

Michelle immediately answers. "Decent coffee." I bark out a laugh. I can't help it. We've been living on rot gut for the last few days.

"Em," Jenna says immediately. I clench my teeth.

"Let me see if she's up for it, baby." Jenna's head nods slowly.

Fueled by an overwhelming urgency, I leave the hospital for the first time in three hellishly long days. Even though it's dark out, the air seems cleaner outside. I stop to inhale deeply and smell the sea. I wonder if I'll be able to smell it in the middle of winter.

Driving slower than I want to, it takes over twenty minutes to drive the eight miles back to the house. When I get there, the heartache that shoots through me when I don't see Em's Rover in the driveway almost causes me to crash my own vehicle through the closed garage door. I turn off the engine and just sit with my head on the steering wheel. Tears start flowing, and there's nothing I do can stop them. I almost lost them both, and then to find out Em saved Jenna?

I don't just owe her an apology. I owe her my life.

Trudging up the stairs to the apartment, I'm surprised when I see the curtains closed and a lamp lit. I expected to find her sitting on the lounger watching the ocean. Trying the slider, I frown when I find it locked.

Walking back around the deck to the side, I knock and wait. Giving her a few minutes, I knock again. Still nothing. Calling the apartment, I warn her, "Em, I'm worried you're injured in there. I'm coming in."

Disconnecting the call, I pull out the spare key. When I open the door, I'm treated to the largest shock since being told of Jenna's accident.

Nothing.

There's nothing of Em's in the space.

It looks just like it did the day before she got here.

No! My heart shies instinctively away from what my mind is screaming at it. I enter the space and call out, "Em? Emily? Are you okay? Where are you?" I'm opening doors along the way.

The laundry room where Mugsy slept. Nothing.

The bathroom. Everything's gone.

The bedroom. Every trace of her has been removed. Except one. Propped up on the bed is a large envelope with "Jenna" scrawled across it.

"No..." I sink to the floor clutching the only proof that Emily Freeman ever actually was in this room. That she opened her arms to me. That she allowed me to love her.

No matter the risk.

"What did I do?" I whisper to the empty room. But I know damn good and well what I did.

I proved her right.

Only she had the wrong theory.

It wasn't people who died because she loved them. It was her heart that kept dying time after time for being broken.

By people who abandoned her.

Like me.

52

JAKE

Jenna's face when I walk back into her hospital room without Emily is probably what mine looked like when I realized she was gone.

It's the kind of pain that tears won't even solve, so you don't even try to cry.

Handing her the envelope, I whisper, "She left you this."

And for the first of many times in the upcoming weeks, my daughter turns her face away from me without saying a word, making me understand the true depth of my mistake.

And the painful screaming that can be heard in silence.

53

JAKE

"Mr. Madison?"

"Yes?" I sigh into the phone.

"This is Stacie at Offshore Animal Care." My body jolts. I haven't thought of the animal hospital since I savaged Emily over trying to get Mugsy's remains. My brutal behavior keeps coming back to haunt me. "I'm terribly sorry to bother you, but we've been trying to get a hold of Ms. Freeman..."

I cut her off. "She was involved in a wreck." What else am I supposed to say? I have no idea where she is because she ran away from my brutal behavior?

"Oh! I'm terribly sorry to hear that. It might explain why her number's out of service," she muses.

Emily's number is out of service. Another thread between us has been cut. My hands are shaking so hard, I can barely hold on to my phone. "Is there something you needed, Stacie?" I'm surprised by how calm my voice is.

"Well, when Ms. Freeman didn't come back to pick up Mugsy's remains, we became concerned. Will you be coming to get them for her?"

And just like that, any energy I've been holding on to since the accident leaches out of me.

Emily left without her beloved dog. She never made arrangements to pick up his remains. She must have been so desperate to get away...

I think I'm going to be sick.

"I'll make arrangements and have someone contact you," I barely manage to get out weakly.

"Thank you. Our hours are eight to five, Monday through Friday, until noon on Saturday. And we're closed Sundays. Have a great day!" I don't respond. I just hang up the phone.

If I hadn't wronged her so badly, I'd drive over to the animal hospital to pick up Mugsy's remains in order to see if Emily would talk to me, but I can't. I have to do what's right. And what's right is letting her move on without me, finding a better man. Someone who may never love her as much as I do, but who will never hurt her the way I did.

Still on the floor, I press the heels of my hands against my eyes.

I can't breathe.

I miss her.

I have no right.

"Jake, what are you doing on the floor?" Dani snaps at me. She's been staying with us—Jenna, Michelle, Jenna, and our families—since she arrived from her photo shoot after Jenna's accident.

"I need to get a message to Em," I whisper hoarsely.

"I already told you, I'm not getting involved." Dani practically clawed my face apart when I admitted what I'd done to Em. Even without the details of Em's past, she was rightfully infuriated.

"Dani, listen," I plead. I don't know if it's the utter defeat in my posture or something she hears in my voice, but she pauses. "That was the animal hospital. They've been trying to reach Em. Mugsy's remains are still here."

Dani's face takes on a weary cast. "Ah, hell." Letting out a long sigh, she drops next to me. "Jake, they're so pissed, I don't know if they'll talk to *me*, that's how pissed off Em's family is. But I'll try, okay?"

"Thank you."

Reaching over, she takes my hand. "I love you, Jake. But what you did..."

"It cost me everything," I finish for her.

"Maybe it's time to try to figure out why you did it?"

My brow furrows. "What do you mean?"

"I think everyone's drowning, Jake. And not just because Em left. Jenna went through something traumatic. She won't talk with you, because...well..."

"Because I fucked up," I say grimly.

"Yeah," she says softly. "And while Michelle being here has been good in some ways, it might just not be the time for her to make the inroads into Jenna's life. Jenna found a woman she loved, a woman who saved her even before the accident, and she lost her. It might be time for you both to talk to someone, even if it's only to help her."

A million thoughts run through my head. Jenna's anger moving to the island. My anger knowing Emily was going to be in the apartment. The bond that developed between my daughter and the woman next door. Our spark that turned into an inferno. The beginning of trust with both of them I shattered by shoving away when I should have held on.

And suddenly I can't take the emptiness where there was once Jenna's joy.

I can't take noise where there was music.

I can't take life where there was once Emily's love.

A love she tried to speak but I shoved back at her. But she did. I knew it and I felt it and I threw it away.

I turn my head away and nod.

Dani lets out the breath she's been holding. Squeezing my hand, she says, "Let me go make a few calls."

"Okay." Leaving me to my solitude, Dani stands and walks away. I sit exactly where I am for God knows how long until I hear my mother call us all to dinner.

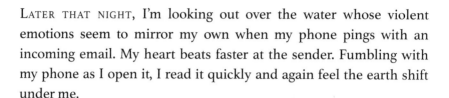

LATER THAT NIGHT, I'm looking out over the water whose violent emotions seem to mirror my own when my phone pings with an incoming email. My heart beats faster at the sender. Fumbling with my phone as I open it, I read it quickly and again feel the earth shift under me.

FROM: Alison Freeman
To: Jacob Madison
Subject: Emily Freeman

MR. MADISON,

We've made contact with the animal hospital regarding Mugsy's remains. They will work directly with us in the future.

On behalf of all of us at Amaryllis Events, we hope your daughter is healing quickly. All medical expenses for Jenna's hospital stay have been paid for by our company to apologize for any belief you may still hold regarding the responsibility of one of our employees. If you find you need further assistance with costs such as rehabilitation, please contact the hospital administrator. They know how to reach me.

Cordially,

Alison Freeman

PLEASE BE ADVISED, *this email address will be blocked immediately after you receive this.*

I STUMBLE BACK at the polite vitriol in the simple message. I expected Dani to get a call and to be able to pump her for something, anything, about how Emily is. These few lines tell me nothing other than Emily feels she has a debt to pay—one I made her think she owes. Which couldn't be further from the truth.

God, help me. God, help us all.

I'm far from perfect, but I love her and I'm willing to do anything to get her back.

Anything.

Even if it's just to hold her to tell her it wasn't her fault so she can walk away into a future believing she's worth everything.

54

JAKE

"I take full responsibility for what happened, Dr. Thurman." My hands clasped between my knees bounce up and down. "I hurt a beautiful woman—a woman I love—all because of what?"

"It's called transference of anger. You weren't really mad at Emily. You were viciously furious at the driver for being drunk behind the wheel, and most importantly, you were mad at yourself for not taking Em yourself. You let loose emotions which are very human, Jake. You just did it at the wrong target."

"And I've lost the love of the two most important women in my life in the process," I say grimly.

"I wouldn't quite say that." Leaning over to his desk, my psychologist lifts his phone. "Linda? Can you send Jenna in please?"

What the hell? My head snaps around as the door opens to my daughter. I hope I hide my cringe when I see her still hobbling toward us using her cane.

Guilt.

It wasn't Emily's fault. It was mine.

All told, Jenna was fortunate. After Emily saved her life, and once she was cleared by neurology after banging her head on the dash caused her to slip into a temporary coma, Jenna managed to escape the accident with a few bruised ribs, a sprained wrist, a torn-up ankle that will take months to rehabilitate, and a body covered with cuts and bruises.

The worst thing she ended up with was the same thing I did though: a broken heart.

"Hi, baby," I say softly. I don't expect her to say anything back. After all, she's barely said anything to me unless she's been forced to.

But today? There's something different in her eyes. "Hey, Dad."

I close my eyes as the beautiful pain at hearing that simple sentence washes over me. Dad. "God, Jenna. I'm so sorry, baby." Standing up, I take the few steps to stand in front of her. "I made so many mistakes," I choke out.

"Then fix them," she says simply.

"It isn't that easy, Jen."

"Dad, the biggest issue you have to conquer is in this room. It has nothing to do with anyone else," she says wisely.

I stare down at her in shock.

Placing her cane aside, she lays her hand on my heart. "Aren't you the one who taught me there has to be a baseline to go with any melody? Well, you have to fix your head and your heart, Dad. It won't be easy, but if you're not in rhythm, how do expect the rest of us to join in? Besides," she jokes with tears in eyes that mirror my own, "we all know Em can't play a tune worth shit. You're going to have to be the one to teach her. You have to make her understand we're worth another chance."

"You're the best miracle I've ever been given," I whisper, gathering her slowly into my arms.

"Then don't you think it's time to forgive the other person who helped give me to you? I started to the minute I woke up. Just because she wasn't meant to be with us doesn't mean she's a horrible person."

"Do you mean your mother, Jenna?" Dr. Thurman asks.

She nods against my chest. "I've hated her for years for leaving. But in light of what I went through—what we've all been through—I realized she isn't a bad person; she just wasn't meant to be a mother, a wife. She wasn't meant to stay. And that's all right. There are people who are meant to be temporary in our lives."

"Not Em," I say firmly.

"No," Jenna says softly. Moving to one of the two chairs in front of Dr. Thurman's desk, she reaches inside her bag. Pulling out an envelope, I seize up, recognizing it immediately.

The message she left Jenna.

"Go ahead, Dad," she whispers.

With trembling fingers, I fumble it open. Reaching inside, I pull out a single piece of paper. After studying the sketch of me and Jenna laughing in the music room, captured in silence, I flip it over and let out a choked sob. Passing it back to Jenna, I'm surprised when she hands it to Dr. Thurman. He reads it aloud. "Jenna. I can't stop what I feel. It's forever. I'm so sorry. Emily."

"I don't know when she drew it," Jenna whispers.

"I do." One night when Jenna was sleeping at Lynne's, I saw Em with her personal journal propped on her lap. She had an almost dreamy smile on her face. I remember her closing the book and then snuggling down in bed before I rolled on top of her to make love to her again.

It was a few nights before Mugsy died.

"Dad? If Em feels that deeply, she can't cut us out that easily, can she?" Jenna's voice holds a note of panic.

"Baby, I think if you showed up tomorrow, she'd welcome you. If I walked in the door..."

"It was that bad?" she whispers.

Ashamed, I just nod.

"Because of me?"

"No, Jenna, because of me. Because like with all the times with you when you tried to talk with me and instead ended up talking to Grandma or Dani, I shoved her away."

Silence descends upon the office until Dr. Thurman clears his throat. "Well, I think you have a lot to think about before we talk again, Jake."

I nod. "Can I say one thing before we go?"

"Of course."

I turn to my daughter, whose face is a mix of sadness and pain. "This is on me, beautiful. You need to celebrate the second chance you've been blessed with. I will do anything—and I do mean anything—to make certain you are protected and happy. You survived, Jenna. You're a miracle every day. And I'm so sorry for everything I've ever said or done to make you think otherwise."

Jenna struggles to get to her feet, though it's easier now due to all of her physical therapy. "I love you, Dad."

Pulling her into a hug, I whisper, "I love you too, baby."

And I'm whispering my thanks to Emily that she gave me a chance to say that, even if she never gives me the chance to thank her in person.

55

JAKE

School started a few weeks ago. For the first time since I've become a teacher, I barely remember each day what I'm teaching my students.

Each day is blurring into the next with the exception of Jenna's excitement about senior year punctuating through the bleakness.

I've tried to send Emily letters. They've been returned —unopened.

I've tried to ask Dani about her. She's can't give me information about what she doesn't know.

I don't even have music in me anymore. I haven't been down to the studio in months.

I'm existing in a shallow grave of emptiness because I know she's out there likely still blaming herself for everything that happened when there's no fault.

No blame.

Except for what I did to her.

Then the only blame belongs to me.

56

EMILY

I've been back from Nantucket for about two months. The physical injuries I sustained took a few weeks to heal. I know the emotional scars will be there forever.

Three weeks after I returned, I had to fly to France. In my...obsession with everything on the island, I lost track of time. I forgot it was almost time for me to leave anyway. I had to be in Paris with Lara Fredericks's wedding gown ready to play stylist. Getting away, even for a week, was good. I was too busy to be brooding about what happened, and I wasn't home to be missing my normal routine with Mugsy. After helping the new bride through her wedding, I wandered the streets of Paris after and stumbled upon Tissues Reine on the Place Saint-Pierre, an extraordinary fabric store where I purchased bolts of ivory and cream silk and organza to come back with me to the States.

Then the real work began. It's been nonstop work preparing for my first showing at Fashion Week. I've consulted and hired lighting artists, DJs, and caterers for the after-party. While Cisco is contracted to be providing the alcohol—something that I will survive in my frozen state—I've left the final decisions on food up to Corinna. I've also been working with Caleb, Keene, and Colby on security because nothing can happen to compromise the venue, the dresses, or the models. All of the entrances will be protected by Hudson so I can focus on what will be going on inside.

The setup is unusual for a bridal show. Since bridal gowns are so heavy, I'd have likely chosen somewhere other than the Skylight since the runway is so long, but this may work to my advantage. If the models walk at an average pace, each gown will be able to be seen for almost two minutes before the next makes its way onto the runway. Appreciating more what Barnes was saying about the dealing with Patrick's location selection is a challenge, but not an insurmountable one. It just means I'll have to get creative.

I'm dealing with so many details, I don't have time to think about Jake. No, that's a lie. I can't go to sleep without remembering the feel of his arms around me. I still cry into my pillow every night realizing I fell in love with this complex man and he closed me out as surely as if I'd never existed. Doesn't he realize I was just as devastated by the accident as he was? Doesn't he understand I love Jenna too?

In the end, I came to the conclusion I was as the hydrangeas he left me the first morning: I was nothing but dead from the moment I was first touched.

It's a cold realization to accept my future holds barely a whisper of the things I imagined in it. Sure, I'll have my family, but I will never have a family. I'll accept love, but I will never go looking for love again. I'll never put someone else through that danger, that pain.

Desperately wishing Mugsy were still alive to snuggle, I pull mounds of blankets tighter around me. They're a poor substitute for the last warm body that lay in this bed with me. As I drift off to sleep, I wonder if there's ever been a case of someone dying from a frozen heart.

Or if I'll be the first case.

I'VE BARRED off my part of the mansion for anything but urgent interruptions. My show is a month away, and I have three days to finalize my designs. This will barely leave me enough time to get them completed in time. Even though I feel like my soul is supposed to be on display for the whole world to see, it doesn't matter anymore. My soul is as blank as the paper in front of me.

Glaring down at my sketchbook, a sudden unwelcome flood of emotions fills me. I heave my sketchbook across the room. The charcoals I'd laid in the crease fly in every direction. Even as they land with a gentle *plunk* against the hardwood floors, tears burn in the back of my eyes.

Damnit, it shouldn't be this hard to live in a world when you're already dead.

I scrub my eyes with my fingers when I hear a hesitant voice from behind me. "Em? I was told it was okay to come in."

Turning, I see Holly standing in the doorway. I open my mouth to speak and instead burst into tears. My body heaves with uncontrollable sobs I can't rein in. I've been holding in the trauma for months, pretending it was just another breakup.

What a time for the pain to unleash.

Holly races forward. "Men are so damn stupid. I swear to God, Em." Her arms wrap tightly around me as the emotional dam finally bursts.

"I...I..." Stuttering, I start over. "I'm so sorry. I don't mean to unload on you. I don't want to be a burden."

"Screw that."

Taking a deep breath, I wipe the tears with fingers smeared with charcoal. "He...he told me what he thought of me. He made his decision. Now I'm the one who has to live with it."

Pulling me, she drags me over to my chaise. "Are you?"

"Am I what?" I'm confused.

"Living. Since Jake...ended things."

Lifting my chin pugnaciously, I lie as convincingly as I can. "Of course. Didn't I get to travel to France a few weeks ago? For some people, that's more than just living."

"Where apparently, you bought the most amazing fabric we've ever seen that you haven't done a damn thing with," she retorts.

That stings. "I've been working."

"Let me the sketches, then," she demands.

I glare at her. "No one sees them until they're done."

"No?" Standing, my baby sister strides to where I've hurled my sketchbook in anger. "You're a month out from Fashion Week, Em. Is anything new in production? Since the last stuff you sent to Ali?"

I bow my head in shame.

"Are you going to let a broken heart ruin your chance of a lifetime, or are you going to use those emotions to yell 'fuck you' to everyone who dared to tell you couldn't do this, weren't good enough, or aren't loved enough?" she taunts me.

Chest heaving, I shove to my feet and I stride over to my desk where I keep my private journal locked up. Blindly grabbing it, I fling it at her. "You try designing wedding gowns when these are the images seared in your mind, Holly. You try believing in the magic of love when everything about you says everyone you love will die if you even dare to hope for it, when everything you believe tells you you'll never fucking deserve it. Then when I feel it for the first time, it's ripped from my heart. It bled my soul. Being in love stole everything from me. Even my ability to create. I'll never get it back!" I scream.

Holly looks down at the book in her hands. This book has never been seen by anyone in my family. It was something I used to show Jake my world, my life. It was the only voice I had to talk about my past. She flips it back to the beginning, studying each picture. With each turn of the page, I can read her expressions as clearly as if I was telling her the story myself. I can tell when she's seeing Aunt Dee versus my father. There's heartbreak when she's looking at a young Cassidy versus the judge who granted us emancipation. Shock and then tenderness at the images of Ali, Corinna, and herself as we first found them, and then on their graduation days. Memories locked in my head over the years, transposed permanently into that book. My ex-fiancé in anger and then the image of him in bed with another woman. My first impression of Jenna at the coffee shop. When Holly turned to the page I captured of Jake after the first time we slept together, her face takes on the same pain I'm feeling. Then when she sees the one I did of him yelling at me, telling my love essentially killed everyone who it touched, she hisses.

I expect empathy. Instead, her face hardens with anger.

"Are you going to let them steal your voice?" Closing the book, she hands it back to me.

"What?" Shakily, I lean over to accept it.

"That book isn't just about capturing images in your brain, Em. That book is about capturing the emotions you can't let out using the words that were stolen from you as a child. Are you going to let Jake be the final person to take away your voice? You worked too hard to get it back." I sway in place as her words penetrate. My knees almost buckle under the impact. I grip the edge of my desk tightly.

Holly comes up to me and brushes her lips against my forehead. "Speak up, Em. Speak now. If this is your only shot to use your words, what do you want to say?"

I choke out the words. "I want to tell my father I hope he's rotting in hell. I want to rub the judge's face in it—the one who didn't believe that three kids could make a life together on their own. I want to kill the bastards who took my sisters hostage." I take a deep breath.

Holly urges me. "Go on."

"I want to slam my head against a wall for being weak and accepting Bryan's proposal. I was giving in and settling. He made me feel trapped, and I hate that. And as for Jake?" This one is the hardest, but I plow on letting my emotions carry me. "I'd want him to know I'll survive. No, better yet. I want him to look back with regret because I...I'm gone, and I will live this life." I dash away the falling tears.

"All of that, Em. Now here." Holly shoves my sketchbook at me. "Harness all of that power and draw the designs we've been waiting for. The designs your soul's screaming for."

Snagging it from her hand, I begin frantically looking around for the charcoals I flung around the room earlier. Spying one at my feet, I grab it and touch it to my page.

The familiar tingle begins in my head, my hands, and my heart. First, I draw the outline of a face and the long, lean body of the model type I want. Tapping into the long-buried pain, I begin to place patches of lines over the spots to indicate intricate detail where I was held back by the intruders from getting to my mother and father when I was a young girl. The banded arms held me over the chest and up one shoulder when the other came at a slant from the opposite side banding down over my hips. I can see it in my mind's eye already. Sleeveless, sheer underlay, it will be screamingly provocative.

When the masked monsters made it so I couldn't speak, this dress will finally give me the chance to scream.

I look up only when I feel the hand on my shoulder. "You have three days," Holly murmurs. Bending, she drops a kiss on the top of my head. With that last piece of news, she leaves me in my studio with something I didn't have an hour ago.

An ability to talk one of the few ways I know how.

~

"I DIDN'T THINK it was possible for you to outdo yourself, Emily, but these designs?" Alison lets out a low whistle. She's scanning the final designs into her computer so she can submit them for expedited copyright. "You're going to blow the roof off of the place."

"If they get completed in time." Now that I've finally completed the designs, I know the difficulty in executing them up to my standards. "I've left a hell of a burden on the people who build my samples because I couldn't get my head on straight."

"Do you need to go with another company? Multiple companies? To hell with the cost." Alison's fierce reply astounds me and then melts another small place in my frozen heart. Normally a huge penny-pincher when it comes to the bottom line, the fact she's willing to throw profit out the window tells me she's just been waiting for the moment to intercede.

Because that's what the family that loves you does.

"Let me call them," I offer. Pushing the sketches around, I pull out one in particular and hold it up. Alison's breath catches. "I'll be doing this one myself."

"Sweet Jesus, Em. That will take you hundreds of hours," Alison breathes reverently.

"About two hundred," I estimate. "But if I take this one off the table, I think I can keep everything else at our predicted cost and on schedule." Frowning, I warn, "I just won't be able to take any appointments since I'll be working on this dress day and night in the studio."

Taking the paper from me, Ali declares, "If you can make this dress come to life in four weeks, we'll divide your appointments between us or have interns take them. This dress is..." Her voice trails off.

Swallowing hard, I try to give the words to what this dress is to me. "It's everything, Ali," I whisper. "It's the storm, the passion, the anchor, the wreckage, and the rescue."

Coming out from around her desk, Ali carefully takes the drawing from my hands before she pulls me into a hard embrace. "We'll get you through this," she vows.

Dropping my chin on her shoulder, I tell her, "You already have."

For a long time, we stand there holding each other close. I know the future doesn't have any other love planned for me, but at least it gave me this. A family forged of a bond so strong, that though it will be tested, it will never be broken.

Unlike what I thought I found on Nantucket.

I went there with damaged pride. I came home with a pulverized heart. Not the kind of souvenir you want to bring home.

Who knew that sand wasn't the only thing the ocean could damage beyond repair?

57

JAKE

Days turn into weeks. I dream of Emily every single one of them.

It's the big things, the little things. Everything from the way she'd stare out at the ocean, to the way her laugh would turn into this adorable giggle, to the look of unbridled shock the first time I sang to her, to the way our bodies fit when we danced; everything was perfect with her.

I still see Dr. Thurman once a week. He made me realize I wasn't just lashing out at Emily because of the accident. He's made me see I also used it to push Emily away before she could walk away—like Michelle did. We've spent so much time working through long-buried issues, particularly about Michelle abandoning our marriage. He even conferenced Michelle into one of our sessions where I finally got to tell her what I thought about being left with a daughter to raise and a woman who left us both angry and terrified.

It wasn't the easiest phone call I've suffered through, but it was necessary.

Dr. Thurman's worked with both me and Jenna separately. We've conquered hurdles I don't think we would have ever approached without his help. Now, we now have a communication system firmly in place so we both respect each other's boundaries. On days when Jenna doesn't want to open up, I don't push. And since she gets that respect from me, the same goes both ways. I honestly don't know what I'm going to do when she goes to college next year. We've talked openly about all her school choices—including, to my chagrin, RISD.

I want to share all of this with Emily, but I can't. So, every night I sit in my bed and whisper in the darkness everything I wish I could say. More often than not, it ends up with me telling her how much I love and miss her.

And it ends up with tears raining down my face.

I hold on to my memories knowing it's practically futile. If there was a chance of a reconciliation, she'd have done something to reach out to Jenna at least. Wouldn't she?

It's mid-October now. Jenna's supposed to be going out shopping with Lynne later today for a homecoming dress. Trudging past her room, I hear her on the phone. "I don't know, Dani. I have no problems with missing the dance, but I'm guessing there's no way Daddy goes for it."

I pause. I know she might think I'm breaking our communication rules, but her door's partially open. Knocking, I call out, "Jen, is everything okay?"

There's a deadly quiet before I hear, "I'll call you back in a little bit." Jenna's at her door a few moments later. "Hey, Dad."

I lean against the jamb. "Hey, baby. I didn't mean to eavesdrop, but I was walking by..."

"No," she says anxiously. "Want to come in?" She bites her lower lip.

"Sure, honey." I follow her into her room. Sitting on her bed, I ask, "What's going on?"

Jenna begins pacing back and forth, her agitation evident. "I don't know how to bring this up to you."

"Jen, you can talk to me about anything. But if it's going to hurt your ankle, will you at least do so sitting?"

Sitting next to me, she turns to me and bring up the one topic I never expected her to.

Emily.

"Daddy. Dani says she hasn't talked with Em. She's so focused getting ready for Fashion Week." Hesitating, she adds, "She has talked with her sisters though. They want to do something big for her. Dani called to asked me if I want to go to New York to see Em. She was going to call and ask you next." She scrunches up her face.

Pulling Jenna as close as I can, I whisper, "You should go."

"Really?" Jenna's face transforms and begins to glow for the first time in months.

"If her sisters think it's a good idea, Em obviously still cares about you, baby." The words feel torn from me, they're so hard to say. "You know she'll welcome you with open arms," I say hoarsely. Unlike me. After everything I said to Em that night in the hospital, there's no way she'll ever let me back into her life.

Jenna's vibrating with joy. Tampering down my agony, I listen to her ramble on about calling Dani and making plans to get to New York, right before she leans up and gives me a kiss on the cheek. "Thank you, Daddy. Thank you for everything." Pulling back, she looks wise beyond her years. "Have I ever said thank you for giving up your dreams to give me the world?"

I certainly did that, I think somberly as I watch her bounce as best as she can while she calls Dani back. *Forget the music, Jenna. I stupidly gave up the only thing you need to make life worth anything.*

Love.

58

EMILY

It's close to ten and I'm still at the office sewing away. The finale dress is taking shape. Even I'm starting to feel a modicum of excitement.

"Jesus, Em." Holly whistles as she walks around with her camera. "It's devastating. I don't even know that photos can do it justice."

I'm too busy swallowing to reply. Once I finally can, I give her a tired smile. "The construction has been a bitch. But it will be worth it."

With a bark of laughter, Holly moves over to my work table where I've constructed thousands of miniature amaryllis flowers out of organza and crystal. Lifting her camera, she takes a picture of the pile to immortalize the journey of how I sweat blood and tears on the way to Fashion Week. "Do you feel any different making this dress?"

I think about the question. "Part of me feels like I've been playing my designs safe." Looking at the creation in front of me, I snicker. "No one can say that about this dress. Hell, about the entire collection."

"Where's the rest of it?"

"At Keene and Ali's in the city." I didn't want to bring them back here when I'll be moving into their place for the foreseeable future as soon as I'm done with the monstrosity in front of me.

Holly lowers herself into the lounger while I pull on white gloves to protect the dress as I attach each individual flower. I refuse to allow a single imperfection to mar the thread, the flowers, or the delicate fabric underneath. Threading the needle efficiently, I affix the next flower in the cascading waterfall from the deep V in the back.

When it's done, the dress will look like a woman ran through a field of flowers—amaryllises to be exact. My model will be covered from head to midthigh in the tight little buds. The twenty-foot train, which starts at her shoulders, will give the impression of floating flowers that are flying off her body as she runs away.

This isn't just a dress. For me, it's a statement of war against whatever curse is being held over me. It's a battle for my life. It's a fight to not drown in my grief. It's the determination to not lose myself in the demons that constantly plague me.

There's no choice anymore but to believe I will win.

Holly's talking, but I miss what she's saying as I've been robotically adding flowers to the behemoth of a dress. "Sorry, love. What was that?"

"Who's modeling the dress?" Holly asks again.

I shrug. "I don't know. I have to do casting auditions next week."

And then I hear a voice I never expect to from the door. "How about I give it a try? It looks about my size?"

Turning, I openly gape at Dani Madison as she walks into my workspace unannounced. "What on earth are you doing here?"

"I come bearing all kinds of interesting news." Using her critical eye, she walks around the dress. I find I'm surprisingly nervous. Forgetting who she is to Jake, Dani is still one of the world's greatest supermodels. Even a kind word of hers after the show would solidify my standing in the community. "Jesus, Em. You're a genius."

My breath comes out in a whoosh.

Dani walks around the dress again. "I came in on the tail end of your conversation. You know, I'd be honored to walk the runway wearing this dress."

I'm blown away by the offer, but I'm realistic. She's only offering because of what happened with Jake. Remembering our bet, I can't accept the pity. "Just because Jake and I aren't..."

"Jake has nothing to do with this, Em," she states calmly. "This has everything to do with staking a claim on you before some other model has the chance to do so." Tossing me a wry glance, she continues. "After next week, you're going to be inundated. I'm using our friendship to plead my case."

I'm overwhelmed with the emotions coursing through my system. Between the devastating end to my relationship with Jake, finding the ability to pull from the dredges of my soul to develop this collection, and now this praise, I suddenly feel a tidal wave coming.

I just don't want anyone to see it.

"Then come back in three days. I'll have the rest of these attached, and we can do last-minute adjustments." My voice is gratefully cold.

Reaching for another flower, my back is to Dani when she says to Holly, "Can I talk to Em for a moment alone?"

Shit. The crystal-accented bloom in my hand starts to shake. I just know this is going to be about Jake. I've managed to pull the ice princess mask back on successfully. Hell, Corinna's even been talking to me about setting me up with a guy she used to date. For the last few weeks, I haven't let it slip. I know it will if Dani merely says his name.

Don't go, Holly, I silently beg. But the rolling of my office door tells me Dani and I are alone.

"You told your sisters you'd would have loved to have shown Jenna Fashion Week."

And just like that, I'm bleeding. I glance down to see if the bright white petals I've been attaching to the exquisite dress are stained with crimson, rather like the ancient myth of how the amaryllis flower came to be. "Yes, I would have," I reply quietly. "If this is what she wants, she should see what it really involves, not just the glitz and glamour portrayed in the magazines."

Dani nods. "I've tried to tell her over the years about the hell I went through when I first started. About the crass insults, the handsy photographers, the times I'd try to starve myself to make sure I'd fit into a certain sample size. She didn't believe me." Stopping in front of me, Dani grabs my wrist above where the glove covers it. "I think she'd believe you."

I try to wrench my hand away, but it's held too tightly. "The time for that's past. It would be impossible."

And then I hear a voice I thought I'd never hear again. "It's not so impossible, Em. Daddy said it was okay if I came. He thought you might want me here."

I rip my wrist away from Dani with a gasp. Turning, I face the girl who holds the same dreams in her eyes that I had in mine at the same age. Who I feel I breathed part of my soul into when I was pushing air into her lungs. "Jenna." Tears run unchecked down my face.

She runs across the workroom so fast that even using a cane, you'd never know she was injured in a car wreck only a few months ago. Her body slams into me. For moments, we clutch each other. Her head lies on my shoulder, mine on hers, our sobs mingling. Not even finishing the signature dress in the collection matters as much as this.

Nothing matters as much as this.

It isn't until I hear Dani murmur, "Good surprise?" that I pull back and cup Jenna's face. I fell in love with Jake's daughter as much as I did him. But until this moment, I didn't realize I was mourning not one, but two people.

Stroking her blonde hair back from her face, I murmur, "The best." Shaking my head, a shadow of a smile crosses my face. "I don't know how you all managed to pull it off."

"Well, after your sisters talked to Dani, I talked to Daddy and the rest is history." Jenna giggles, wiping her eyes. I inhale sharply. Hearing even the slightest news about Jake is a new wound I'll have to sew up later.

Dani interrupts. "I think that's about all Em wants to hear about your father for tonight, Jen. I'll talk with her about the rest soon. Right now, she has to finish the dress I'm going to wear for her, and we need to get to Corinna's."

Jenna jumps up and down with teenage enthusiasm. "Oh my

God! Dani's wearing your dress? This dress? It's *stunning*! I have a million questions. I can't wait to come back and help tomorrow. I can help, right?" She looks at me anxiously.

I'm looking at another four hours of work minimum tonight, but I think I just found a temporary intern. "You'll help, Jenna—" She beams. "—but if you think you're touching a single stitch on this dress, you're insane." I smile as her face falls. "You will be assisting me running errands, going for more fabric, things like that."

"I came down from Nantucket to be a gopher," she grumbles.

I cup her chin. "No, you came down from Nantucket to see me and to intern for Amaryllis Designs. You want to see the craziness of Fashion Week from the inside out? Then buckle up, buttercup, because I have three days to finish this dress before we move to New York City. That's where the real stress begins." I let her face go. "Be back here by seven—that's a.m. And although you'd better have coffee from The Coffee Shop with you, it'd better not come anywhere near this room. Corinna can tell you where to put everything in the kitchen."

If I didn't feel the excitement pulsating off her, I'd let her go play with Dani for a few days. But Jenna's one of the rare few I've met who doesn't just want to draw pretty pictures. She wants to feel the ache in her fingers, her shoulders, and her heart as her designs are judged by the world.

And if I can help this child of my heart, the child I helped breathe life back into, I'll do anything.

59

JAKE

"How are you doing, baby?" I've barely talked to Jenna in the past few days. It's giving me an early preview of what college is going to be like next year. It sucks.

"Daddy, you won't believe how amazing it is here!" she squeals excitedly. "Right now, we're in Em's sister's penthouse in New York City in a place called Tribeca. It's enormous! Dani and I are sharing a room because Em has all of her dresses hanging up in Ali's daughter's room. And no one's allowed in there until tomorrow when we head over to the studio to start fitting models."

When Dani filled me in about how they were going to surprise Em, I prayed it didn't end in heartbreak for my daughter. It turns out, Em welcomed Jenna with open arms and a lot of tears. "It sounds like you're having a lot of fun," I manage to get out.

"It's a lot of hard work, Dad." Her voice turns serious. "Em hasn't had more than three hours of sleep since before I arrived in Connecticut. First, she was working on the final dress, then she's been handling all of the details that are critical for this show to go right."

I frown. "Is that all the sleep you're getting?"

"No. Em's being a pain. She's making sure I'm down for at least six a night," she quickly tells me.

"Is Em doing okay?" I ask casually. I've stooped to a new low. I'm asking my seventeen-year-old about the woman I love but destroyed.

There's silence on the other end of the line. "Jenna?"

"I...I was just trying to figure out how to answer. She's brilliant, always, but Daddy?" Jenna's voice is regretful as if the words she's about to say are going to hurt me.

There's someone else. I brace myself to hear it, but what I hear is far worse.

"She isn't happy. It's like she's dead inside." Jenna's voice is a whisper. She's talking rapidly as if she's afraid of being overheard. "I think if you told her today her collection was the best in the world in comparison to every other designer, she'd still be wearing the same look she wears every day."

"What look is that?"

"Like none of it means a damn," my daughter tells me bluntly.

On the other end of the line, I close my eyes as the pain ripples through my body. My fault. All of it.

"Wait a second, Daddy." I hear the phone clatter to the bed. In the background, a loud commotion is going on. I hear a male voice drawl, "Did you honestly think we were going to leave you here by yourself? Please. That's not what we do."

A female voice chimes in. "That's not who we are."

Suddenly there's music playing, and I can't hear any voices until Jenna comes back on the line. By then, I've worked myself into a frenzy. Em's exposing my seventeen-year-old to a party? What the fuck?

"Daddy! You'll never believe this, but Em's entire family just drove in from Connecticut tonight. All of her sisters, her brother, and their husbands and kids. It's like a ready-made party. And guess what? Em laughed. I heard Em laugh!" Jenna's choked up.

Her family who's always been there for her is there now when they suspect she's burned out and breaking. I swallow past the lump in my throat. "That's great, baby. Go have fun with them."

"Do you have anything you want me to tell Em?" She asked me that before she left. The problem is I have too damn much to tell Em, and I can't use my daughter to do it. I'm also fairly certain the door would be slammed in my face if I tried to do it on my own.

"I…" I don't even have a chance to deny the request because I hear Dani call Jenna to join the party.

"I have to go, Daddy. Love you."

"Love you too, Jenna."

Jenna hangs up. I drop my phone next to me before I surge to my feet and begin to pace. I owe Em an apology so huge. Underneath that cool exterior beats a heart that feels too much and bruises too easily. And I took a bat to it the last time we saw each other.

I need to see Em one more time, even if it's for her to tell me to take the express train to hell. Walking back over to my phone, I dial the number of the only person I know who might help me.

One ring.

Two.

Three.

"This better be good, Jake. I'm about to head out onstage," Brendan warns me.

"I need to know how to get a hold of Corinna Freeman," I say in a rush.

The silence on the other end of the line tells me I don't have to explain. Either Dani or Em's family already have. "If I give you this number and you break her again, I'm going to be losing a close friendship. So will my nephew," Brendan says angrily.

"I plan on sewing up the wounds I caused. Then, if it takes me the rest of my life, I plan on begging her for another chance to prove I'm not a complete asshole."

"That might take you the rest of your life," Brendan snaps, right before he hangs up.

Seconds later, I have an incoming text with a 203 area code and a message that says, *Don't screw up.*

I don't plan on it.

I can't.

Too many people are depending on me to get it right.

"I'm sorry, Mr. Madison. After everything you put my sister through, you expect me to hand over her location as if it's available for public consumption?" Corinna Freeman's voice could freeze hell over on its hottest day despite its honeyed drawl. "I can't believe Brendan gave you this number. It's not as if you don't have a way to reach your daughter," she adds bitingly.

Jesus, Brendan wasn't kidding when he said Corinna might hold this call against him. The woman on the other end of the phone sounds like she'd cheerfully chop me up with a meat cleaver and then feed me to a ravenous pack of mountain lions.

"Ms. Freeman, you have no reason to trust me..." I begin.

"Trust you?" she says scathingly. "I had no reason to accept this call except Brendan assured me you might have something to say I might want to hear. If it weren't for him, I'd have laughed over what I'm sure would have been your pathetic excuse for a voicemail."

"And I'm sure you've never made a mistake?" I retort, my temper slipping a bit.

"I've made them, Mr. Madison. I also owned up to them the minute I knew I was wrong. You brought my sister to her knees, you bastard." There's heavy breathing on the other end of the line. I keep thinking Corinna will stop, but she goes on. "Do you know the last people who did that? They shot her parents. In front of her. That's who this family associates you with. Want to hear about why we prevented *your* daughter from staying with Em when she first got here? Because she still couldn't stop crying over you. That's the Em we're trying to save. And you think I'm going to tell you where she is." She snorts derisively.

"I love her."

"Obviously." Her sarcastic drawl is followed by an acidic laugh.

"Goddamnit, my daughter was in a coma!" I roar. Launching myself to my feet, I begin pacing my New York City hotel room. I left Nantucket first thing this morning. I'm exhausted, but I want to settle this as soon as I can. For Em. For me. For us. "I was out of my mind. I wasn't thinking. I was barely surviving. I was lashing out at everyone: doctors, nurses, my ex-wife. And yes, Emily. Has nothing like that ever happened to you?"

"Did you ever give her a chance to tell you what happened?"

"I was wrong. I know it. I had to get to Jenna at the hospital first. Then when she finally woke up, I went to find Em to apologize. Do you have any idea what it was like when I got there and instead of being able to beg for her forgiveness, I find nothing but an envelope? I never had a chance to say I'm sorry."

"That's just too damn bad. Because what she really left you with was a child who was breathing. Because I do believe it's my sister who —while concussed—still managed to breathe life into your daughter's lungs until the EMTs arrived."

"You're right, Ms. Freeman. And after, I had to help that daughter get well. I was torn between caring for a daughter who was just out of the hospital and..." Fixing my heart and soul so when I approach Emily again, I don't make the same mistakes over and over. But that's not for Corinna. That's for Emily to know. "I thought I did the right thing by focusing on my daughter until she advised me I was an idiot."

"Didn't you get the message when your letters were sent back, Mr. Madison?" a voice that doesn't sound familiar asks me. Crap. I've been on speaker.

Scrubbing my hand down my face, I ask wearily, "How many of Em's siblings are there?"

A different voice answers calmly, "I think the better question would be, which ones of us aren't?"

"And what questions we'll have for you to determine if you'll ever get close to Em ever again," a third voice says.

"Apparently, Jenna's the smart one of this family," Corinna says scathingly.

"I will talk to whomever I need to in order to get to see Em. I just want to see her before her show Friday." You'd have thought I dropped a bomb in the room with that announcement. The outbursts of *Are you insane?* mingled with *He must be kidding* would almost be humorous if a male voice didn't come over the line. "Please hold, Mr. Madison."

I can only assume it's her brother, Phillip. No one's introduced themselves.

Several long minutes later, the first voice unknown voice comes on the line. "Mr. Madison? This is Alison Freeman. I'm the corporate lawyer for Amaryllis Events."

Shit. The one who emailed me. "Yes, Ms. Freeman."

"You're in Nantucket?" she queries.

I go for broke. "Actually, I came to New York this morning."

I hear some papers shuffling in the background. The purr of satisfaction in Alison Freeman's voice comes through the line and scares the shit out of me. "Then be at this address no later than 9:00 a.m. tomorrow morning." She quickly rattles off an address. "The guards will give you a pass to the executive floor. Be there at one minute after and they won't see you."

"Who won't?" I ask cautiously.

"The people you need to get through to get to us. And Em." Alison promptly disconnects the call.

Though I'm left wondering what the hell I'm going to find—and don't think I'm not googling that shit—at least I know I'm one step closer to getting to Em.

And maybe finding a way back to what we were.

60

JAKE

When I searched the address last night, I learned I'd be going to a place called Hudson Investigations. Even though Em never gave me their last names, I quickly recognize the owner profiles on the site as her brothers-in-law. Their first names are so distinctive, there's no way it's not them. There's also no way after reading about Hudson operations online I don't recognize I'm not headed into an interrogation.

It's a quarter to nine. I glance up at the receptionist, who looks like he could take me down with one hand tied behind his back. I haven't seen anyone enter or exit since I came up the elevator with a security escort ten minutes ago. I wonder if one of their techniques is going to be to make me wait while they're all late.

Behind me the elevator pings with a soft ding. My head swivels so fast, I might have given myself whiplash. It's not anyone I recognize from the website. In fact, the person doesn't look to be much older than Jenna. He's carrying a thick white envelope almost reverently. Placing it directly into the admin's hands, he hands over a piece of paper to be scanned and signed. Turning, he doesn't glance my way before striding rapidly back to the elevators.

The man behind the desk stands with the envelope in hand

before heading toward one of the closed doors. Less than a minute later, he's back at his desk. I'm dying to check my watch again, but some gut instinct tells me not to.

Within the next few minutes, the door the admin went in flies open and the man I recognize as Keene Marshall steps out. I immediately stand. He smirks. "Anxious to get this party started, are you, Madison? Tony, when Caleb's off his call, have him meet us in the conference room. Once he's joined us, you can show Mr. Madison in."

"Absolutely, Keene. Do any of you need anything?" Tony asks. He leans back in his chair to include the men in Keene's office.

"We might need tarps," a dark voice calls from within the interior.

"Colby, you can't kill anyone," a smooth voice says exasperatedly.

"You're a killjoy, Jason."

"I'm a doctor," he retorts.

"Children," Keene says mildly, still staring at me. "It's so much more...*fun* just to talk. After all, words have so much power."

The other office door opens. Caleb Lockwood steps out, his face carved in granite. "I couldn't agree more, brother."

It's then I realize I wasn't sent here to be able to get to Em.

I was sent here so I could never see her again.

"WE ALL KNOW who you are, Madison. This told us quite a bit." Keene taps the thick file he pulled out of the white envelope I saw being delivered earlier. "But I believe in being cordial whenever possible."

Jesus, they ran a background check on me? I don't let my discomfort show even as my lower stomach begins to cramp. And the day I believe this man believes in being cordial is the day I sell my sax. "All right."

"Everyone here is associated with the Freeman family to an intimate degree. To my left is Colby Hunt—Emily's younger sister Corinna's fiancé. To his left is Jason Ross—Emily's brother Phil's husband."

"Good to meet you both," I offer. I receive a look from Colby Hunt that could slay me if the silver of his eyes could become daggers. From Jason Ross, his face is blank, but he nods.

Keene resumes talking. "To my right is Caleb Lockwood, Emily's older sister Cassidy's husband. And next to him is Charlie Henderson."

"Caleb." I nod even as I meet his frosty stare. "Mr. Henderson? I'm afraid Em never mentioned you."

Charlie goes to speak, but Keene interrupts him. "She wouldn't have until you were fully brought into the fold. It appears she started to do that, and she was shunned. I felt Charlie should understand we might have a security risk at hand."

Woodenly, I parrot, "Security risk?"

Keene ignores me and continues. "Let me finish the introductions and tell you how I'm related to the family. Cassidy Freeman isn't just Caleb's wife—she's my biological sister. Additionally, I'm married to Emily's younger sister Alison." My eyes widen a bit.

Suddenly, this meeting takes on a whole new life. There are secrets within secrets in this family. Em trusted some of hers to me, and due to the way I blew us up, her family can't trust a thing I say. "It's going to take a lot more than the abject apology I owe Em, isn't it?" I say warily.

"First, if we allow you to get close enough to Em, that apology will be on your knees so she can kick you through your balls right to your ass if she wants," Caleb sneers.

"Second, boy, if you think this will be less painful than what that woman has been living with the last few months, then you are severely mistaken," the man named Charlie growls.

"Not to be offensive, Mr. Henderson, but what do you have to do with the Freemans?" I ask boldly.

"He's their guardian angel," Colby states.

"He saved them when few others would," Jason says softly.

"He's defended them from even us," Keene warns.

"And he sides with them over us to this day," Caleb adds. Flipping open his own copy of his file, he scans the page. "For the record, before we get started, I want to say you've done a hell of a job raising

Jenna. She's a remarkable young woman. I know you did that mostly on your own." For a moment, I see a softness in Caleb's dark eyes. Then his eyes turn almost black. "What I cannot reconcile is how a man who raised such a strong woman could hurt another so easily? You never even gave her a chance to defend herself."

"Amen, brother," Colby mutters, flipping open his own file.

Jason just keeps his focus on me.

"So, Jacob. Since we're now all nice and acquainted. Would you like to start by telling us your version of what happened? Or would you like us all to lay out the reasons why we're inclined to never let you get close to Emily ever again?" Keene's face takes on a menacing cast.

Swallowing hard, I push myself to my feet. And I begin to tell men who are all but strangers essentially everything that happened between me and Em leading up to that final night.

IT'S BEEN HOURS. I've been questioned, requestioned, cross-examined, and yelled at for the better part of the day with no break. I've been asked about everything from the moment I met Em, to what I'd been told about the accident, to conversations I've had with my daughter. I've been asked the same question time and time again in different ways with different slants. I've retold these men everything— including the fact I'm in love with Em.

And they still haven't budged.

Colby Hunt says something which slashes at me. "Even through all the challenges we all faced when falling in love, it was never our love that was in question." And suddenly I go a little insane.

"My daughter was in a coma. The minute, the very minute she was awake, I went after Emily. Some of you have children—what would you have done? You would have lost your minds. All I wanted was for my little girl to wake up. I'm her father. My job is to protect her and I failed."

"Fine. I'll accept that," Caleb says cuttingly. The other men in the room nod. I let out a breath. It may have been too soon when he tacks on, "Now, explain why our Em is sliced so deep with wounds that may never close." He stands and slaps his hands on the table. "Why should we let you near her when she might never recover from the next blow?

I sink slowly back down. "I've been working on that," I whisper.

Jason Ross—Phil's husband—speaks for the first time. "Have you?" He pushes to his feet and stands. Walking toward me with purposeful strides, he gets close enough so I have to tip my head back and stare at him. "Can you tell me right now it's never going to happen again? Because minutes after she opened the door to us, she collapsed crying on the kitchen floor of that apartment. She didn't stop sobbing even as Keene and Caleb packed up her stuff. She didn't stop crying when the Uber got there taking them to the airport and her sister, Holly, Em, and me to the ferry because I refused to let her get on an airplane with a concussion. Which she obviously had." I feel ready to throw up hearing how wrecked Emily truly was.

Nothing I imagined was this bad.

Unfortunately, Jason doesn't stop talking. "For me, I've been watching Jenna all week. This isn't a girl who doesn't have love. She's open about the fact she's been in counseling. My problem is without knowing if you're going to do it again, we can't just let you near her. What you did almost destroyed Em. What they're not telling you, but I will, is she came back unable to draw. Unable to create." Feeling the blood drain from my face, he brutally continues. "This week almost didn't happen for her until one of her sisters managed to get through to her. We're not trying to be assholes..."

"Some of us are," Keene mutters.

"But Em needs to have this moment of glory on her own because she earned it with every ounce of pain and every tear she shed. If we allow you to see her before she receives every accolade she earned by fighting through that, how are we helping her?" Leaving me gaping like a fish, Jason goes to sit back down.

Charlie Henderson clears his throat. "I need to know who you told about Emily's past, Madison."

I bristle. "No one."

"Not even your daughter? Not your psychologist?"

I shake my head. It was far too devastating. "It's Em's story to share."

"Anything about her brother, her sisters, anything?" he persists.

"Nothing. She only told me her part of the story a few days before things went to hell. She said their stories were for them to share."

"And another piece falls into place," Caleb mutters.

I tilt my head. "What do you mean?"

"She's entrusted no one with her past—including that dipshit fiancé she was engaged to for months. No wonder why she looks like she's bleeding to death slowly inside. You didn't just reject the woman; you rejected the child she was. She finally chose the person to give all of that to and she was turned away," Jason says simply.

All the blood leaves my face. "No, it wasn't like that," I whisper. I crush the heels of my hands into my eye socket.

No one says a word around the table.

The sound of the door opening behind me doesn't cause me to lift my head until I hear a new male voice say, "Actually, Mr. Madison. What you did to my sister was exactly like that. So, let's wrap this up so we get back to healing the heart of a woman who may never be the same ever again?"

My head shoots around. I see him lounging negligently in the doorframe.

Phillip Freeman.

61

JAKE

"You're her brother," I murmur. Of all her siblings, even knowing they're not biologically related, Emily looks the most like the man standing before me.

He glares at me. "Phillip Freeman-Ross. What the hell are you doing here, Madison? She's starting to heal."

I stand and face Phillip head-on. "If you think she's healed any more than I have, then you are completely wrong."

Two quick strides and he's in my face. "What makes you think you know her better than me? What makes you even think she might still give a damn about you?"

"Em told me she would sooner burn her journal than show it to another human. That's how she told me about you. She showed me pictures about her parents' murder, her Aunt Dee." Shock drains the color from Phillip's face. "There were pictures of the day she met her 'new' brother and sister and the day they all tried to stand before a judge to become a family."

"Shit," I hear Caleb curse behind me. I don't turn from Phil to look anywhere else.

"She showed me her pride the day her sisters graduated college and pictures of Mugsy through the years. But above all of that, do you know what she *told* me?" At the wordless shake of his head, I plow on. "She told me she was prepared to live without love so all of you can survive."

The room explodes behind me. "What the hell do you mean by that, Madison?" Keene growls.

"She thinks she's the catalyst of her parents' death. Her aunt's death. The night she opened that journal and told me her story, she told me it was eight days before her eighth birthday. Which is on August eighth. And then she asked me if I knew that the number eight means death. She's not living." Turning my back on Emily's brother, I sit back down.

Jason drops his head in his hands. "Jesus Christ."

"I fucked up. I am well aware I've lost the second-best thing in my life—Jenna being the first. That is entirely on me, and I've been working with someone to fix that in the smallest hope in hell she ever lets me back in. But I *need* her to know it isn't her fault. She has to live." Taking a deep breath, I add on, "Whether that's with or without me."

My head drops into my hands. There's nothing more I can say.

"Madison, can you give us a minute?" My head snaps up as Caleb stands along with Keene. They make their way over to a still-stunned Phillip. "Brother, come with us for a minute. Everyone else, we'll be right back." The three men make their way out the door.

It closes softly behind them. There's absolute silence for a long time while I try to regain control.

"Jacob," Jason says quietly. "From a medical standpoint, Jenna says she's okay, but I notice she's still limping. Is everything going well with her rehabilitation?"

Even though I'm mentally and physically drained, I appreciate the quiet conversation to take my mind off what's going on outside the door. "Her therapist says everything is on track. She has a few more weeks, and I'm sure the winter won't be great, but they expect a full recovery."

"That's good to hear. I had the names of a few specialists I was going to recommend if things weren't." I offer him a small smile in gratitude.

"Actually, that reminds me." I reach into my jacket pocket. Pulling out an envelope, I slide it to the center of the table. "The reimbursement of Jenna's medical bills for the hospital."

Colby sputters, "The family paid for those."

"The family assumed I blamed Em for something that was never her fault. I never would have expected you all to do that."

"They're not likely to take it back."

"Then donate it," I tell him. "But it's not coming home with me."

Charlie reaches for the envelope. Slitting it open, he whistles. "Damn, son. That's a check for the entire bill."

"Yes, it is."

Cracking the first joke of the day, Charlie asks, "Can you still send your kid to college after that?"

"Mr. Henderson, you've read the report in front of you? I assume everyone has?" At his nod, I continue. "I'd appreciate if no one mentions I cowrite songs with Brendan to my daughter. It's bad enough when Dani's around to curb her shopping tendencies. If she knew there's a trust in her name..." I shake my head.

"Did Em know?" Colby asks, bringing us back to the here and now.

"No. It's another thing I never got the chance to tell her." I wait for the debasement to start again, but he surprises me.

"When Corinna and I first started dating, she told me holding things back was more dangerous than finding them out later. If you get a chance to fix things, don't hold back."

I blink at him. "Thanks for the advice."

"No prob—" The doors open behind us. Keene and Caleb take the seats they were in before. I'm shocked when Phillip Freeman sits down next to me.

My heart is pounding out of my chest. This is it. Phillip turns to be before he begins talking.

"Have you ever read the legend of the amaryllis, Jacob?"

"No."

His mouth quirks into a sad smile. "You should. When I studied it in school, I found it to be both a beautiful and tragic story. Much like the lives of me and my sisters. The amaryllis is a symbol of pride, determination, and beauty. I've tried to make certain each of my sisters knows they are allowed to feel all of those things after the lives we've had."

I nod. "Emily's tattoo."

Phillip reaches for the button on his shirt. Rolling it back, he shows me his wrist. "All of our tattoos. Each of us bear the mark somewhere." He carefully flicks down his shirtsleeve while I come to my own conclusion.

And the blood flows from my heart as red as the ink on his wrist.

"You're not going to let me see her, are you?" My voice breaks, and I frankly couldn't care less.

He shakes his head. "It wasn't the decision of the men in this room. Nor was it just my decision. I called my sisters. They believe down to their souls, Jacob, that she needs this moment where she stands on her own two feet for the first time since everything happened."

Even as the burn hits the back of my eyes. "Will...I have no right. But will you please do two things for me?"

"What?" Phillip and I are talking as if there isn't anyone else in the room.

"Make sure she understands this isn't her fault. It's mine. I..." My voice begins to break.

He nods. "And the second?"

"Please understand, I'll respect your wishes for tomorrow, but I'm not going to give up unless she's the one who tells me to go away."

Fire burns in Phillip's eyes. "We'll see how long that takes."

62

EMILY

It's four fifteen in the morning. I never went to sleep last night. I can't even find solitude in my dreams anymore. They're filled with ghosts. Night after night, new nightmares have taken residence in my mind. My mother and Aunt Dee are walking down the runway with tears on their faces as all the bastards of my past sit in the front row jeering at them. It isn't until I step out onto the runway that they stop. Then Jake comes up onto the catwalk and viciously attacks my work in front of everyone in the room. They're all still laughing as I run off the runway.

It doesn't take years of therapy to realize I'm afraid of this last piece of my life being ruined the way everything else in my life has been by that indolent bitch, love.

I lean my head against the cold glass in the living room of Keene and Ali's penthouse. There's no peace to be found anywhere anymore. Not in sleep, not in my designs, not in silence. I'd rather the room be filled with noise so I don't have to think. It takes so little effort to murmur a word here or there in the middle of a big gathering and paste a false smile on my face than to be left alone with the ache in my chest.

"Couldn't sleep?" Keene comes out of his and Ali's room.

I shake my head against the glass.

"Excitement or nerves?"

I shrug. Let him think what he wants. It will be over soon enough.

Keene says something and I just stand there. He reaches out to clasp my arm. I react violently. "Don't. Please don't touch me." If no one touches me, no one can hurt me.

Keene curses under his breath. "I should have gotten in one good hit when that fucker was in my office today."

I'm confused. "Who?"

"You know damn well who. Ali said the sisters talked when we called earlier."

"And I also said we didn't tell Em he was there, Keene," Ali says exasperatedly from behind us both. Turning, we see her in sleep shorts and a tank, running both hands through her hair.

Keene winces. "Shit."

"Why don't you go check on Kalie while I talk with Em?" Ali suggests.

"Right." Pausing beside her, he reaches down and cups her jaw. I can't watch. I turn back to the window and lose myself in the emptiness of the New York skyline.

I feel Ali slide up next to me. For long moments, we stand there saying nothing. "Where do you go when you're this quiet, Em?" Ali finally breaks our silence to ask.

I think about how to answer her. "I go to the place where my life is shattered."

"Do you try to put the pieces back together?"

I shake my head. "I don't know how."

"What if someone else is trying to?"

Blankly, I look at her. "Who would want to?"

"Me. The family. Our men." She takes a deep breath. "And Jake Madison."

The sound of his name coming from Ali's lips is like a knife through the bubble of protectiveness I've been keeping around myself these last few weeks. "No..." I deny it instinctively.

"Do you trust me, Em?" Ali asks me, fervently.

"Right now, you're one of five people in the world I do trust," I admit wearily.

"Then come away from that window and listen to me. I'm not saying it's not going to hurt, but you have a right to hear everything I'm about to say."

~

AN HOUR LATER, I've cried more than I have since I first left Nantucket.

It turns out when your heart has been shredded, putting it back together requires more than just fabric glue. It requires a backstitch, a serger, and maybe some delicate topstitching to hide the repairs.

I'm still hurting. I'm still in pain. But now I feel something else.

I feel angry.

I've never felt angry before when love died because I killed it.

Maybe it's because this time, it wasn't me who did.

It's something for me to think about after I get through the show tonight.

Jenna stumbles out of Kalie's room at five fifteen. She takes one look at me and mutters, "Uh-oh. Did you sleep at all?"

Ali barks out a laugh while I shake my head.

"Great. Let me get dressed and figure out where there's coffee." Jenna starts to make her way back into the bedroom.

"I suspect you're going to need a few more today, sweetheart," I call out. She pauses and gives me a quizzical look. "I imagine your father's going to be pretty tired after the day he's had with my family trying to convince them to let him see me. You might want to tell him there will be a pass waiting for him with security. I imagine he's been up most of the night trying to figure out what to do next since my family told him he couldn't come to the show yesterday. He's probably going to need a caffeine boost."

The shock on her young face can't be faked. Jenna has no idea Jake is in the city.

"What on earth are you talking about, Em? Daddy's in Nantucket."

"No, Jenna. He isn't. He came to the city yesterday wanting to talk to Em before the show," Ali tells her gently.

Jenna whips her head toward me. "And you said no?" Her voice is tragically sad.

"Actually, I have quite a few things to say to your father, but I wasn't told he was here until an hour ago. I do, however, refuse to say them before what may end up being the most important day of my life." My voice is arctic. Ali squeezes my shoulder.

"Oh-okay. So, should I call him or something?"

"No, Jenna. Your job today is to staff Em. I'll call him once you both have left for the show. You've only got fourteen hours until the lights go up," Ali soothes her.

Her brown eyes, so like Jake's, begin to glow. She comes hobbling toward me. Before I can stop her, she slides her arms around me and hugs me tightly. I swallow convulsively. It's the first time Jenna's hugged me since the first night she arrived.

And just like that first night, I just want to bawl like a baby when she does.

"Go get ready." My voice is husky, even to my own ears. "We have to leave soon."

"Right!" Ali's arm around my waist props me up when I would have fallen down crying again.

"Are you sure about this?" I know she's concerned about my decision to let Jake into the show.

"Yes. Is it the right thing? I don't know. I just refuse to let him think for one more second I'll never recover from loving him. Even if I have to fake it, he'll walk out of there believing I'll forget about him the minute he does."

"Em?"

"Yeah?"

"Come home to cry, okay?" Her arm tightens around me.

I lean my head on her shoulder. "It's the only place that's safe for me to go, Ali. I'll be home."

63

EMILY

I t's quiet backstage. I've just called everyone together to thank them for all of their hard work under some crazy deadlines. I'm about to take the microphone from the stage manager when Jenna grabs my hand. "Dani wants to talk with you before you go out."

I say a quick prayer this isn't about my allowing Jake in to the Skylight. To say my family was drastically unhappy when they heard about my decision—something Holly relayed to me while she was backstage earlier—is an understatement. "If you think it's tense back here, you should be in the front of the house. I can't tell who's going to snap first, Cass or Phil."

"Great. Just great. Tell them if they get blood on the dresses when they're being paraded, I'm going to kill them," I said before stalking off to make sure a model's hair and makeup were being applied correctly.

Now, as I make my way to my finale dress—more importantly, to the woman wearing it—I can't help the churning of my stomach. I refuse to let any of that show on my face. "Dani, Jenna said you needed to see me?"

Giving me a head-to-toe perusal, she nods. "I was wondering

what you were doing when you agreed to let Jake in. I think I get it now. You're going to show him the life you're going to lead without him."

Ignoring her statement, I specify, "Was there something you needed pertaining to the show?"

"Come with me." Dragging me away just a few feet, she looks down at me from her enhanced height due to the four-inch heels she's wearing. "I'm not supporting a single thing he did—not one. He should have turned to you and not from you. I just want the right to say one thing."

"What's that?" I ask coldly.

"Don't let him steal your ability to love, Em. No matter what, don't let him have the part of your soul made for believing in love."

I step backward. "Don't you see, Dani? All Jake reinforced was that love is a game of how long someone can endure another person before they leave. Or die. He didn't take away my ability to love. He just reminded me I was never meant to have it."

"Ms. Freeman, one minute," the stage manager calls out.

I smile briefly. "If you'll excuse me, I'll be back to walk you down the runway soon enough." I turn and walk away.

"Em!" Dani's yell causes me to pause. "It's limitless. It's timeless. It forgives everything."

I turn around slowly. "Maybe when you're lucky enough to be cherished, Dani. Instead, I've only found the kind that wants to shove me to my knees begging." I shake my head back and forth. "Not anymore. I'd rather go stone-cold dead inside than ever feel like that again."

Without another word, I move back to the stage manager. I shrug on the cape I'm wearing over my finale dress.

"Get them quiet out there. I'm ready."

From the wings, I watch as the lights flicker on and off. Soon, a spotlight displays the Amaryllis Designs logo in white against a black backdrop, and the music drops until there's nothing but silence. They're waiting for me.

Handing me a microphone I was warned in advance would be live, he whispers, "Knock 'em dead, Ms. Freeman."

Stepping from the wings, I'm at first overpowered by the thunderous applause as the spotlight hits me. Giving myself a moment to adapt to its blinding heat, I attempt to pick out my family in the second row. Except Holly. I ensured she has one of the coveted front-row seats.

There. I see Cassidy's long hair in a braid over one shoulder. She's holding Phil's hand on one side and Ali's on the other. Ali's got Corinna's hand. Corinna's arm is draped over Holly's shoulder. Holly's camera is already raised and trained on me. They're all there for me.

Just like they always have been. Just like they were while I've been healing. Just like they always will be.

And in my soul, I know I won't break over what's happened. I will go on. I can do this. The words just flow from my lips.

"Thank you for coming. I'm Emily Freeman. On behalf of Amaryllis Designs, I'm honored for you all to be here for our first show!" After I wait for the applause to die down, I continue. "Before we start tonight's show, I'd like to tell you a little bit about my collection, 'Silence.'"

My voice strong, I continue. "Because of a family tragedy when I was a young girl, I didn't speak for years. It was through my art that I actually communicated. It was my healing, my therapy. It became the only way I could speak." I try to calm my racing heart. "I found my voice. I fought for it back then. Recently, there have been some events which tried to steal my voice." I pause in astonishment at the uproar of support from the crowd. "I refuse to let that happen. Then. Now. Ever again." I pause as the cheering starts again. "The dresses you are about to see are what rescued me from my silence, from my despair, from myself. It's stronger than a ring. More lasting than a picture. It involves vows, solemn ones, spoken between people who know what the words 'Till death do us part' truly mean. So, with that, I'd like to dedicate this collection to the brother and sisters of my heart. Phillip, Cassidy, Alison, Corinna, and Holly, there are no greater vows than the ones we spoke together." The only one whose tears I can't see are

Holly's because her camera is in front of her face. But I know they're there.

"I now give you the last time you'll ever see my silence. Because let me assure you, if you can't be yourself, if you can't speak freely with the ones you love, you'll never be free to love. Enjoy the show." I step behind the wings and hand the mic to the stage manager.

Three.

Two.

One.

Katy Perry blares through the Skylight as the first model steps out on the stage in the mummy wrap dress I designed so long ago when I first arrived in Nantucket after I ended my engagement to Bryan. *It feels like a different me walking down the stage*, I think critically. I hear the gasp of the crowd as the model turns and the deep asymmetrical V in her back is shown.

Perfect.

As she saunters down the runway heading back in our direction, a little of the knot in my stomach releases.

One down, twenty-nine to go. Including the dress that my heart and soul are presently sewn into.

As the second model heads down the runway to Kelly Clarkson, the gasp is immediate. The sheer gown that is essentially the reenactment of my being dragged out of my bedroom by my hair looks provocative. Suggestive.

What it also does is scream out loud the words I couldn't say when I was seven years old.

Finally.

~

EVERY TIME A MODEL walks down the runway, the knots in my stomach are moving closer to my throat. Finally, it's just Dani in the wings. Standing next to me, she reaches over and links our pinkies together as the final model before her poses at the end of the runway.

"You didn't just break your silence, Em. You shattered it," she whispers.

"That was the point," I murmur back.

She takes a deep breath and lets it out slowly. "Let me be the first to tell you, I am so proud of what you accomplished under circumstances most people would have buckled under." Cutting fierce violet eyes toward me, she murmurs, "I'm honored to be wearing any dress of yours, but particularly this one."

"Dani..."

"This dress is the physical manifestation of your love, Em. It's wrapped all around me. Every stitch you sewed was to prove your heart was still beating—that my asinine cousin didn't take it from you. And the song I'm walking to?" She shakes her head, causing ripples of tiny amaryllis flowers to sparkle. "Perfection."

My voice cracks when I admit, "It's all I can do to prove it to myself."

We're both watching the model who's almost made her way back. It's almost time. "What's that?"

"That I'm not drowning without him. Without Jenna."

The opening notes of the song play. "Let me help pull you from the waves, Em. None of us are going to let you sink into the abyss." Turning, Danielle Madison hits her cue and takes the spotlight in my finale dress just as Avril Lavigne's guitar strums pick up its pace in the song "Head Above Water." As I see her long legs eat up the runway, the veil with the amaryllis-filled crystals takes flight behind her. Dani poses during the coda of the song, the lights illuminating her dress spectacularly, before turning and heading back toward the stage entrance, her face regal, her head held high.

Filled with beauty, strength, and pride. Everything an amaryllis should be.

Tears run unchecked down my face. As the music changes to Avicii, a celebratory cheer can be heard from the crowd. I let loose a smile—a real one. Damn, it feels good to know that if I have nothing, I'll have this. Dani wraps her arms around me and starts swaying back and forth laughing. "Take off this cape, and let's get you ready to walk the runway."

Spinning around, I unsnap the cape and reveal the short sparkling, long-sleeved minidress I slipped on earlier in crimson red. Exactly the color of my amaryllis tattoo, which is on full display across my lower back due to the deep V in the back. I reach up and unsnap the clip holding back my curls. Flipping my head over, I fluff them out a bit. "How's this for a statement dress?" I taunt sassily.

"I think the statement you're trying to say is 'Fuck you.'"

Grabbing Dani's hand, I wait for the stage manager's cue. Just as we step into the spotlight and Dani and I raise our hands jointly, I spy Jake, now standing along with the rest of the audience at the Skylight, a few rows behind my family. His mouth is agape. Ignoring his penetrating stare as I wave my arms back and forth, I murmur to Dani, "You'd be one hundred percent correct."

Holding out her arm, she says, "Then sell it, my friend. Let's take your victory lap so you can celebrate."

And I start down the runway after my first successful fashion show.

Partway down the aisle, I'm stopped by Phil, who steps over the photographers to hand me a bouquet of flowers. "We're so proud of you, Em. So damn proud of you."

Grinning, I tell him, "Save it for the party backstage. I have a lap to finish." Then I pull out a perfect amaryllis from the bouquet and hand it to Dani. She transfers it to her left and holds it high.

The crowd goes nuts again.

We finish our way around with a lot of shutters snapping, flashes popping, and enormous cheers both in the front of the house and backstage.

I hear the first cork pop and call out, "No one in any of my dresses better be drinking!"

Everyone laughs.

And the party begins.

64

JAKE

From the fourth row, even I can feel the oxygen leave the room when Dani steps out onto the runway in her dress. For me, every dress that walked the runway was like watching Em's personal sketchbook come to life. First was the mummy wrap dress with diamonds on the edge of each hem representing the suffocation of her engagement. Then the sheer dress that wouldn't mean anything to anyone except someone who saw her drawings. That one depicted where she had been held back by the monsters who yanked her from her idyllic world as a child. Another dress that was so soft you wanted to wrap yourself in it—Mugsy. The high-collar lace dress for her Aunt Dee; the ballgown for her mother. Dress after dress of her private memories finally exposing her deepest secrets, her silence finally broken.

The world spun around me as Dani stood there in the spotlight. I don't know what image inspired this dress, but I can suspect. As Dani strides down the runway, the train of the dress, which attaches at the shoulder, floats behind her as if she's running away from something horrid and into the arms of something beautiful.

Away from pain and toward love.

This dress is the visual embodiment of every mistake I made. I figured it out within days of the accident, and regaining control of my emotions. I knew down to my soul that Emily would rather it have been her in the coma than Jenna. I knew the moment I went to go find her at the apartment and found her gone. I knew then—as I know now—Emily doesn't give up on those she loves.

Now, she's telling that to the world in a way that floats and twinkles under the lights as it moves.

"Oh, God, that's the Legend dress," I hear whispered by a woman sitting next to me excitedly.

"The Amaryllis Legend? Didn't I read in the prep materials she sewed every stitch of that dress herself?"

"Yes," she hisses. "Now, hold on. I'm sure there's going to be something... Ah, there it is."

And suddenly at the end of the runway, the spotlight turns bright red on Dani as she poses. Turning the Legend alive. I swallow convulsively. After I left Hudson Investigations the other day, I read as much as I could about the legend behind the amaryllis flower, learning more about Emily's tattoo and why her family chose that symbol to bind their vow. Just like the flower, her dress is conveying that, much like Alteo turned Amaryllis away, the legend will go on.

Just like Emily will do without me.

I can barely breathe.

I'm surprised Dani hasn't slipped on my blood as it begins pumping out of the hole in my heart. While I'm sure many are astounded a model of her caliber is walking in Em's show, it's the dress that holds me captive. Soon, she's made her way back down the runway with her head held high.

The music trails off, and suddenly the models come out one followed by another. Em's life journey begins walking down the runway again to an incredibly upbeat song. Everyone jumps to their feet applauding. Finally, Em and Dani come around the corner, and they raise their joined hands in victory. The room goes ballistic. The sound is almost deafening. There's a small grin on Em's face as she and Dani begin their walk down the runway. My breath catches when she stops practically in front of me, but it's only to receive flowers from her brother. They hug fiercely. Em removes a single glorious red amaryllis from the bouquet and hands it to my cousin. Dani holds it aloft, to the crowd's delight.

It isn't until Em disappears backstage does anyone sit back down. I collapse back in my chair, lost about what to do next. I brace my hands on my knees as I bow my head.

"Mr. Madison?" I hear a familiar voice next to me. Warily, I turn my head. There's a stunning blonde who's been a few rows in front of me most of the night.

Slowly, I push to my feet. "Yes?"

"This is for you. I was asked to deliver it once the show was over." She places an envelope in my hands, and I watch as she makes her way back down the stairs toward a few recognizable faces. Since she moves directly into Keene Marshall's arms, I can only presume I just met Alison Freeman.

Looking down, I see an envelope with an amaryllis embossed on the back. Slowly, I unseal it. Pulling out a piece of card stock, I'm shocked to see Em's handwriting.

I'll be out to speak with you after I'm finished.

Flipping it over, I don't see anything else written. Just one line, ten words, that could mean a new beginning or the end of everything.

Knowing I have nothing I can do but wait, I sink back into my seat and let the accolades about Em's show flow over me.

I wonder if I'll have the chance to tell her how damn proud of her I am.

65

JAKE

It's hours later when the media finishes talking to one another and interviewing guests. I've overheard nothing less than the highest praise for any of the dresses. According to the buzz around me, Em didn't just make a mark on bridal fashion, she redefined it. Any number of camera spotlights have been shined on the members of the Freeman family. I'm surprised they're not blind.

At one point, the entire clan headed backstage with a gaggle of photographers trailing at their heels. They emerged a half hour later laughing hysterically, holding champagne glasses.

It must be one hell of a celebration going on. A well-deserved one.

I don't pull out my phone to pass the time. I don't check my watch. I relive every moment from the first time I saw Em in Dani's apartment, to our squabbles, to our first kiss. I remember the first time I touched her beautiful body, the first time her head lay on my heart. I scrub my hands down my face, remembering when she screamed Mugsy's name.

And I remember her down on her knees as she begged for me to listen to her about the accident. Pleading with me to accept her—accept her love.

Like a fool I denounced them both as cursed.

What a fucking asshole I am.

The lights go dim, and suddenly a spotlight appears on the stage. Still wearing the sparking red dress she wore when she walked the runway earlier, Em steps from the wings with a bottle of champagne in her hand. She walks with an innate grace about a quarter of the way down the runway. "You have five minutes. They're waiting on me next door at the party."

Quickly making my way down the stairs to the runway, I realize we're farther apart than I initially thought, both physically and emotionally. "Thank you for allowing me a chance to see you tonight."

She shakes her head. "I didn't do it for you."

"Then why did you?" I've been wondering that since I received the call from the hotel concierge earlier today.

"I did it because you allowed your daughter to be a part of this, and she deserved her father here to recognize she was a part of something enormous this week. I'd like to think if she chooses to pursue a career in fashion, you'll support her after this. Now, if you'll excuse me, my presence is requested at the party next door."

Emily turns to walk away, raising the bottle of Veuve Clicquot to her lips.

I'm going to lose her unless I say something. Anything. "Don't go. Please. I beg you." My voice cracks on the last words.

She stops in place, the bottle of champagne slowly dropping. Turning on one heel, she hisses, "You dare to say that to me? I was on my fucking knees for you. I cried enough for you in that moment and in the minutes in between to fill an ocean."

"Then let me swim across it to get back to you." I step toward her and die a little as she backs away.

"I would have torn my arms from my body and my eyes from my face before I let Jenna get hurt, yet you said I was cursed. That being around me was what hurt her."

"I wasn't thinking rationally." I wasn't thinking at all. But now I am. And I'm silently begging for a chance to explain.

"Did it ever occur to you I was injured too? Did you want me to die for your daughter? I was willing to. Do you know who I had to call for help to make sure my own head injury wasn't going to kill me as I scrambled to get off the island? After being so ill it took me almost a damn hour to climb the stairs to get to the apartment, I managed to call the only people on the planet who I knew would come save me, and they dropped everything to do so. My family." I blanch. "That's right. It took them four hours on a private jet to get to me. Jason wanted to bring me back to the hospital to have me looked over, and I refused. I'd rather have died than seen your face again." Em's words pound at me like physical blows. In some small way, this is how I made her feel.

And it's unacceptable.

She turns away from me again. I know this is the end. The last time I'll see her. Abruptly, she stops. "I'll always believe one thing you said to me."

"What's that?" I manage to choke out.

"That I'm going to kill anything I love. So, after tonight, keep Jenna the hell away from me so I know both of you will live." Tears clog her voice. "Goodbye, Jacob."

"Goddamnit, Em. You're wrong!" My voice echoes in the cavernous room.

She shakes her head in denial.

I cross to where she's standing. I'm behind her, but I don't have the right to touch her. Not anymore. "I am so sorry. I was afraid. I lashed out at anyone who could feel anything beyond scared that night. But you're wrong too. You don't bring upon death to those you love."

"Some of us don't have the right to feel." Her voice is so remote, it's as if she's entombed herself inside her walls for her own protection.

"You're wrong. You taught it to me," I argue. "I've been talking to a doctor. I swear to you. He helped me realize I didn't know how to love —how to trust—after Michelle. You showed me love isn't just the moon and the stars, but the earth, the sun, the clouds, and the rain too. It's the good, the bad, the pain as well as the pleasure. It's about finding the person to get you through all of that and still be without on the other side. You taught me love is all of those things, Emily." In disgust, I mutter, "I'm the one who should be on his knees."

Silence envelops us both. I hear her harsh breathing in synchronization with my own. It's a hope, a small one, but she hasn't walked away.

Slowly she turns to face me. We're less than a foot apart when I see her face. From a distance, I couldn't see the wear and tear. Now, I can see it's been ravaged by months of pain. Up close, I can see the fatigue in her dark blue eyes. Her cheeks are gaunt behind the expert makeup job.

Her lips part before she says, "Then why aren't you?"

66

EMILY

Shock holds me in place as Jake lowers himself first on one knee, then the other. Sitting back on his heels, he tips his head back at me. His face is wet even though tears aren't actively falling.

I can't process the way he's humbling himself before me. I have to give him a few truths so I can move on with the life I'll allow myself to have. Which won't be much of a life at all, but at least I'll survive.

"I want you there while you listen to what I have to say."

He nods his head.

"I refuse to ever be a whipping post for anyone ever again. My heart has to beat for myself first, and it's been doing a crappy job of that." I begin pacing back and forth. Champagne sloshes over my hand. I lift my hand to my mouth and sip it off.

"I learned I'm willing to go to the ends of the earth to be able to love without fear, but I'm not willing to fear love. If it means not loving anymore, I'll do that. Because it's easier than protecting myself from it." Jake's eyes darken at my words, but he doesn't say anything. I continue. "And I'm stronger than I give myself credit for, even if I shouldn't love someone for their own safety," I end bitterly.

Jake lunges for me and pulls me toward him. Burying his head in my stomach, he shakes his head back and forth. "I should go to hell for ever adding to your fear of that. People didn't die because they loved you, Em. You just felt that because your heart kept breaking. Stop the cycle with me." Lifting his head, he rests his chin against me. "Please, Em. Please, listen to me."

I place a hand on his shoulder. "Jake, I've accepted who and what I am. Just let me go." I take a step back. He follows me on his knees. I shake my head. "Stop, please. This isn't why I came out here." I move backward again.

"Then why did you?"

"To show you I'll live, damn you. To show you didn't completely bleed me dry." A sob hitches in my throat. "To make you beg the way you made me beg before I consign you to hell."

"I'm already there, Emily." Now, I can see the tears in his eyes, and they infuriate me more.

"Liar!" I scream. "You told me I was enough to send you into a rage. To get the hell out of your sight. You told me that. Why did you really come here? To ruin the most important night of my life?"

"No. That's impossible considering how much I love you."

My hand is cracking across his face before I can stop myself. I toss the bottle of champagne aside as I start to hit him. I vaguely hear the hiss of the bubbles as it spreads across the runway I was so triumphant on hours before. I don't care as I unleash the pain and fury bubbling up in me like an overflowing teakettle. "Damn you, Jacob. Damn you!" I shriek. "You can't come here and do this to me. I was going to be okay."

Stopping my next hit simply by wrapping his arms around me, he pulls me to him. "No, lady, you weren't. Neither am I. Not without you. You made a world where the only thing that makes sense is loving you."

"You said I was a curse."

"A curse, a blessing—what's the difference when you're so woven in my soul I can't rip you out without damaging myself?" His head tips up, and the pain he's suffered right along with me is etched there. I'm completely unable to hold back the hurt I feel from him being in pain. Just as I was unable to resist Jenna's when I saw her pain over Lynne for the first time.

I collapse onto him.

"I want to believe you," I sob as he strokes my back. "I just can't right now."

"It's going to take time to regain your trust, Em. Please give me that time to try," he whispers hoarsely against my ear.

Looking up into his handsome face, I touch his lips. I pull away as I stand. I start to walk away.

"Please, Em," he begs. Tears track down his face.

I've never felt pain like this before because I never loved like this. With my back to him, I'm standing on the precipice of two destinies. The first is a fortress of my own making where I refuse to live, to feel out of fear. The other is jumping into the ocean where I may drown in my own tears.

"I told you I cried an ocean of tears for you," I whisper.

"Yes." His voice cracks on that single word.

"I am sick of crying." My voice holds the exhaustion I've been living with.

"Tell me if you want me to try to fix it or if you want me go." The words sound guttural as they are torn from him, but in that instant, I know he'll do whatever I ask to give me back what I need.

Isn't that its own measure of love? Being able to walk away?

"The thing is, if there's enough sun, water evaporates back into the sky, Jacob." Turning, I roll my lips together to prevent them from trembling. We stare at each, each afraid of making the next move, when I blurt out, "I want to feel the sun."

"I'll find it every day."

"I'm tired of my nightmares."

"I'll hold them at bay however you let me."

"I want to believe I'm worthy of love." Now my tears begin to fall.

Untucking one knee, he pushes up. Rising to his feet, he stands before me. "You always were. The truth is, you're the reason I believe in love at all."

"Then where do we go from here?" I whisper, unable to cross the line between us.

Unable to take that first step.

Jake steps toward me. When he sees I'm not backing away, he comes closer until he stands directly in front of me. Touching my cheek gently, he murmurs, "Hi, my name is Jake Madison. You put on a hell of a show tonight. Would you like to get a bite to eat and tell me about it?"

My lips tremble as I look at him. *It's now or never, Em.*

Or forever.

"I...I think I'd like that."

His arms seize me against him, and when my head is tucked against his neck, I can feel the pounding of his heart. Against my cheek, I feel the damp wetness of his tears.

"There's so much to say, Em."

"And we'll say it," I whisper. "But tonight, do you think we can just go out back, eat some food, and begin tomorrow?"

Lifting my face toward his, he rubs his cheek against mine softly. "I think that sounds just about perfect."

Sliding an arm around me, he asks, "So, what should I be prepared for when we walk outside?"

"I honestly don't know." Because the press is all over and Jenna is there, my family will behave. It doesn't mean they're going to accept my decision easily.

Stopping, he turns and cups my cheek. "Em, I deserve whatever it is they want to dole out at me. It will take time, but I'll win back your trust. I'll earn theirs. I promise."

Like an uncertain butterfly, I raise my hand to touch his fingers on his face. My first step on the path to forgiveness.

Toward the future.

To maybe believing again.

67

EMILY

"Hey, baby."

I hear Jake's warm voice through the phone, and it sends shivers down my spine even in the warm Atlanta sun outside the bridal salon where I'm giving a trunk show. "Hi. What are you guys up to?"

"Jenna wants to go out on a date with some screwball I've never met. He's on the football team. Worse yet? She wants me to let him drive her alone in the car. This is definitely not a good communication day."

I can't help the grin that spreads across my face. Jake scowls back at me in our FaceTime chat. I can't help the giggle-snort that escapes. His face softens when he hears it. I ache to reach for my journal. But that will have to wait until I'm in my hotel room later.

In the month since Fashion Week ended, I've been on the road more than I've been at home. Within a week of the reviews of my show appearing in the paper, Ali was jubilantly dancing around the office as appointment after appointment was coming in for Amaryllis Designs. And not only that, the calls were for me to fly with my dresses to meet with brides all over the United States and all over the world.

I'm astounded people believe in me enough to take a chance on me. I'm humbled by every compliment I receive. Every time a bride has tears in her eyes as she tries on one of my dresses, I feel each one wash over me. They clean a piece of my soul I didn't know I needed.

Jake and I have talked every single day since that night in New York. Even though his reception from my family has been polite at best, he hasn't let that deter him from our new beginning.

"Where did you go?" he asks softly.

"Just thinking about you," I answer honestly. One of the first things Jake did when we started talking was introduce me to the psychologist both he and Jenna had been working with. While we've only talked on the phone, I look forward to actually meeting Dr. Thurman.

If for no other reason than to say thank you for consulting with my own doctor.

My anger at Jake sharing my secrets with my family abated when I realized he did so out of concern for my mental and spiritual health. Phil—still not one hundred percent Team Jake—said it was pretty damn obvious even to him this man loved me when he begged for my family to get me help. The day my brother handed me a list of names for people who dealt with childhood post-traumatic stress disorder and begged me to talk to someone, I took them knowing that I had no excuses left.

My counselor, Sam, is sharp, dry-witted, and willing to work around my crazy schedule—even scheduling sessions via FaceTime while I'm on the road. She knows her shit and makes it a point to get to know mine. After I mentioned Jake was in counseling, she immediately asked for permission to contact with Dr. Thurman. "I won't reveal anything personal, Em, but if your ultimate goal is to be heart whole, then I need to be able to coordinate with him to make sure we're working together to get you both through the same trigger event that started all this."

Since I didn't want Jake to think I was betraying anything he told me in confidence, I asked him. He was all for it. "Baby, whatever you need to get to where the sun shines every day. That's what I promised you."

The warm glow that gave me, it lit my sky for days even through the rain I was suffering through in LA at the time.

Now, Jake and I are so much more open about our communication, even when we only have a few minutes.

"It's just beginning, sweetheart. You'd better get over it now before she goes to college." And in the next second, I'm giggle-snorting as our video shows him banging his head against the kitchen counter repeatedly.

"Thanks, Em. I needed that mental image right about now."

"Can I ask a question without you getting upset?"

His face focuses completely back on me. "Of course. You know that."

I bite my lip. "Is it the idea of the date, or is it the idea of the boy being an inexperienced driver after everything that happened?"

His face freezes. For just a minute, I think it's our video connection. I'm just about to start calling out when his face shifts in pain. "It's both, but Em? Truthfully? It's probably the second," he admits.

"Then talk to her after she's lifted her no-communications ban, Jake. Jenna can't read your mind. Tell her what your feeling and why you're so concerned."

"It's completely irrational—"

I cut him off. "No, it's not." Taking a deep breath, I admit, "I still have panic attacks every time I'm in traffic."

"Damn, baby. What does Sam say about that?" Now his concern has transferred to me.

"That once I'm home and driving again, it will ease up some. It's part of being out of control."

He thinks about that. "It makes a lot of sense."

"What? Feeling the way you do about Jenna?"

"No, what you're still dealing with. All the travel, new cities where people drive recklessly, and you weren't driving when you were in the accident, Em," he concludes softly.

"Worry about fixing things with your daughter," I advise him.

"I'm in a perpetual state of worry about fixing both of my women. I'm used to it," he retorts.

Okay, it wasn't the Atlanta heat that just melted my heart. It's the man on the other end of the phone. "I have to go soon," I say regrettably. "Tell me something that made you happy today." It's how we end each call now.

"Jenna submitted her final application for college, so I'm not going to go into the poorhouse anytime soon."

"Like that was going to happen." My voice is full of derision. Shortly after New York, Jake admitted to me he helped cowrite some of Brendan's songs. He wasn't just a musical genius who could seduce me by opening his mouth, his brain allowed him to secure an excellent future for his daughter while still allowing her to grow up comfortably.

"Tell me something that made you believe today, Em." His husky voice comes back at me.

I don't have to think. "A bridal party came in today. The bride wanted high-end design but has a sister whose measurements don't conform with the rest of the party. They all fell in love with 'The Lynne.' I was meant to be there with you all, to design that dress."

"Yeah, you were." The deeper register of his voice tells me my words mean so much to him. "Where are you off to next?"

"Tomorrow, I fly home for Thanksgiving. Then..." I hesitate. "What would you think if I flew up to see you and Jenna for a quick visit before I head to Toronto?"

"I think you just found the perfect way to end this call. Go back to work, sweetheart. We'll talk tomorrow."

"Night, Jake."

"Night, honey."

I disconnect the call before heading back in.

68

JAKE

I am officially a mess. Em's plane is an hour late due to high winds. I'm pacing the waiting area at Memorial Airport waiting for her flight from JFK to land so I can hold her in my arms for the first time since New York.

"Dad, will you calm down? Everything is going to be fine." Jenna is completely over me losing my cool.

"I just want her to get here safely," I mutter.

Standing, she walks over and plants her hands on my chest before shoving me in a chair. "Calm down before we have to call someone to give you a pill or something. Jesus. It's not like she's never been here before."

While that's true, it's so different. This is a new beginning with the woman I've visited in my dreams every night since we've been apart. This is the woman whose forgiveness has made me become a better father and a better man. This is the woman who showed me that the storm of the ocean felt so right because she was on the other side, that music was worth making because she couldn't make her own, and that love was worth any risk. As long as it was with her.

This is Emily.

I'm about to open my mouth when I hear something over the PA system. "Flight 5921 arriving from JFK operated by Cape Air has now landed. As soon as the plane has a spot to park, the passengers will be able to disembark."

I close my eyes in relief.

"Now will you calm down?" Jenna demands.

Reaching out, I hook an arm around my daughter. "Will you?" I finally recognize my daughter's constant nagging for what it really is: her own concern.

Slipping an arm around my waist, she mutters, "When I see Em come through security."

Throwing back my head, I laugh.

"Did they say what the delay was, Em?" Jenna asks from the back seat of the Pilot as we drive back to Sconset.

Em twists in her seat. "High winds in New York. We couldn't take off. I was on the cell with Caleb pestering the hell out of him to ask if his jet was available for me to use. He laughed and said if they weren't taking off at JFK, it was unlikely they'd be taking off at Teterboro."

"Caleb has his own jet?" I jump in to the conversation.

Em twists back and nods. "His business does."

"I'm surprised they didn't run over me with the jet when I came to New York, then," I mutter under my breath. Or at least I think I do until Em whacks me in the arm.

"Stop that. They're getting better about this."

Jenna, my little snot of a daughter, outright asks, "Who's on Team Dad this week, Em?"

"Wait? What? There're teams?" I'm amused, appalled, and intrigued all at once.

"Dad, there's a betting pool on who will be the last you'll win over."

I very briefly take my eyes off the road to shoot a killing look at Emily. "And you're aware of this?"

She shrugs. "It keeps them from betting on sex."

Jenna laughs while I groan. "Fine. Tell me. Who is for and against?"

"Completely in your corner? Holly. Swear, that girl has some inner eye none of us can figure out. But the day after the show, she was all Team Jake."

"I didn't say more than two words to her." I'm stunned.

"With Holly, you don't have to. It's what she *sees*."

"Okay. So, Holly. Is that it?" I demand.

"Surprisingly, no. Jason, Ali, Cass, Colby, and Charlie," Emily concludes.

"Which leaves, your brother, Caleb, Keene, and Corinna," I conclude.

Em waves her hand. "Corinna's already falling. She wanted to know how many to cook for over Christmas. When I told her you already had plans to go to your parents, she wanted to know where to send a special package."

"Whoohoo! Corinna baked goods!" Jenna yells from the back seat.

"And the others just need...my blood?" I conclude.

"Time, Jake. Time. I predict Caleb, Phil, Keene," Em confides. "Normally, I'd say Phil last, because he's my brother, but frankly, Keene can just be a prick who holds a grudge."

I chuckle. "I kind of got that impression."

"I'll tell you all the good stories later."

Since we're at a stoplight, I reach over and squeeze her hand. "I look forward to it, sweetheart."

Her smile stops my heart, even as the car behind me honks at me to go.

IT'S FREEZING cold on the beach. There's nothing worse than the gusting wind coming off the ocean making the low forty-degree temperature feel much colder, but Emily has something she needs to do.

She wants to spread some of Mugsy's ashes here.

Emily has borrowed a pair of Jenna's high laced-up L.L.Bean boots to keep the freezing cold, wet sand out. Between that, her own coat, and scarf, she should be warm enough. Sliding into my own coat, I reach for her hand. "Are you ready?"

She nods, but it's with a sad smile on her face.

Quietly, we make our way out the back door and down the deck stairs to the beach. Once we hit the sand, I wrap my arm around her to give her more support, both emotionally and physically. "Do you know where..." My voice trails off.

"Closer to the apartment? This way he'll always be right where he first fell in love with the beach," she chokes out.

We walk for a few minutes in the uneven sand until Emily says, "Here's good." Digging around in her pocket, she pulls out the packet of ashes. "I guess...I guess I just throw them?" she says uncertainly. Tears are falling behind her glasses and freezing to her cheeks.

Slowly, I shake my head. Softly, I begin to sing to her a song by Luke Bryan about dogs growing old. Even as I'm changing the words to suit her and Mugsy, Em sobs as she lays her head on my chest. When I finish, I ask, "What's your favorite memory of Mugsy, Em?"

"There are too many. It would take me forever to tell you all of them."

I kiss her forehead. "Then let's add that to our talks each day. You can tell me a Mugsy memory each day."

Her breath catches and doesn't release. Did I say something wrong? I begin to panic until her mitten-covered hand slides up to my jaw.

"And that right there is the reason I took a chance back at the Skylight." Rising on her toes, she brushes her first kiss since she left the island against my lips. Falling back on her heels, she gives me a wobbly smile. "I'll be right back."

She strides away to say goodbye to Mugsy here where so many hurts were perpetrated and maybe are starting to heal.

69

EMILY

"I am freezing cold," I declare to Jake.

His laughter is followed by "It isn't a picnic here either, baby."

I frown. "What do you do on the island when it's that cold?" I'm on what should—thank God—be my last trip before I head home to Connecticut until after April's Bridal Fashion Week. Where all this will begin again.

He shrugs. "Stay inside. Drink a lot of hot drinks. Read a lot. Grade papers."

Something has bothered me for months, but I haven't asked him about it. "Have you been playing?" Other than Jake singing to me when we spread Mugsy's ashes, I can't think of a single time he's mentioned music other than teaching. And we've talked every single day.

He opens his mouth and then closes it. "What is it, Jake?" I ask, concerned.

"You know how you have to be inspired to draw?"

"Yes." Boy, do I understand that feeling.

His eyes can't meet the phone's camera. Uh-oh. What on earth?

"Em, I haven't been able to play since the accident. After the first few weeks, I just stopped trying."

I freeze in the act of taking a drink of hot chocolate to choke out, "And this hasn't come up before, why?"

"Because the most important thing in this world was to heal what I did to you, Em."

I close my eyes. Conflicting emotions are raging through me right now. I whisper, "Why are we so far away right now?"

"Because your dream is coming true." His voice is tender. "And right now…"

"Right now, I don't know if I would punch you or kiss you for saying something like that to me!" I yell.

"What?" he asks confused.

"I am so mad at you. We're supposed to be building an *us*. That means fixing you and fixing me. You don't get to give up on fixing you until I'm better!"

"I just want you to realize I will always be your sun to evaporate your tears, Em. I promised you that."

"What makes you think I don't, you jackass?"

There's a deathly silence between us. "Excuse me? Do you mind repeating that?"

"What makes you think I don't? If you loved me any more, someone would wonder why there are two suns orbiting in the sky instead of one."

Now he's the one getting angry. "You're saying this to me when you're thousands of miles away?" His voice is incredulous.

"Damn straight I am. I'm going first tonight. You know what made me believe today, Jake? You. You made me believe. Because I love you and I'm not afraid to tell you that," I hiss out.

"I'm about to hang up on you, Emily. Because I suddenly want to go beat the shit out of a drum set."

"Good."

"I'm glad you think so, because the most beautiful thing of my day is those words. I love you too, Em."

And even through our stupid anger, his voice saying that to me cleanses every part of my soul. "I know, Jake." A sob hitches in my throat. "Got any plans for winter break?"

"Even if I did—which I don't—what have you got in mind?"

"Come to me. Come to the farm. Come to my home."

The convulsion of his face is so beautifully twisted and horrifically ugly, it causes another sob to come out. "We'll work out the plans tomorrow, love. Go rest. You have an early flight."

"I don't want to hang up," I whisper. His smile is so tender, I can feel it everywhere.

"I know. But the woman I'm in love with just told me to get my ass to the basement to make her some music."

I hiccup as I brush the tears from my face. "Yeah. You better get on that."

"I plan to. Night, baby."

"Night, Jake." When his face disappears, I jump from my seat. Grabbing my new journal, I turn to the current page and start sketching.

And in my mind, I can hear, *All you have to do is believe, Emily.*

And quietly I tell her back, *I finally know that, Aunt Dee.*

Before I go to sleep, I make two calls. The first is to the airline to add an additional flight from JFK to Nantucket. The second is to my family to tell them I'll be home a few days later than I expected.

It's Caleb who asks me if I want to fly commercial instead of taking the Hudson jet.

I'm a wreck sobbing when I hang up.

70

EMILY

It's been four of the busiest months since Fashion Week, and sales for Amaryllis Designs are off the charts. In between flying all over the globe for trunk shows, I've had to hire two full-time bridal consultants to work the showroom. Ali is purring like a cat with saucers full of cream after she checked the bottom line for sales. Even with the new staff, I have more than enough money to plan my next show in April, October, and the April after that. I could even consider expanding into boutiques in other stores if I wanted to begin opening up our presence to other cities, though she cautioned me that would be a huge effort and even more time away from home.

I'm not sure I'm ready for that just yet. But maybe in the future.

Jake and I have talked every night. I can't determine which of us is more excited for his trip to Collyer. In the meantime, Nantucket has been abuzz with news. Jenna's college acceptance letters are coming back in, and she got into her number one choice—UCONN.

In an amazing turn of events, she's decided against RISD. After spending time talking with Ali, Corinna, and Holly, she realized the larger school with a broader selection of studies would be a better fit. Turns out, Jenna has a huge head for marketing. I was pleasantly surprised by the number of ideas she bounced off me during her time with me over Fashion Week, ideas I'd never even thought of to market the business. She plans on minoring in studio design to keep her interest in art alive. Interning with me over the summer and during long breaks will incorporate her love of fashion with a much more practical future. Jake privately couldn't be more thrilled, though he told me he would have supported any decision she ultimately would have made.

After I got home from Toronto—and my impromptu trip to Nantucket—I shocked the hell out of Jenna when I pounded on the door. She grinned and pointed down to the music room. When I walked in, Jake jumped up from the piano and wrapped me tightly in his arms. He didn't let me up for air for quite some time.

Later that night while we were curled in front of the fire, Jake told me he knew his cruelty set us back emotionally to the beginning. He was willing to wait as long as it took for me. I was floored by his declaration.

"I betrayed your trust in me as surely as if I'd cheated on you," he admitted quietly, holding me tightly in his arms.

I thought about his words before carefully responding. "Yes and no. It's hard to express. My love didn't disappear, which it would have if you had cheated on me. It was just harder to open myself up again."

"Rightly so, Em." He hugged me to him for a few moments. "I'm just glad you gave me that second chance."

"My heart wouldn't let me do any differently," I whispered.

As much as I know Jake's it for me, I haven't been ready for this final step until now. Jake understood. He gave me the space to be as much of a part of their lives as I could handle between my new success and the emotional challenges I was learning to overcome. We've built our new relationship based on friendship instead of the burning heat over the summer. It's a solid foundation that's just going to get better over time.

I know we have so much to look forward to. We'll have a chance to watch the bogs be filled with water to float the cranberries to the surface for harvesting. We'll drink more beer at Cisco Brewery. We'll celebrate Jenna's birthday at Cru again. And we'll make even more memories in Connecticut.

Jake has a contract to teach at Nantucket High until the end of the school year, but he and Jenna have the next few weeks off for winter break. Until I knew where my heart was, where his was, I wasn't ready for him to invade my last sanctuary—the farm. I'm ready now.

So, here I am waiting for them to arrive. The lights are twinkling outside the stained-glass window in my studio in the mansion. Caleb —having come over to Team Jake and knowing how important of a step this is for me—offered to fly Jake and Jenna on the Hudson corporate jet into Teterboro where they'll be brought directly to Amaryllis Events.

Standing in front of the illuminated glass, the fireplace crackles behind me, sending off a warmth that removes the chill inside the large room. There's coffee, cocoa, some of Corinna's homemade caramel, and an assortment of cookies waiting. Really, the only thing it's missing is Mugsy. I feel a pang deep in my heart knowing that while he'll always be with me, I'll never feel his silky head butt up against me again in these precious moments.

The door slides open behind me on well-oiled wheels. Turning, I see Cassidy stroll in. "Are you anxious because you want them here, or are you anxious because they're coming?"

With a twist of my lips, I reply, "Can't it be a little of both?"

Her long hair falls down her back as she throws back her head. "Of course. Caleb just called. ETA five minutes."

Five minutes. Pressing my hand to my stomach, I look around. I wanted Jake to be brought to the mansion first, the same way Jenna was. I want him to finally be able to visualize my space the way I can see his when we're talking on the phone. I need for him to under-stand Collyer from the inside out so maybe when we're at a point where it's time for decisions to be made, I won't be looking at the hardest decision of my life.

Because for him, I already know I would leave.

I've learned life is best lived where the clouds touch both the sun and the sky, in that simple place where tears are shed from both joy and sorrow. Because what I said to Jake a few months ago is true. I have cried an ocean over him. And I'm sure I will cry more tears in this lifetime over the love I've once again found faith in. Because love isn't as simple as the words happily ever after. It's fabric that, yes, may be torn, but it can be fixed. But only by those careful enough with the tears who handle it delicately and don't rush the repairs.

I have that patience. And I found a man willing to give love that care.

"Any idea of how much hell the family is planning on doling out to him?" I murmur to my older sister as she sidles up next to me.

Jake hadn't just spent time repairing his relationship with me. Much to my surprise, he quietly contacted Ali to act as an intermediary to distribute letters he'd written to each of my family members and Charlie for his breach of trust. While none of them would tell me what they said, the words went a long way toward closing still-open wounds.

"Let's just say, I overheard Phil talking about taking him out for a run," Cassidy says drolly.

I choke. "Now, if you said Ali, I might find that more of a threat."

We both laugh as we lean against opposite sides of the window.

"You make me proud to be a Freeman, Emily," Cassidy murmurs.

My mind blanks. "Excuse me?"

"All the things we overcame, all the love we shared, that's the one thing I don't know if I ever told you. My heart relied upon yours to keep going in those early days." Cassidy's voice shakes as she blindly reaches for my hand. "If it wasn't for you and for Dee, believing that two brutalized children deserved love, none of this would exist."

"Cass..."

"There's one lesson Dee taught us I think you forgot along the way though."

"What's that?"

"That love built on respect, trust, and faith is the everlasting kind." Her face wet with tears, she looks up at me. "After all, isn't that the kind of love we have for Dee? The love we have for each other? The love we've fought for?"

The powerful burn in the back of my eyes can't be held back. Tears spill down my cheeks. "Yes."

"Then remember that kind of love transcends death, sister. You can't kill that kind of love." Cassidy reaches up and brushes away my tears. "So, this will be the only time I say this. Stop believing you're not worthy of it, Emily Delores Freeman, because you are."

Cassidy's words and ensuing emotion must have distracted me from Jake and Jenna's arrival because my ears catch the sound of something that has my breath stopping while my heart pounds furiously in my chest. I'm stunned so completely, I don't notice the gentle smile on Cassidy's face. The sound has me so entranced because it's something I haven't heard since the week of the accident—Jake teasing out seductive notes on the sax.

Jake playing to the entire mansion isn't just to entertain them. Down to my soul, I know it's a statement of intent. It's to show them he's not afraid to lay his heart out on the line for the Freemans to see it. He's telling them—me—he's telling me his heart's in the spot where the sax is how he wants to express himself.

A little bluesy.

A little sexy.

A lot in love.

"Oh, God." I'm sobbing. My hand comes up over my mouth just as Jenna bursts into the room.

"Em! You have to come... What's wrong?" she demands.

As I race past her without saying a word, I hear Cassidy say, "Nothing, baby. Let's give them a minute of privacy."

"Ugh, that's what Caleb said you'd say." Jenna's voice is barely registered as I throw open the mansion door.

And there he is.

In a dark green fisherman's sweater and jeans, Jake's on our front porch playing his heart out. When he sees me, he winks, but his lips keep blowing.

I'm desperate to throw myself in his arms, the anticipation making it worse as he moves around me, occasionally nudging me. I stand there shivering in the freezing cold, awed by the talent of the man before me.

I'm even more shaken by the love.

When he finishes, he carefully detaches the sax from his neck. I don't say a word as I wait for him to put the shiny instrument in its case and stand in front of me. When I feel his arm slide around my waist, I quiver. When his hand slides through the curls at the nape of my neck, my lips part. Which must be exactly what he wanted as he lowers his head and his—warm from the workout he gave them on the mouthpiece of the sax—touch mine. Sliding my hands up his chest, one of mine cups his jaw. The other threads through his thick hair.

When we pull away, the cold air leaving our mouths swirls between us like smoke from the chimney atop the mansion. In the lights strung around the portico, I can see the crinkles in the corners of Jake's eyes as he smiles down at me. "If that's the kind of greeting I get when I visit you at work, I'll pick you up every day I'm here."

Sliding my trembling fingers from his jaw to his lips, I feel him kiss them. "Only for those I love, Jake."

His eyes close as his head bows. Shoulders shaking, he whispers, "What did I do to deserve you?"

I duck so I can see his face. His eyes are as wet as mine were when Cassidy just handed me these words. "Love is built on respect, faith, and trust. You've always had the first, we can only pray for the second, and you fought for the third. As long as you keep doing that, I don't know how I won't love you."

Jake buries his head into my shoulder while swaying me back and forth. His choked "If it's all right, I'll always love you" comes out as we're swaying in each other's arms on the porch to music only we can hear.

It's a long time before we go inside to join the others.

And that night, my bed holds a man who will go to any lengths to make me believe.

EPILOGUE - EMILY
FOUR YEARS LATER

J ake and I are standing in the Gampel Pavilion as Jenna crosses the stage to accept her degree in business from UCONN. Michelle is on the other side of Jake wiping tears from her eyes, leaning against her new husband, Eric.

Freely letting my own tears fall, I'm trying to hold the phone as steady as possible so my family can watch on FaceTime while crowded around Cassidy's computer in her office.

Jenna shakes hands with the university president, posing for a picture that I'm sure Holly will complain about later. My heart aches with how mature she looks with her hair curled down her back over the cords announcing to the world she's graduating magna cum laude. Privately, she griped to me about not getting summa. I outright laughed in her face and asked her if she had fun in college. When she rolled her eyes and replied, "Duh?" I said that was just as important as getting the extra tenth of a point of a GPA.

Especially since her new boss didn't care.

Ali made Jenna an offer to come on board at Amaryllis Events working directly for her. I can't say I'm not disappointed to know my stepdaughter won't be working for me in the salon, but she'll be taking over marketing full time from my sister. With her innovative ideas, we're sure to attract a new generation of brides, and—Jenna mentioned impishly the other night at dinner—international ones as well. She's already called dibs on travel, much to everyone's dismay. Then again, with everyone having families, it's probably better we leave the traveling to someone who has the freedom to do so.

Jake began looking for teaching positions around Collyer pretty much the second he left that winter break. Even with all his experience, breaking into the Fairfield County school system is the holy grail of teaching assignments, so he expanded his search. We both were pleasantly surprised when he found a position at Rochambeau Middle School in Southbury, about thirty-five minutes away. The students seem to soak in the lessons he imparts through music.

I'm also certain every middle school girl—and a few of the boys— have a crush on my husband if the volume of mean mugs and envious stares I get when I go to school productions are any indication.

Jake and I married two years after the awful accident that almost took Jenna's life. In a quiet ceremony at Dani's home on Nantucket, I walked on Charlie's arm along the beach behind the house where Jake and I first met to join my life to the man who made me believe not just once, but twice in the power of love. My something old was decoupaged photographs of Aunt Dee and my mother wrapped underneath the handle of my bouquet before Phil attached satin ribbon wrapped around the mix of hydrangea and amaryllis flowers. My something new was the lacy high-necked gown I designed, where I pinned a cameo Jason once gave me of my Aunt Dee. My something borrowed was Cassidy's mother's pearl earrings. My something blue was Corinna's sapphire bracelet. All of my sisters, Dani, and Jenna stood up for me. Jake asked Brandon to be his best man, with Jason, Caleb, Keene, and Phil at his side. I'm not entirely sure who cried more during the ceremony, Jake's mother and aunt or Phil and Cassidy. It really was a toss-up.

The beach was littered with people it seems like we've loved forever as well as people who'd more recently joined our circle of trust, like the principal of Jake's school, our newer employees at

Amaryllis Events, Charlie's latest girlfriend. But the most important thing was, it was filled with love. Even Mugsy was there in spirit as we'd spread his ashes there that long-ago day. And for the rest of my life, I'll never forget the look on Jake's face when he repeated the vows we'd written together, including the words that have come to symbolize love to us both—respect, faith, and trust. After we were pronounced husband and wife, his whispered "I believe I'll love you forever" is a moment I know I'll never forget.

I drew it in my journal soon after our honeymoon was over.

Like I imagined so long ago, I spend my life living in that space between the ocean and the sky. Life isn't perfect.

"Mommy, I saw Jenna!" I hear shrieked through the phone. I press the button to turn around the image so I can see Jake's and my children, Jonah and Talia.

"Yes, sweetheart," I tell my exuberant daughter, who's sitting in Cassidy's lap. "You did."

"I'm gonna be like her when I get old." Jonah rolls his eyes at his younger sister. I give him a disapproving look while Cassidy gently corrects my four-year-old gently. "I'm going to be like her when I get older."

"That's what I said, Aunt Cass," Talia says, exasperatedly.

Cassidy looks at me behind her little pigtails and smiles.

One of the hardest days of our marriage was finding out I had endometriosis to such a degree that if I wanted to have children, I would not only have to undergo surgery, I would likely have to take fertility drugs. My heart was crushed at the idea of not being able to carry Jake's child. For weeks, I operated in a blind depression until Jake reminded me that Jenna was alive because I put my air into her body. That made her as much mine as his. Even while I was contemplating that thought, he hit me with another. There were kids in the foster system around the nation who would sell their souls to be a part of our family. "Isn't that what Dee would want you to do? Build your own family by looking for the right hearts? No matter who gave birth to them?"

We started looking soon thereafter.

Now, all our children light up our lives: Jenna's almost twenty-two, Jonah is eight, Talia, four. Jonah and Talia's birth father is in prison for murder; their mother died of an overdose. But I know more than anyone that environment and nurturing plays one hell of a role in the way a child will grow up.

When I met Jonah, he was in the process of trying to steal food from the back of a Stop and Shop near Jake's school before he went back to his foster home. He thought I would turn him in. Instead, I bought him food from the bakery.

"You're not like normal adults," he said as he powered through the second donut.

"What do you mean?" I asked quietly, but I was all too afraid I knew. I lifted my hand to touch his hand. He jerked away. My heart cracked open into a million pieces.

Embarrassed, Jonah shrugged before turning his attention back to the sprinkles. "I don't know."

I offered him a ride home since he missed his bus, and I saw the squalor he and his sister were living in. I remember turning to him and whispering, "Jonah, this can't be where you live."

He shrugged before reaching for the handle. "This is all kids like me have, Miz Emily. Nobody wants someone who's my age, and T—that's my sister—she won't let me go. We make do."

"Jonah..." I started to say, but he was already out of my car.

"Thanks for the donuts, Miz Em. I'll be sure to share some with T." Slamming the door, I felt like someone had just slammed the door on a prison. Whether it was Jonah's or mine, I wasn't sure.

I drove to Jake's school in tears. Jake took one look at me and flipped.

"What happened?"

"We have to go get them," I babbled incoherently.

"Who, baby?" He rubbed his thumb over my cheek.

"Jonah. His sister. I can't leave them there. Not like that. Not when..." And I proceeded to explain everything that happened, everything I saw and suspected.

It was Jake who called our social services coordinator. We waited anxiously while she agreed to look into the situation. "Go home for now. Unfortunately, these things take time."

This did nothing to ease either of our hearts, but we ceded defeat in that moment. "He has your eyes. He—*they* have to be ours. I just know it."

"Baby, I don't doubt it. After all, it took Dee one look for her to find you your family the first time." Jake held me as I cried in his arms.

Through the determined work of our social worker and a miracle, Jonah and Talia were moved to the farm within days. We were told there was clear reason to remove the children from their current situation. Jake and I had already gone through classes to be able to foster a child as part of the adoption process, so that was one less hurdle we didn't have to cross.

In our minds, we've been a family ever since, but it was only six months ago that Ali sat by our side in the courtroom and Jonah and Talia's last name was changed to Madison.

Just like mine.

"You have a lot to be proud of today, Jake. You did a wonderful job raising our daughter," I hear Michelle tell Jake. He squeezes my shoulder. Hard.

"I have to go, baby. Daddy and I will see you at home," I tell my little girl. Every time I look into her brown eyes, I see her father.

He was right: It doesn't matter who gave birth to our children. They're ours.

"Okay, Mommy. Love you!"

"Love you too." Disconnecting the call, I curl under Jake's arm.

"Everything all right with T?" he asks, with a warm smile.

I nod, smiling at Michelle and Eric. "She was excited to see Jenna graduate."

"Is Cass's office still in one piece?" I laugh, but we know the little whirlwind who has settled into our home and our hearts so beautifully can also destroy a room in point two seconds.

"For now." Leaning forward, I explain briefly, "I brought Talia with me to work one day after she had shots instead of bringing her to daycare. While I was working with a bride, she was supposed to be resting in my studio. Instead, she managed to pull down a dress and drag it on. Considering it had about a thousand pounds of beading on it, I'm still not sure how she managed to wander out with it on."

Michelle slaps a hand over her mouth to stifle her laughter. Eric doesn't have as much luck. His guffaws fill the air, prompting all the other people around us to "shh" us.

"Jenna occasionally tells me stories about her baby sister." Sadness crosses Michelle's face. "Every time she does, it makes me realize what I missed with her. What I hope she'll forgive."

"Michelle." Jake reaches over to squeeze his ex-wife's hand. "If there's one thing I've learned is that love has an unlimited capacity for forgiveness. You just have to work hard to earn it."

"I hope she sees it that way."

"Since the accident, you've been the mother she needed. And you've never given her reason not to believe you love her." He lets her hand go. "You just have to have faith in the relationship you're building with her."

Even as Michelle settles deeper into Eric's arm, she gapes at Jake. "Since when did you become the expert on love?"

Turning his head to fully look at me, there's a smile on his lips that frequently play the saxophone at home that silently tell me I shouldn't plan on getting much sleep tonight. "Since I realized that Dani did me the biggest favor of my life by being a pain in my ass. As usual."

Pulling me close so only I can hear, he whispers, "I love you, Emily. Forever."

Laying my head on his should, I whisper back, "I believe I'll love you too."

THE END

WHERE TO GET HELP

Most people recover from traumatic events such as the death of a loved one. With time, the grief passes, the pain lessens, and life eventually gets back to a new normal because the reality for most people is that normal is never quite the same ever again.

Unfortunately, some experience severe distress and anxiety that lasts for months or years. They re-experience the event through thoughts, reminders, or nightmares; to the point where even everyday activities can become challenging. Even being a part of a warm and loving family, people can often feel detached or estranged. These may be symptoms of post-traumatic stress disorder, or PTSD.

According to the Anxiety and Depression Association of America (ADAA), PTSD is a serious, potentially debilitating condition that can occur in people who have experienced or witnessed a life-threatening event, such as a natural disaster, serious accident, terrorist incident, sudden death of a loved one; war; or rape or other violent personal assault. Four main types of symptoms characterize it:

1. Re-experiencing a traumatic event through intrusive distressing recollections, flashbacks, and nightmares

2. Emotional numbness and avoidance of places, people, and activities that are reminders of the trauma

3. Feeling cut off from others and other negative alterations in cognitions (ways of thinking, understanding, learning, and remembering) and mood

4. Marked changes in arousal and reactivity, including difficulty sleeping and concentrating, feeling jumpy, easily irritated, and angered

If you suspect you have PTSD, seek professional help. Most people who receive treatment for PTSD see significant improvement and enjoy a better quality of life.

This is not to say you or a loved one have PTSD. Maybe, you need a helping hand to get you through a rough patch. Don't we all? I know I have on several occasions. Moreover, I've been grateful for the assistance.

Visit the ADAA at www.adaa.org to find qualified mental health professionals in the Find a Therapist directory.

ALSO BY TRACEY JERALD

Midas Series

Perfect Proposal

Perfect Assumption (Coming April 2021)

Perfect Composition (Coming Summer 2021)

Perfect Order (Coming Fall 2021)

Amaryllis Series

FREE - AN AMARYLLIS PREQUEL

(NEWSLETTER SUBSCRIBERS ONLY)

FREE TO DREAM

FREE TO RUN

FREE TO REJOICE

FREE TO BREATHE

FREE TO BELIEVE

FREE TO LIVE

FREE TO WISH: AN AMARYLLIS SERIES SHORT STORY - 1,001 DARK NIGHTS SHORT STORY ANTHOLOGY WINNER

FREE TO DANCE (COMING SPRING 2021)

Glacier Adventure Series

RETURN BY AIR

RETURN BY LAND

RETURN BY SEA

Sandalones

CLOSE MATCH

RIPPLE EFFECT

Lady Boss Press Releases

CHALLENGED BY YOU

ACKNOWLEDGMENTS

To my husband, you are the reason I believe each and every day. I love you so much.

To my son, keep smiling that beautiful smile. And never stop giving Daddy and I hugs and kisses even when you become a teenager. We love you.

To my mother, for giving me the life lessons I am able to pass down. I love you.

To my father. You are missed every single day I'm without you.

Jen, for being my best friend, my sister, my therapist, and for holding my head above the water, I love you.

My Meows, there's nothing we won't do for each other; together, we've celebrated love, cried over death, fought battles, and triumphed. If some of us could avoid pneumonia while we're doing all this, that would be fabulous. XOXO! I love you all.

To Jennifer Wolfel. So, I vote we do a beta read at Disney. Doesn't that sounds like a great idea? Thank you for everything you do to help me simply by never holding back your thoughts.

To Sandra Depukat from One Love Editing. One of these days, I'm going to write a book just based on the comments in my edits. Flipping popcorn...I love you so much!

To Virginia Tesi Carey - V, thank you for being you and for adding your special touches! Love you!

My cover and brand designer, Amy Queue of QDesigns, you once again spun your magic for me. I know this one was so much more of a challenge but that's because we both know who inspired Jake! Love you!

To my team at Foreword PR. Linda Russell – there isn't anything I wouldn't do for you. I love you!

For my Facebook group — Tracey's Tribe. I'm sending my love to you, always.

To all of the bloggers who read my books, thank you from the bottom of my heart.

To my readers, I love each and every one of you. Thank you for your love and for choosing to read my words.

And to everyone who helped me get through writing Em's story while I was suffering through not one, but two concussions, THANK YOU! There were so many days when I wanted to curl into a ball because looking at a computer made me physically ill. You got me through the pain, the stress, and helped me to recover.

And to the real Mugsy, I love you. Always.

ABOUT THE AUTHOR

Tracey Jerald knew she was meant to be a writer when she would re-write the ending of books in her head when she was a young girl growing up in southern Connecticut. It wasn't long before she was typing alternate endings and extended epilogues "just for fun".

After college in Florida, where she obtained a degree in Criminal Justice, Tracey traded the world of law and order for IT. Her work for a world-wide internet startup transferred her to Northern Virginia where she met her husband in what many call their own happily ever after. They have one son.

When she's not busy with her family or writing, Tracey can be found in her home in north Florida drinking coffee, reading, training for a runDisney event, or feeding her addiction to HGTV.

To follow Tracey, go to her website at http://www.traceyjerald.com. While you're there, be sure to sign up for her newsletter for up to date release information!

CPSIA information can be obtained
at www.ICGtesting.com
Printed in the USA
BVHW041116080721
611406BV00008B/229